The Social Context View of Sociology

The Social Context View of Sociology

Marty Zusman
PROFESSOR OF SOCIOLOGY
INDIANA UNIVERSITY NORTHWEST

David Knox
PROFESSOR OF SOCIOLOGY
EAST CAROLINA UNIVERSITY

Tracie Gardner
LECTURER
CALIFORNIA STATE UNIVERSITY, NORTHRIDGE

CAROLINA ACADEMIC PRESS
Durham, North Carolina

Library of Congress Cataloging-in-Publication Data

Zusman, Marty E.
  The social context view of sociology / by Marty Zusman, David Knox, Tracie
Gardner.
     p. cm.
  Includes bibliographical references and index.
  ISBN 978-1-59460-572-7 (alk. paper)
  1. Sociology. I. Knox, David, 1943- II. Gardner, Tracie. III. Title.

  HM585.Z87 2009
  301--dc22

2008019581

Carolina Academic Press
700 Kent Street
Durham, North Carolina 27701
Telephone (919) 489-7486
Fax (919) 493-5668
www.cap-press.com

Printed in the United States of America

This book is dedicated to the thousands of university students who have been exposed to the social context approach. Over the years they have praised the approach as giving them immediate insight into what sociology is as a discipline, what meaning the context approach has in their lives and how they have applied it to their lives. Their encouragement has resulted in bringing the social context approach into mainstream sociology.

Marty Zusman—"I dedicate this book to my wife, Jane. Without her insistence and encouragement this book would not have seen daylight. I also thank my family; Rochelle, Amie, Steven, Andrew, Jackie, Julie, John and Jennifer. I would also like to thank Kristie Gilmore who typed the early chapters of the manuscript. Finally, on a personal note, I was a student of Marvin Olsen who once told me, 'If you want to learn what sociology is all about, think of the levels of social organization.' Thanks, Marv, as a teacher and scholar, your ideas live on."

David Knox—"To Cameron Emmott who is taking her first steps into the world of social context."

Tracie Gardner—"To my daughter, Ellen Rose, who continually inspires me with her innocent wisdom."

Contents in Brief

Contents

Part IV
More Organized Contexts

Part I

The Sociological Approach

Chapter 1

The Social Context Perspective

A mind once stretched will never go back to its original dimensions.
Oliver Wendell Holmes

How many of the following statements do you believe are true?

I am an individual and make my own decisions.
Whether or not and whom I marry is my decision.
I am in college because I worked hard in high school.
I choose the foods I eat based on my own individual preferences/taste buds.

Most U.S. college students believe all of the above to be true. They reason that they are individuals, in control of their own choices, and their decisions simply reflect personal preferences. However, the statements above are only partially true; most (if not all) of the "choices" we make in life are determined by the social context/social organizations of which we are a part.

Social Context: An Aid to Understanding

People tend to make decisions their close friends and parents will approve of. Most groups socialize their members to date and to marry within their same race, which largely explains why most U.S. marriages are between individuals of the same race. Fewer than five percent of all marriages in the U.S. are interracial and less than one percent consists of a black and a white spouse (*Statistical Abstract of the United States: 2008*, Table 59). People are hardly "free" to marry whomever they want. Rather, their decisions are largely controlled by social context.

Similarly, the "decision" to go to college is influenced by a number of social factors. What if you lived among the 2.5 billion people—one-fourth of the global population—who survive on less than $2 a day? Would going to college even be an option? Probably not. Your "choice" to go to college is not just a reflection of your free will. Rather, your choice has been influenced by the fact that you live in a society where going to college is an option. Even if you, or your family, do not have ample funds to pay for college, our society has a number of systems in place that are designed to assist low-income students with funds, grants, and loans.

Regarding your food choices, what you eat, how you eat, and how much you eat are all influenced by social context. If you lived as a Hindu in India, you would be socialized to consider cows as sacred and not a source of food. If you were French, you would probably cut your pizza with a knife and fork, as that is considered the proper way to eat pizza in France. In addition, the portions of food served and consumed in the United States are much larger than in other cultures. These examples illustrate the central theme of this book: social context has a powerful impact on who we are and the choices we make.

Individuals are born into, live in, and die in social contexts. We are not born into a vacuum, but into a family, which is part of a particular social class, community, and society. At our birth we are assigned a racial identity and a gender. We live much, if not all, of our lives with other people, such as parents, siblings, roommates, spouses, and children. We attend school, work, worship, and play in social groups. At death, there is the gathering of family and friends for memorial and funeral services. This pattern exists throughout the world as people everywhere live in families, groups, communities, and societies, rather than alone as isolated individuals. Sociologists focus upon these and other social contexts in order to understand the world in which we live, as well as ourselves and others.

Psychologists look within the individual to explain human behavior: homeless individuals living on the street are seen as lazy; high school dropouts are viewed as rebellious and lacking motivation; divorced people are seen as unable to maintain intimacy and commitment. Sociologists examine the social context to explain why people behave as they do. The social context limits alternatives, restricts decisions and creates outcomes. The thoughts and behaviors of individuals have more to do with social context than any inherent personality characteristics. Individuals may be homeless because they live in a society that does not have enough employment opportunities and/or fails to provide mental health care services to those who need it. High school dropouts are often discouraged by an educational system that fails to help them realize their potential. Divorced individuals in the United States live in a societal context that fosters individualism rather than familism, and which includes legal and cultural acceptance of divorce.

In this chapter we present the unifying theme of the social context perspective used throughout the book. This theme is focused on nine social contexts. Rather than present a series of unrelated sociological topics, concepts, and theories, we unify the various chapters with the overriding theme of social context (also referred to as social organization).

Sociology is the study of social organization. The term **social organization** or **social context** refers to the patterns of human relationships and interactions that characterize social life. The world into which you were born has families, schools, churches, hospitals and other organizations. These organizations have been developed by human beings in response to their needs. For example, the family ensures the reproduction and socialization of new members to replace dying members. Schools function to teach youth basic language, rules, and skills so as to be productive members of society. Churches exist to provide explanations and meanings for the existence of life. Hospitals exist to respond to health crises and return the body to normal functioning. Indeed, all of life is organized. The three hundred million people in the United States cannot function without organized patterns of behavior to meet various social goals.

Sociologists believe that social organizations provide the context that largely determines what a person does in life. For example, at this moment you are reading and not interacting with anyone. If you look up from this book and begin to talk with someone, the person with whom you interact will help determine the nature of your behavior, because that interaction forms a context. This context will differ according to whether the person you interact with is a sibling, roommate, lover, parent, professor or police officer. Interacting with each of these individuals will create a context which will elicit a different set of behaviors from you. You are not a "personality" that engages in behavior independent of your social context. Rather, your behavior is largely determined by the social context of which you are a part. As your social context changes, so does your behavior.

Similarly, your behavior depends on your race, social class, and marital status. All of these involve different social contexts which will create different behaviors on your part. For example, as a young black unmarried female, if you experience a pregnancy, you are more likely to have the child than if you are an unmarried white female (who is more likely to have an abortion). A person from the upper class is more likely to read the *Wall Street Journal* than a person from the lower class. A spouse is more likely to carry life insurance than an unmarried person, etc.

Sociological Theories

A **theory** is an organized way of explaining something. There are three major theories which will be used throughout this text: functionalism, conflict and symbolic interactionism. While we will go into greater depth in explaining and using these theories in each chapter, a general understanding is given at this point.

One of the ways these theories differ is in the degree to which they suggest that human behavior is determined by social forces. Theories are seen as **deterministic** or **non-deterministic**. If a theory views a human being as merely an object that is determined or forced to act in a particular way because of the context they are in, that theory is deterministic. If a theory views a human being as someone who is an active subject and can determine his or her own destiny then that theory is non-deterministic.

Functionalism

Functionalism views society and other social contexts (e.g. family, school, church) in terms of the function it serves. For example, the family functions in society to provide new socialized members to replace those who die. Functionalists use the terms manifest and latent functions. A **manifest function** is the anticipated/intended function such that the manifest function of education is to teach youth the language and rules of society. A **latent function** or unanticipated/unplanned function of education is that it keeps youth occupied so as to reduce the crime rate. Another example is that the manifest function of college is to provide a credential to get a job, while the latent function is to provide a context where students can find a marriage partner with a similar level of education.

Conflict Perspective

Conflict theory focuses on the aspects of context that are conducive to struggle and conflict. In that struggle some people/groups are able to exercise more power and achieve greater rewards. As a conflict theorist, Karl Marx saw the struggle between economic classes of people as persistent and inevitable. Conflict theorists today look at all contexts and ask who is benefiting from the present social organization. Those who benefit will attempt to protect their advantage. The Democrats and Republicans are in repeated conflict over control of the House of Representatives and the Senate. Each is trying to control the other to its own advantage.

We will discuss in later chapters on race and gender inequality that conflict theorists see conflict as normative. Some conflict is channeled into courts, arbitration, and labor negotiations. Conflict may also be ongoing as between men and women, blacks and whites, the old and the young. Conflict theorists view people as having competing interests that lead them to use power to achieve their goals at the expense of others. It is a deterministic approach in that it views social context as creating the outcomes.

Persons who have power and money will act to maintain their advantage. Indeed, real estate developers (who have both power and money) run for political office to be voted onto the city council. Once they achieve a position on the council they approve the rezoning of various lands in the community from "residential" to "commercial" to advance their own power and income.

Symbolic Interactionism

Symbolic interactionism believes that human beings are social actors that create and determine the world around them through the use of language (symbols). The person, therefore, not only reacts to context, but actively creates it. Events are not determined or caused by the context, but rather individuals are active in creating their own outcomes by use of communication. As the term "symbolic interaction" suggests, people use "symbols" in "interaction" which determines the context. For example if you are walking from class and see a stranger, you will look down and pass on by. But if you see your lover, you will establish eye contact, talk, flirt, and touch. Your mutual behavior depends on your responding to the symbols (words/touch) as you interact with each other.

Throughout the later chapters of this book we will return to these major sociological theories which help to explain why people behave the way they do. To further our understanding of the sociological perspective we must also look at some of the important terms that sociologists use.

Social Organization Terms

All social organizations can be described using four terms—the focus of this section.

Position

Position refers to social location in a social organization. For example, in the family, there are the positions of wife, husband, and child. In a society, president, surgeon general, and senator are examples of positions. In an association such as a baseball team, there are the positions of manager, catcher, and bat boy or bat girl. The position a person holds affects how others will interact with that person. A 25-year-old divorced single parent on a date with a never-married, childfree 25-year-old person will be viewed differently (and vice versa) than if the position is the same for both. A disabled person in a classroom and on the playground will be perceived and related to differently than an able bodied person. You will talk differently to the peer riding in the car with you than to the police officer who just stopped you for speeding.

Status

Every position is associated with a status. **Status** is the ranking of a position in a social organization from low to high along some criteria such as power. Parents have more status than children, the president has more status than the surgeon general, and the manager of a baseball team has more status than the bat girl.

Role

A **role** is the way a person in a particular position within a social organization is expected to act. Parents protect their children, the president makes a State of the Union Address, and the batboy retrieves broken bats. Roles are important not only because they make social interaction predictable but because they influence psychological well-being. If you are in the role of a newlywed you are likely to feel better about your life than if you just became a divorced person. When one's role departs from what is socially expected of a given age and gender, distress results. For example, a person in the role of unemployed husband and father and a woman in the role of mother with no employed husband are likely to report high stress levels.

Norm

Positions, statuses, and roles are associated with norms. **Norms** are expectations of behavior associated with the various positions, statuses, and roles in society. A person in the position of child with little status who is assigned the role of "the youngest" may be expected to do very little around the house. A mother with moderate status who is assigned the role of economic provider will be expected to work.

The president who has high status is expected to behave with the utmost grace when interacting with foreign dignitaries. The manager of a National

Football League football team is not expected to spy on the other team. New England Patriots coach Bill Belichick was fined half a million dollars, and the Patriots were ordered to pay $250,000 for spying on an opponent's defensive signals. Table 1.1 uses football as a context for the terms of this section.

Table 1.1
Football Game Described in Sociological Terms

Position	Status	Role	Norm
Referee	High	Rules on Plays.	Attend game sober and have 20/20 vision.
Coach	High	Hire/Fire.	Take responsibility for preparing the team for each game. Don't spy on other team.
Quarterback	High	Execute plays.	Provide role model for team, maintain training schedule (e.g. don't break curfew which will result in probation).
Rookie	Low	Sit on bench.	Stand up and yell when team scores.
Waterboy	Low	Provide Gatorade.	Make sure ample liquid is present.
Fan	Low	Observe game.	Avoid throwing cans and paper on the playing field.
Sportscaster	High	Relay game.	Avoid bias in reporting the game.

Social Organization Framework

Social organizations may be described according to their structure and process.

Structure

Sociologists sometimes examine the world as though they were taking a still photo of a social organization. By doing so they discover the social structure which exists at a given time. **Social structure** may be defined as the way positions, statuses, roles and norms are organized in a social organization at any given time. The structure of the social organization of a university is illustrated in a flow chart which shows the positions of chancellor, an assistant to the chancellor, deans of various schools, departmental chairs, and faculty. Each position is associated with a status, a role, and a set of norms.

Families also have structure. A family with an infant, or a family with an adolescent, or with only an aging parent, all have different structures due to differences in the positions, statuses, roles, and norms. These different structures create different outcomes.

For example, alcohol use is related to structure. Being a member of a sorority or a fraternity as a college freshman involves a social structure which lends itself to considerably more alcohol consumption than being an 18-year-old that lives at home with one's parents (Borsari, Murphy, and Barnett, 2007).

Structure also affects school performance of adolescents. Tillman (2007) analyzed national data on 13,988 adolescents to identify the effects of passing through different family structures (married parents, single parent family, and stepfamily). She found that, compared to youth who have always lived with both biological parents, adolescents who live in a stepfamily (married or co-habiting) or in a single mother home have lower GPAs and more school behavior problems. The stress of transitioning from one context to the other or the existence of negative characteristics like poor emotional/physical/psychological health of parents who are going through a divorce are the likely culprits. Regardless of the exact factor, structure affects outcome.

Process

Sociologists not only look at the structure of social organizations but also its process. **Process** refers to how social organizations change. Heraclitus said "Nothing endures but change." Everything is always in a state of change. At one point we are young, at another we are middle age, at still another we are old. We change social classes (from lower to middle), marital status (from being single to being married to being divorced or widowed), and employment (from being unemployed to being employed to being retired). We also change the groups to which we belong (from clubs in high school, to work groups, to community associations such as church).

Every time there is a change in social context, there is a subsequent change in behavior. When a spouse becomes a divorced person, the new position is associated with a new status, a new role, and a new set of norms. The divorced person drops in status (married people have greater social status than divorced people in our society). The new role may involve spending more time alone and/or going to singles' bars. The new norms usually involve very limited contact with the ex-spouse (and such interaction is likely to be hostile). It is the new context which dictates the changes in behavior the person exhibits. Much of sociology is concerned with the process of our changing social groups which is accompanied by changes in our behavior. As our social context changes, so we change.

When we describe the population of a group or society, we are describing an aspect of the structure of that group or society. If we study a particular social organization (families) over time we will observe change (process). Examples of these changes in the last fifty years include divorce replacing death as the endpoint for the majority of marriages, marriage and intimate relations as legitimate objects of scientific study, the rise of feminism/changes in gender roles in marriage, and the decline in remarriage (Amato, Booth, Johnson, and Rogers et al. 2007). Other changes include a delay in age at marriage, increased acceptance of singlehood, cohabitation, and child-free marriages. Even the definition of what constitutes a family is being revised with some emphasizing that durable emotional bonds between individuals is the core of "family" while others insist on a more legalistic view, emphasizing connections by blood marriage or adoption mechanisms. The family at one point in time with its various positions, statuses, roles and norms is its structure; the changes across time represent its process.

Types of Social Organization

Using the framework of structure and process, we now present a typology of the nine types of social organizations (Olsen, 1968).[1] Each of these types represents a subfield of sociology. An analysis of each of these types will provide a basis for understanding not only the varieties of social organization but will provide a way to link the concepts, theories, methods, and knowledge of sociology into a unified whole.

Each of these nine concepts are areas of specialization for sociologists. You do not find "sociologist" in the classified ads. If you want to be a sociologist, you specialize in population and get a master's or doctorate in demography and work as a demographer for the Bureau of the Census. Or, you get a degree specializing in associations, like medical sociology and work for the American Hospital Association studying patient outcomes. After defining each of the social organizations, we provide examples.

Populations

Population is the study of characteristics (e. g. sex, age, and race) of individuals in a geographic area which impact the development of social organizations. For example, in the college or university you attend, the various

---

1. The nine areas of social organization, first identified and defined by the late Marvin Olsen (1968), include populations, collective behavior/social movements, social class, groups, families, communities, associations, networks and societies. (Olsen also identified a tenth context, confederation.)

populations include men, women, blacks, whites, students, teachers, and administrators. Looking at our society as a whole, some of the various populations include Republicans, Democrats, spouses, widows, the employed, and the unemployed. Population involves the study of demography from the Greek language, meaning "description of people."

The important insight that sociologists contribute to understanding human behavior is that changes in social organization result in changes in social life and the way in which people behave. For example, crime increases in a society when there are a lot of people in the population between the ages of 16 and 30 and decreases as the people in the population age. Hence, most people tend to give non-sociological explanations for crime such as "people are selfish and criminal." Sociologists studying population know that crime is a demographic issue and can predict a society's increasing or decreasing crime rate just by knowing the changes occurring in the age of its citizens.

Collective Behavior/Social Movements

This area of social organization is best defined as a **collectivity** or **aggregation** and involves engaging in collective action. Collective behavior is usually spontaneous and unplanned, unstructured and short-lived. Myanmar (formerly known as Burma), in the fall of 2007, was the scene of Buddhist monks leading 70,000 protestors to end 45 years of military dictatorship. This was the largest collectivity uprising in Burma in decades.

In contrast to collectivity, **social movements** are usually planned, structured and enduring. In effect, there is some action which unifies large numbers of the population into an action which is not yet accepted as "normal." The women's movement has focused on the elimination of oppression and inequality. These goals are similar to those of the gay liberation movement including the legalization of same-sex marriage.

Mobs at any given time (structure) may be made up of individuals who are religious, married, family men with no criminal backgrounds. Yet, in the spontaneity (process) of the mob (context) they may kill a human being or commit other acts which, as individuals, they might otherwise regard as unthinkable.

What sociology contributes to our understanding of human behavior is the focus on social context, which is more important in explaining a lynching than studying the several individuals that make up a mob. It is the context or social organization that influences the outcome and not each unique individual. As individuals, married, religious, family men may never commit murder. But in the context of a mob, individuals are more likely to become killers.

Social Class

Sociologists describe people as belonging to different social classes. A **class** is a ranking based on the extent to which people share in characteristics of wealth, power and social position. One's class may be achieved through the combination of effort and opportunity. Class may also be ascribed, or determined, at birth.

How a person thinks and behaves is greatly influenced by his or her social class (lower, middle, upper). We need not ask if upper class individuals, like the president of the United States, drink cheap wine, buy their clothes at thrift shops, drive used cars, or attend state colleges. Nor need we ask if street people eat caviar, drive BMWs, or attend Ivy League schools. The behavior of individuals may be understood, explained and predicted by knowledge of their social class.

The term **social stratification** refers to the division of people in a society according to their social class. Sociologists are concerned with the structure of social class in America. For example, what percent of the U.S. population belongs to which social class? Sociologists who specialize in this area also study the processes involved in social stratification, looking at, for example, how individuals change social class and how the distribution of those in the respective social classes changes across time.

Where a person is in the class structure will impact the person's self concept, anger, and level of frustration. Dolan (2007) studied working class men in the United Kingdom to garner their perceptions of having lower incomes than those living in affluent areas. The research was qualitative so that men were encouraged to talk about their perceptions. The results emphasized how, for these men, it was not the differential income but the negative ways in which they were perceived and treated that impacted them. They were angry, frustrated and felt "dents" to their self-esteem.

> *They look down their noses at you.... They judge you not to be a decent spender. They think scruffy car, scruffy bloke.... I know they are thinking that or I feel they are thinking that.... It does get me angry because I have been there, done that and all the rest of it (Richard 43, affluent area/non-affluent household).*

One's social class also has implications for one's health and remaining alive. Upper class individuals have better nutrition, better health care, and can afford more expensive medications. One's social class and life chances were dramatically illustrated by the sinking of the *Titanic* in 1912. Of the 700 people who survived, a disproportionate number were living on the upper deck. Those in the lower decks had less access to lifeboats.

Groups

A social **group** is defined as two or more people who know each other and develop a pattern of interaction based on common expectations. Groups are the smallest category of organized life. To many sociologists, groups represent the core study of the discipline. The smallest group, called a **dyad**, consists of two individuals. The dyad is sometimes considered to be the strongest of all social organizations. The dyad is often weakened when a third member enters, as when a couple has a child or when a wife or husband has an affair.

Sociologists study groups at a given point in time (structure) and as they change (process). Following a couple from courtship through living together through marriage to divorce or widowhood involves examining both structure and process. Some sociologists argue that when an individual enters a group, he or she gives up his or her individuality and becomes a social actor who "fits in." Notice how your behavior changes depending on whether you are with your roommate, sibling, parents, religious leader, or professor. The study of groups is important because groups help shape the attitudes and behaviors of those who belong to the group.

Families

All societies have one or more forms of **family,** which has traditionally been defined as a context consisting of men and women connected to each other on the basis of kinship to produce, nurture and socialize children. The sociological study of the family examines the structure of different types of families such as the nuclear family, (e.g. husband, wife, and child) and the extended family (e.g. not only the married couple but their parents, grandparents, married children and cousins). In addition to family structure, sociologists study family process or change within and among families. Over the last 50 years, spouses have become more egalitarian, more wives have worked out of the home leaving young children in day care, and more single parent families have come into existence.

Families are influential in determining the attitudes and behaviors of their members. For example, "individual success" might be predicted by knowing family background. Upper class families propel their offspring to attend Ivy League universities. Working class parents may encourage their offspring to get a stable job in a factory. These are sociological correlates of individual success. Psychological explanations, by contrast, focus instead on the individual's I.Q. and motivation rather than family structure or dynamics.

Communities

Communities are social organizations characterized by a contiguous geographic area wherein people have organized to meet their needs and concerns as they carry out their daily lives. Community is a single term that encompasses everything from metropolitan areas to rural towns. New York, Miami, Atlanta, and Stillwater, Oklahoma, are all communities. Even within the larger communities (e.g. New York) there are smaller communities—Chinatown, Harlem, Upper East Side. Communities can be studied at any one time (structure) as well as analyzed across time (process). The ninth ward of New Orleans was a community which was devastated by Hurricane Katrina (and the aftermath continues—Tierney, 2008). Sociologists argue that by knowing the community (social organizational context) in which a person lives they can predict the attitudes and behaviors of that person. Persons who were forced to move out of the community to Houston or other cities experienced change due to their new context. Not only were they separated from extended kin, they were dependent on strangers in their new communities for jobs, food, and clothing. If you were to move to Harlem or Malibu for the next two years, you would most likely change many of your behaviors because of the social forces operating in the context of each community.

Associations

An **association** is a social organization formed in pursuit of some specific common goal. Associations may be small or large and are sometimes considered to be a special type of context. Hospitals, universities, churches, the military, and human rights/animal rights associations all exist for the purpose of achieving certain goals. Paxton (2007) studied membership in voluntary associations and found that members in those organizations that were connected to a lot of other voluntary associations (e.g. Human Rights, Animal Rights) tended to have higher levels of trust in humankind.

Institutions are patterns of activities which are seen as crucial and important to the society. There are many institutions. Some basic institutions are religion, politics, health, education, the military and economics. Institutions are larger structures within which there may be smaller associations. For example, the military is an institution which includes associations of various types. Marines, sharpshooters, Navy, Seabees and others all exist for the common goal of protecting our society.

We can predict a person's behavior by studying the various associations in which a person becomes involved. For example, the Enron scandal where stock investors were lied to about the viability of the company occurred when corporate executives conspired to "cook the books," inflate the price of the stock and sell their own shares. On the floor, workers were encouraged to 'increase sales" with the threat of losing their jobs. These individuals had become part of an association which led to the end of Enron.

Networks

Networks tie together social organizations concerned with similar activities in their pursuit of goals. **Micro networks** are social organizations that link together large numbers of individuals, rather than organizations. Match.com and Facebook tie together individuals interested in connecting with each other. **Macro networks** tie the social organizations of the world together and help to coordinate social life. The airline industry has international networks which allow planes to leave one country and land in another.

Networks enable individuals to move smoothly through social organizations. For example, a six-year-old in America can start in public, private, or parochial school and eventually earn a Ph.D., even as he or she moves from New York to Boston and finally to Raleigh, North Carolina. This is because networks exist that link together the various educational institutions.

Examples of networks include medical networks (clinics, hospitals, laboratories), communication networks (television and radio stations, newspapers, magazine and book publishers), socialization networks (families, nursery schools, youth groups) and legal networks (courts, law firms, police departments, prisons). Notice that each association within a network link is interrelated with the other associations. Regarding legal networks, law firms prepare cases heard in courts where police officers take the convicted to jail. Similarly, in reference to socialization networks, families provide initial socialization which is reinforced in schools, Boy/Girl scout clubs, and churches.

A given association may contribute more than one network link. Schools are part of the educational network linking grammar school to graduate programs just as they are part of socialization networks linking families and schools.

Societies

A **society** is characterized by autonomy, geographic boundaries, a shared culture, greater self sufficiency and independence in decision making. The United States is a society and it is the most powerful of the social organizations that affect our lives. Societies such as Iraq, Iran, and Jordan represent different social organizations. By studying these complex social organizations we gain an insight as to the importance of "context" in our lives. If we were to move to another society, our "normal" behavior patterns would be significantly altered. To understand what we would become we need to understand the society into which we migrated. Our future success, failure or very survival would depend upon understanding and adapting to the social organization of our new societal home. The study of societies helps us to understand, explain, and predict not only our own day to day behavior patterns, but also the social lives of other people.

For example, the predominant sexual value of college females in the United States is relativism (sexual intercourse is appropriate if one is "in love" and the woman feels secure). However, in Jordan, an unmarried female who has intercourse (even if she is raped) brings shame to her parents and siblings and may even be killed with little consequence to the person who murdered her. For instance, a 20-year-old woman who is raped can be shot by her brother since she has brought shame to her family—the tradition is called honor killing in that she is killed because she brought shame and dishonor to her family.

An example of how the life of a never married U.S. male would be different in another society may be illustrated by looking at norms for remaining single. In the U.S., a male is expected to move out of his parents' house and to marry by his late twenties. Not so in Italy. Single men live at home with their mother until their late thirties or forties. It is their mother who cleans their room and cooks for them and expects them to stay home and not move out. If they do marry, they are expected to live next door. The term is Mammoni or "mamma's boy." Hence, whether a person is married or single is less a function of individual personality and motivation and more a function of social context—in this case, society.

Societies may be viewed at one point in time (structure) or across time (process) to illustrate change. The war in Iraq drags on as there is hope of moving from a society ruled by Saddam Hussein to a stable democratic society. Because of the various factors competing for power, some believe the political unrest will continue.

In effect, a society and its members may be thought of as a context. Many aspects of the social world such as family life, employment, crime, and inequality are influenced by the larger society. A fascist, communist, socialist, or capitalist society will create different outcomes for those who live in them. Industrial and agrarian societies will also have markedly different effects on the lives of their people.

Loneliness is a function of the society in which one lives, not the individual. Research on persons living in Spain reveals much less loneliness than those living in Canada and the United States. "Since Spanish society centers on relationships, encourages interpersonal interactions, discourages divorce, and most of its members maintain strong family ties, it stands to reason that the Spaniards, both men and women, would score lower than the Canadians on the loneliness subscales ..." (Rokach, 2008, p. 62). The same finding was held in reference to the United States with its citizens being more lonely.

Confederated Systems

Although in this book we will concentrate on nine social organizations, there is a tenth; confederations. A **confederated system** is a social organization that ties societies together because of their involvement in a core set of activities. While they remain as separate societies, the larger confederated system unites and integrates the societies. Some confederated systems are global systems such as the "world economic system" which developed with the spread of capitalism. The European Common Market is a confederated system in Europe which is forming a unified Europe. Each of the countries is giving up some of their autonomy to the larger confederation. Sociologists are only recently beginning to look at such global organizations and courses are rarely offered on this topic.

It is important to note that there is some overlap in the above categories. A sociology class may start out as a group but become a collective if there is a decision to protest a tuition hike. Women represent a population but feminists among them may become part of the women's movement.

Table 1.2 summarizes the ten types of social organization.

Organization of the Book

This book is organized with several goals in mind—to provide a cohesive lens through which we can understand and explain human behavior, to discuss how each of the nine areas of social organization/social context can be used (confederated systems will not be discussed) to understand human phenomenon, to emphasize the importance and outcomes of various social contexts, to contrast popular beliefs with empirical research, and to present current research results on the topic of each chapter.

Pervasive Social Organization/Social Context Theme

Social organization/social context is the consistent theme to connect the chapters. Each chapter emphasizes that every aspect of our lives is influenced by each of the nine areas of social organization. Whether we are in a taxi, a

Table 1.2
Types of Social Organization

Type	Definition	Example
Population	Category of individuals sharing similar traits. It is not a true social organization.	Women, Men, Widows, Retirees, Hispanics, Homeless, Employed, Republicans, Catholics
Collective behavior/ Social Movements	Spontaneous, brief collection of people engaged in action.	Riots, Theatre audiences, Gay liberation movement, Passengers on bus/airplane, Individuals in an elevator
Social Classes	Ranking based on similar economic and social advantages.	Upper class, Middle class, Working class, Lower class, Under class
Groups	Two or more individuals interacting as a separate unit.	Roommates, Lovers, Your sociology class, Committee, Sorority, Commune, Cohabitants, Sociology faculty, Basketball team
Families	Individuals tied together by kinship.	Nuclear family, Married Couple, Extended Family, Single-parent family, Blended family
Communities	Social actors in a specific territory organized to meet their needs and concerns as they carry out their daily lives.	Chinatown, New Orleans, Washington, DC
Associations	Social organization formed in pursuit of some specific common goal.	American Medical Assoc., Alcoholics Anon., Phi Kappa Delta, Prisons, Hospitals, Military, University, Human Rights, Animal Rights, Synagogue/church
Networks	Linkages between social organizations.	Educational net, Medical network, Legal network, Communication network, Underground network
Societies	Social organization that has a shared culture and greater decision making power.	Iraq, United States, Canada, Australia
Confederated Systems	Societies tied by core set of activities.	European Common Market

classroom, a family, an airport, or an athletic club we are in a social organization. The structures and processes of the social organizations which surround us daily shape our thoughts, attitudes, and behaviors.

The book is organized around the nine areas of social organization. Once again, these nine areas include populations, collective behavior/social movements, social classes, groups, families, communities, associations, networks, and societies.

For each of the nine areas of social organization, we will examine the various concepts and theories. Sociological **concepts** are ideas sociologists have developed to describe or explain social phenomena. As we discuss each of the nine areas of social organization, we will introduce new concepts. When discussing family, the concepts monogamy, polygyny, and polyandry will be introduced. When discussing associations, the concepts of alienation and anomie are discussed. In the study of class, concepts such as mobility, social strata, and prestige are examined.

A **theory** is an explanation of how two or more concepts are related. For example, suppose our concepts are "**principle of least interest**" (person who has the least interest in a relationship controls the relationship) and "**mating gradient**" (men tend to marry down in terms of education and social class whereas women tend to marry up). A theory linking these concepts might be that men may more often control relationships since they have more resources than the woman.

Unlike the theory just presented, some theories are very general and may be applied across the board to all nine organizational types. As discussed earlier, conflict theory says that competition between groups is a basic process in social organization that can apply to societies (the war with Iraq), populations (blacks against whites) or associations (Democrats and Republicans).

We have already noted functionalism, symbolic interactionism and conflict theories. We will refer to these as we discuss the various areas of social organization.

Outcome Predictions

A major benefit of studying social context is to examine its influence on various outcomes. Rather than look to the individual (which is the focus in psychology) to explain certain outcomes (e.g. unemployment, illiteracy, alcoholism) we look to the social context. Whether or not a person cohabitates before marriage is more related to the social organizations which surround the person than the personality characteristics of the person. The norms for cohabitation in Iceland are such that 90 percent of spouses will have lived together before they marry. Indeed, having children in a cohabitation relationship before marriage is expected. In contrast, only 12 percent of spouses in Italy will have lived together before marriage (Italy is a Catholic country which does not support living together outside of marriage). The issue is social context, not individual initiative. Similarly, illiteracy and alcoholism are products of the social order. Throughout the text we will emphasize how various social organizations produce certain outcomes.

Popular Beliefs and Scientific Data

Various beliefs which are widely held in our society have little scientific support. Sociologists identify popular beliefs, collect data, and analyze the data to find out if the beliefs are indeed true. For example, it is widely believed that if a high school student participates in sports that he or she is less likely to become involved in deviant behavior. Hartmann and Massoglia (2007) used data from the Youth Development Study (YDS) which is a longitudinal survey of 1,000 young men and women from high school to adulthood (10 years later) in St. Paul, Minnesota. They found that high school sports participation is significantly and consistently associated with deviant behaviors—specifically, drunken driving and shoplifting. There is an increase in drunken driving and a decrease in shoplifting.

Other examples of popular beliefs are that the divorce rate is increasing, that children increase marital happiness, and that residential integration is increasing. Yet none of these beliefs has consistent scientific support. It is also assumed that children of divorce will have the highest level of well-being if they have close relationships with both parents. But data from a 17-year longitudinal study demonstrated that children were no better off if they were close to both parents than to one parent only (Sobolewski and Amato, 2007).

In the chapters to follow, as we discuss each of the levels of social organization, we will make reference to some of our society's popular beliefs and point out that there is often little empirical support for these beliefs. In some cases, the data support the opposite of the popular belief.

References

Amato, P. R., A. Booth, D. R. Johnson, and S. F. Rogers. 2007. *Alone Together: How Marriage in America is Changing.* Cambridge, Mass: Harvard University Press.

Borsari, Brian, J. G. Murphy and N. P. Barnett. 2007. "Predictors of Alcohol Use during the First Year of College: Implications for Prevention." *Addictive Behaviors,* 32: 2062–2086.

Dolan, Alan. 2007. " 'Good Luck to Them If They Can Get It': Exploring Work-ing Class Men's Understandings and Experiences of Income Inequality and Material Standards." *Sociology of Health & Illness,* 29: 711–729.

Hartmann, Michael and Michael Massoglia. 2007. "Reassessing the Relation-ship between High School Sports Participation and Deviance: Evidence of Enduring, Bifurcated Effects." *Sociological Quarterly,* 48: 485–505.

Olsen, Marvin E. 1968. *The Process of Social Organization.* New York: Holt, Rinehart and Winston.

Paxton, Pamela. 2007. "Association Memberships and Generalized Trust: A Multilevel Model Across 31 Countries." *Social Forces,* 86: 47–76.

Rokach, Ami. 2008. "Coping with Loneliness in North America and Spain" *Psychology Journal,* 5: 51–68.

Sobolewski, Juliana W. and Paul R. Amato. 2007. "Parents' Discord and Divorce, Parent-child Relationships and Subjective Well-Being in Early Adulthood: Is Feeling Close to Two Parents Always Better than Feeling Close to One?" *Social Forces,* 85: 1105–1125.

Statistical Abstract of the United States: 2008. 127th ed. Washington, D.C.: U.S. Bureau of the Census.

Tierney, Kathleen. 2008. "Hurricane in New Orleans? Who Knew? Anticipat-ing Katrina and Its Devastation" *Sociological Inquiry,* 78: 179–183.

Tillman, Kathryn Harker. 2007. "Family Structure Pathways and Academic Disadvantage among Adolescents in Stepfamilies." *Sociological Inquiry,* 77: 383–424.

Part II

The Basis of Social Context

Chapter 2

Culture

If you see in any given situation only what everybody else can see, you can be said to be so much a representative of your culture that you are a victim of it.

S.I. Hayakawa, former U.S. Senator

An aquarium is a specifically defined territory of water in which various fish, plants, and rocks can be observed. An aquarium allows one to get a look at the total environment of underwater life. Just as the fish are perhaps unaware of the water in which they swim, social actors are often oblivious to the presence and influence of their culture on them. **Culture** is the totality of what a group of people think, do, and create. As an undergraduate who grew up in America, thoughts such as "my career must be fun," behaviors such as text messaging, interacting on MySpace, and creating a costume for Halloween are expressions of your culture.

If you grew up in the Southwest as an Apache Indian in the 1800's, your culture would be entirely different. The image of an Apache warrior with his feathered spear held high, charging bareback on a palomino, and screaming words of war reflects a different culture from you talking on a cell phone as you walk to class. Similarly, Eskimos, gypsies, and pygmies reflect still other variations of culture.

Culture is important to sociologists because each area of social organization (populations, families, etc.) can only be understood by an awareness of the total cultural experience of people in those organizations. Americans, Apaches, and Eskimos (different populations) cannot be understood unless we examine the total cultural frames in which they live. For example, families differ according to whether they are part of a geographic Western or Eastern culture. **Individualism** is a value of Western society whereby what is best for the individual is of prime importance. In contrast, **familism** (doing what is best for the family) is a prime value of Eastern society. The former value results in a high divorce rate, the latter value in a lower divorce rate. The percent of American newlyweds who eventually divorce is 42% whereas divorce in Iraqi families is very rare.

In Chapter One, we emphasized that a comprehensive understanding of social life requires an awareness of the nine types of social organization. In this chapter we focus on the core of each of the nine areas—culture.

Aspects of Culture

Culture can best be understood by looking at its various components, such as artifacts, symbols, values, norms, and sanctions. Each of these aspects can be categorized as material or non-material.

Material vs. Non-Material Culture

If we are to analyze and understand culture, one way to do so is to divide culture into two major categories: the material and non-material. **Material culture** refers to the physical objects made or used by individuals or groups. The cell phone, iPod, and Blue Ray high definition screen are artifacts of the technological world. The clothes of the traditional Eskimo are still made from the skins of animals, their houses are made of blocks of ice, and their fishing hooks are made from the bones of animals.

All social life includes material objects. As we study each of the nine areas of social organization, it is useful to consider the material and non-material of each. The rope of a lynching mob (collective behavior), the photo album of a family (family), and the subways of a city (community) are examples of material culture. **Non-material culture** includes aspects of culture that are not material. The symbols, values, norms, and social sanctions which operate within the nine areas are examples of non-material culture.

Symbols

Symbols are actions, words, and objects that refer to something else. Symbols are important in that members of every social organization must learn to use and interpret the symbols the same way. The guitar is a recognized symbol of country music. George Strait, known as the "King of Country," always holds a guitar when he is singing in public. The fact that he does not play the guitar is irrelevant. He simply holds the guitar since it is the undisputed symbol of country western music. For another example, the thumb-and-forefinger-in-a-circle gesture to and from one underwater American diver to another means "I'm Okay." Michelle Obama's fist bump to her husband when he won the Democratic nomination is another example.

Symbols are a part of a social actor's and group's cultural heritage. Objects may be symbols that represent material aspects of culture. In this context a symbol may stand for a particular social organization. The flag of the United States (society), the wedding ring of spouses (family), and the lapel button of a rotary club member (association) are examples of symbols. Spouses (family type of social organization) develop their own symbols in terms of words they use to address each other: "honey," "sweetie," and "sugar bunny." Symbols vary cross-culturally. Lingering handshakes, handholding, embraces, and sometimes kisses between heterosexual men is normative in much of the Muslim world. But these behaviors create discomfort among American heterosexual men.

The advertising industry knows the value of symbols. The fattened checkmark is the symbol of Nike. This symbol can be seen on hats (Tiger Woods), football jerseys, and windbreakers and reminds the viewer of the presence and status of Nike Corporation.

Values

Values are guidelines for behavior that people believe to be right or wrong. These guidelines are general, and they do not tell us exactly what behavior is correct in a specific situation. We will soon see that norms proscribe specific behaviors for a given situation. Values, however, do guide the development of norms and laws and are essential elements in all cultures.

Each social context has a value system which guides the behaviors of those involved. A lynching mob (collective behavior) feels it is right to lynch a person, the Mormon couple (family) believes it is right to have large families, and members of Jehovah's Witness (association) believe it is right to knock on the doors of people and offer copies of their *Watchtower* magazine.

Societies also have values. Freedom of expression, having children, and two weeks vacation in the summer are traditional American values. Values not only differ between societies but differ within a society. For example, lower class Americans are less likely to value higher education than upper class Americans.

Values also change. In 1967, 83 percent of college freshmen in a national survey reported that "developing a meaningful philosophy of life" was an important life goal. In 2006, only 46 percent reported having this goal (UCLA. Council on Education Survey, 1988; 2006).

Norms

Norms are expectations of behavior which identify how social actors are to behave in a specific context. We expect teachers to teach and protect our children, not have sex with them. We expect the military to use humane interrogation practices, not water boarding. Each type of social organization develops its own system of norms or set of expectations. Different social classes expect different types of behavior. Individuals from the upper class do not shop at the Salvation Army and those from the lower class do not buy their clothes at Neiman Marcus. Different families have different norms. In some families, all the members are expected to be present at the dinner table. In other families, each member eats whenever he or she wants. Different associations also expect different behaviors. In religious associations, the worship service in a Pentecostal Holiness church involves speaking out from one's seat ("amen," "blessed Jesus"), waving one's hands, and clapping to the music of a band complete with guitars, drums, and trombones. In contrast, the worship service of an Episcopalian church is more subdued so that members of the congregation are expected to sit quietly unless singing from a hymnal.

Norms, values, and symbols are part of each of the nine types of social organization. When individuals learn the norms, values, and symbols of the social organizations of which they are a part, they are learning the culture of that organization. The child who brushes her or his teeth before bedtime (norm), says prayers before getting into bed, and has photographs of family vacations on the bedroom wall is learning the culture of her or his family.

Folkways, mores and laws are types of cultural norms. **Folkways** refer to "ways of the folk" or social customs (Summer, 1906). An individual who fails to use a Kleenex, but instead uses his or her shirt sleeve, has violated a folkway. When failure to obey the norm creates anger and outrage, that norm is called a more. **Mores** are highly valued moral norms, the violation of which our society does not tolerate. An individual who sexually abuses a child has violated a moral norm. Because child sexual abuse creates sufficient outrage and concern, such action is usually prohibited by law. **Laws** are formal enforceable negative sanctions for breaking valued norms. Driving while drunk is against the law since the social norm is to drive only when sober. There is also a law against cheating on one's income taxes since the social norm is to pay one's share of taxes. The difference between a more and a law is that the former reflects a serious moral issue (e.g. child sexual abuse).

Sanctions

In order for an organization to have consistency and predictability, norms must be followed. One way society encourages its members to engage in normative behavior is through the use of **sanctions**. These are positive and negative consequences for good and bad behavior. An example of a positive sanction is a promotion by one's employer for good work; getting fired for not coming to work on time is an example of a negative sanction. Folkways and mores are both norms, but they have different sanctions applied when they are violated.

Mild sanctions are used for folkways. Talking in a movie theater is the violation of a folkway and results in others turning around with disapproving glances. Similarly, blowing one's nose and making a loud horn sound may result in glances from others. However, the violation of a folkway is relatively insignificant.

Each type of social organization involves mild sanctions against folkways. Spitting out of one's car window is a violation of a community folkway. In associations such as the Shriners, cutting off one's tassel would be violating a folkway. In an academic study group, not bringing one's notes to the study session would be violating a folkway. Not shaking hands when someone offers their hand would violate a folkway. People are often unaware of how any particular folkway in their culture originated, and social actors learn to obey them without much conscious consideration of why.

Strong sanctions are leveled against the violation of mores. Cheating on exams and shoplifting are behaviors our society does more than glance at. Students are dropped from classes and shoplifters are prosecuted. Even stronger sanctions are leveled against mores such as trying to carry a concealed weapon on an airplane, screaming fire in a crowded theater, and driving while intoxicated. Former governor of New York, Eliot Spitzer, was negatively sanctioned in 2008 by removal from office when it was discovered that he had been a client of a prostitution ring.

Strong sanctions may also be levied against corporations who violate mores. Health Net is an insurance company in California who canceled the health policy of Patsey Bates who had breast cancer and was in the middle of chemotherapy treatment. She sued and Health Net was required to pay Ms. Bates $9 million in 2008 in punitive damages. Attorneys noted that other health insurance companies would be on notice not to cancel the policies of their policy holders who become sick (Girion, 2008).

Some mores are enacted into laws in that they have legal status to regulate human conduct (e.g. taking a gun on an airplane). Not all mores are enacted into specific laws, but some enforcement of those norms which are considered to be based on important social values can be expected. As the values change, the enforcement may change. The law against driving while intoxicated says that you will have your license taken away if you drink and drive. As this value has become more important, the action of drinking and driving has moved from a folkway to a more.

Some mores are also taboos. A **taboo** is a strong social norm prohibiting certain behaviors. Acts that are taboo violate our sense of dignity and propriety. For example, incest, which is taboo in our society, jolts our sensibilities such that we abhor the act. Not only is there an extreme social aversion to incest, there are laws which reflect how seriously we regard incest.

In short, social sanctions are used to regulate and control human behavior to give predictability to cultural life. All types of social organization have sanctions to regulate the behavior of their members. Industrial societies have stop lights to regulate the orderly flow of traffic. Families develop sanctions to ensure compliance. A high school freshman who makes D's the first semester may be told that he or she is "grounded" until his or her grades improve. The various aspects of culture which we have just discussed are summarized in Table 2.1.

Table 2.1
Cultural Aspects of Social Organizations

		Examples of Organizations	
		Collective:	Community:
Cultural Aspects	Family	Terrorists	Commune*
Artifact	House	Guns	Land
Symbol	Crest	Terrorist flag	Walden II
Value	Fidelity	Political	Behaviorism Independence
Norm	Children obey parents	Silence if caught	Work for credit
Sanction	Children can't watch TV	Execution	Disapproval

*Commune example is Twin Oaks Commune in Louisa, Virginia.

Cultural Constraints

The material and nonmaterial aspects of a culture noted in the above section are passed from generation to generation through the use of language.

Language

Language is central to the existence and transmission of culture. A culture cannot exist if there is no language because there would be no way to identify and label different parts of the culture. If you live in a world that has no word for "outer space," it would be impossible to consider developing a rocket to travel there since the need for a rocket exists only if there is the concept for "outer space."

Each time we develop a new idea (portable media player, gas saving car) we develop terminology (iPod, Hybrid) to talk about it. Otherwise, we have no way of transmitting information about this idea to each other. Each type of social organization has its own language. Partners in a courtship dyad (the smallest group) use words specific to each other such as calling each other "honey," "teddy bear," and "sweetie." The meanings Christians and Jews (representing different populations) assign to the word "cross" and "star" also vary.

In the society of the Trobrianders, women rear children who belong to their mother and her brother. When Christians tried to make the Trobrianders aware of Christ, they were not able to make much progress. Since Christ was described as the "Son of God" the concept of a child belonging to a father or a significant male was unheard of. Among the Trobriand Islanders, the child is born into the mother's clan, and the role of the natural father is viewed as very limited in both the creation of the child and future involvement.

Also among the Trobrianders, it is believed that the mother is impregnated by one of her deceased female relatives. Females are significant authority figures along with the maternal uncle. The father is not required for discipline or survival since he takes care of only his sisters. The wife's brother takes care of her. As such, Trobrianders could not imagine Christ or God as male figures, as males were not figures of importance (Malinowski, 1961).

Edward Sapir and Benjamin Lee Whorf developed the **Sapir-Whorf hypothesis** (Whorf, 1941) which argues that what a person experiences depends on the language used in the groups in which the individual lives. Language forces certain ways of thinking about reality. For example, the Eskimo have 20 different words for snow, but no general word for snow. When they see snow, they see it in terms of its graininess, compactness, and wetness whereas those not socialized in their culture just see "white stuff." Hence, the culture we experience is relative to the language used in the various social organizations of which we are a part. This is important because it suggests that there really is not just a world out there waiting to be named, but that *the name creates the world that is out there*. Learning a language structures the way you see the world. The language of any given culture then acts as a constraint to the members of that culture. The Eskimo can't see the world except through their language, and that means that the world they see has many different types of snow.

Culture is transmitted both verbally and nonverbally. **Verbal culture** refers to the words which are attached to objects or concepts and may be concrete/specific such as "tree" or vague/abstract such as "born-again." While the impact of verbal culture is dramatic, language may also be nonverbal. Giving someone the "finger," or "frowning" or moving toward someone aggressively are examples of **nonverbal culture**—ways of communicating without the use of words. "Leaning in" towards a person with whom you are speaking implies agreement just as moving away implies disagreement.

Biology

Culture is a powerful influence that shapes how we think and what we do. Nevertheless, the question is often raised in science as to how much of what we are comes from the culture of the social organization and how much comes from other factors. **Sociobiology** is a discipline which explains social behavior as having biological causes. In reference to language among humans, sociobiologists focus on the biological capability of humans (intelligence, presence of vocal cords, and presence of a tongue to manipulate sound) and the importance of language for the survival of the organism. To the degree that humans had vocal cords and learned to communicate with each other they were able to transmit cultural knowledge, decrease the chance of making dangerous mistakes (e.g. picking up rattlesnakes), and build a social community together. This ability, however, depended on biological capacity.

With the publication of *Sociobiology* by Edward O. Wilson (1975), the issue of how much culture might be a reflection of heredity was explored again by sociology. Sociobiology is a school of thought that attempts to derive specifics of culture and social organization out of genetics and evolutionary mechanisms. Most sociologists agree that genetics produces potentialities, but feel that social and cultural forces determine the extent to which these potentialities are reached.

Environment

The various aspects of any given culture are influenced by environmental parameters. **Ecosystem** refers to the environment inhabited by a group of people. This environment dictates the limits of what the group will create. What individuals think, do, and make is influenced by the environment in which they live. The Eskimo does not develop a jet airplane because doing so is not logical within the limits of their ecosystem. In order to build a jet, they would need steel, electronics, and a technologically sophisticated work force. In addition, the Eskimo has no need for jet airplanes. They travel short distances on sleds pulled by dogs. The term "jet plane" is not likely to become part of the active word pool of Eskimo life because the ecosystem and values of the Eskimo are inconsistent with such a term.

These cultural differences create different social organizations worldwide. To understand the variety of differences both within and between organizations, it is best to consider the wide range of cultural diversity in more detail.

Cultural Diversity

Cultural diversity is evident when we look at subcultures, countercultures, and cross-cultures. These commonly used terms in sociology are used to make clearer distinctions among social organizations.

Subcultures

Subcultures are smaller parts of a larger culture which share many characteristics of the dominant culture. Subcultures have their own language, values, and customs. If we think of a family as a culture, the husband and wife dyad develops their own subculture. They talk about different subjects around the children, have different values than those they display in front of the children, and do things in their adult world that their children do not know about. Similarly, the children become adolescents and develop their own subculture apart from the larger family unit. They have their own language ("awesome"), values ("oral sex isn't really sex"), and customs (tattoos and piercings).

There are many varieties of subcultures including racial, religious, and economic. Blacks, whites, Asian Americans, and Mexican Americans represent different subcultures. Jews, Mormons, and Baptists also represent different subcultures. Similarly, upper class people live in a different subculture than lower class people. The North and South represent different subcultures of the dominant United States culture. Most Northerners do not say "y'all" nor do they regularly eat collards, sweet potato pie, and grits. Yet both Northerners and Southerners share many other aspects of culture that exist in the United States. The homeless represent a subculture where a history of alcohol/drug abuse, poverty, and mental illness are more common (Toro, 2007).

Playing video games reflects another subculture—the gaming subculture. And these cultures may vary by gender. Jenkins (1998) detailed "boy culture" and "girl culture" in video games. He noted a theme of action and adventure for boys in all spheres and a theme of domestication, secrets and romance for girls. Specifically, video games for males are replete with challenges of mastery, levels to achieve, and defeating the enemy. For females, the focus of games is less action packed and more about discovery and relating.

Countercultures

Subcultures do not challenge the basic ideas, values, and norms of the larger culture. Asian Americans, Northerners and the homeless are a part of the larger American culture. **Countercultures** are opposed to the larger culture and develop new ways of thinking and behaving. Countercultures are types of subcultures: those that challenge the fundamental norms, values and beliefs of the dominant culture. The Shakers were an 18th century religious counterculture who believed in segregating women and men and in not allowing couples to have children. Their goal was to set up a heaven on earth and to live in spiritual harmony with each other.

The Twin Oaks commune in Louisa, Virginia, has been in existence for almost 30 years. Developed on the basis of B. F. Skinner's book, *Walden II*, the members of Twin Oaks do not have private ownership of material goods (no one can own a car or a TV), they share what they have, and work for the common good.

The distinction between a subculture and a counterculture is sometimes difficult to make. The Amish support capitalism, monogamy, and Christianity, which are also valued in the dominant culture. The Amish, therefore, are sometimes viewed as a subculture. However, they also reject the dominant culture in that they own no automobiles and desire their children to be educated at home to keep them safe from the corrupt ideas of America. As such, some scholars see them as a counterculture.

An example of a group that is clearly a counterculture is the Westboro Baptist Church of Topeka, Kansas. While the 70 member group is not affiliated with any Baptist convention or association and no Baptist institution recognizes the church as a Bible believing fellowship, the church has symbols (their church) and values (God is punishing America because of its tolerance and acceptance of the homosexual agenda.). The church picketed the funeral of Lance Cpl. Matthew A. Snyder with their posters that he died in a war God intended as a message for America's sinfulness. The father of Matt Snyder sued the founder (Fred Phelps) and the WBC (Westboro Baptist Church) for invasion of privacy/intentional infliction of emotional distress and won more than an $11 million judgment against the church. While the larger culture usually tolerates diversity, the WBC was judged to have crossed the line.

Cross-Cultures

Cross-cultures are comparisons of the dominant culture of our society and those of other societies. Studying life in other cultures (cross-cultural research) provides an opportunity to observe the diversity of cultures in our world. Chinese people generally do not drink milk. Hopi Indians do not have a word that means "future."

An American boards a Continental jet for Europe. Upon arrival, the American will be confronted with a different culture. Some of the cultural differences between America and Europe include the following:

1. In America, a female going topless at the beach is unacceptable. In France, it is normative.

2. In America, public bathrooms are separate for men and women. In parts of Europe, there is no separation of the sexes in terms of bathroom use, although men and women use different separated stalls in the same bathroom.

3. In America, it is unacceptable for men to display any affection other than a brief hug. In parts of Europe, men embrace, kiss each other on the cheek, and hold hands as a matter of course. These behaviors are not associated with being labeled as a homosexual.

Many aspects of our daily lives are determined by the culture in which we live. In the previous examples, whether a female goes topless at the beach, finds a toilet, and whether men express affection depends on the culture in which the person lives. Examples of subcultures, countercultures, and cross-cultures are shown in Table 2.2.

Table 2.2
Examples of Cultural Diversity

Subcultures	Countercultures	Cross-Cultures
Homosexuals	Shakers	Bushmen
Video game players	Amish	Aztecs
The Elderly	Twin Oaks Commune	Hopi Indians
Feminists	Hare Krishnas	Chinese
Mormons	Westboro Baptist Church	Eskimo

Culture Shock

We assume that the way we think, feel, and behave is natural. However, our thoughts, feelings, and behaviors are a product of the culture in which we are reared. Because we assume that others have been reared similarly, we assume that they think, feel, and behave as we do. When we realize that others do not behave the same as us, we sometimes experience culture shock.

One of the effects of experiencing and/or studying other cultures is the discovery that people of different cultures live their lives very differently. People think and act in response to their different cultural learning. An American viewing Lenin's tomb in the former Soviet Union might naturally put his or her hands in his/her coat pockets to protect them from the cold. Soviets regard putting one's hands in one's pockets at a national shrine as utterly disrespectful. Soviet guards attending the tomb will ask a viewer to pull his/her hands out of his or her pockets.

Culture shock exists when one person is shocked by the way something is done in a culture different from his/her own. When Vladimir Putin, President of the Russian Federation, greets a fellow comrade, they kiss each other on the cheek. Americans stand several feet apart when talking while Arabs stand almost nose to nose. Americans shake hands when they greet each other; Saudis never do. When the Spanish conquistadors arrived, they found the culture of the Aztecs and Mayans to be so barbaric that murdering them was considered righteous.

Ethnocentrism

Ethnocentrism is the tendency to evaluate other cultures in terms of one's own. We believe that the way we do things is better than the way others do things. If we eat cows we feel that it is okay for everyone else to do so; we do not understand why some cultures do not eat beef (e.g. India). Similarly, if people in other cultures eat monkeys, as do the Jivaro Indians of Ecuador, we are convinced that something is wrong with them.

An ethnocentric perspective also blinds us to how others experience life. It is difficult for us to appreciate the value of someone's thoughts and behaviors unless we are a part of that person's culture and engage in those same behaviors.

Ethnocentrism also influences the level of discomfort individuals feel in interacting with others different from themselves. Mexican Americans, Asian Americans, blacks and whites often view their differences in ways which suggest that their own way of doing something is better than the way others do something. The result is an artificial social barrier which inhibits groups from comfortable interaction with each other.

Cultural Relativism

Cultural relativism is the perspective that what a person thinks, feels, values, and does can only be understood in the context of that person's culture.

It is important to remove yourself from your own cultural bias, get in the shoes of a person in another culture, and view the world from that person's perspective. Cultural relativism emphasizes that nothing is absolute and that everything is relative to the culture in which you have been reared. What you eat or do not eat or think or believe or feel is a direct result of your having learned those preferences. In Korea, dogs and snakes are acceptable foods. In order to feel that these foods are appropriate, it is important to be culturally accepting to the point of adopting the perspective of the Koreans. Then, seeing dogs on a menu results in a comfortable rather than a nauseous feeling.

Jews and Muslims do not eat pigs. The admonition against eating pigs developed as a response to the importance of ensuring that the pigs did not become domesticated animals such as goats and sheep. To raise pigs would be to encourage a food competitor—pigs eat nuts, fruits, tubers, and grains. In addition, the pig provided no milk, cheese, hides, dung, or traction for plowing. In effect, pork was a luxury meat that the early pastoralists could not afford to keep in their diet.

Cultural Change

There are many aspects of modern American culture that are similar to the cultures of the ancient Hebrews, Romans, Greeks, or early Christians. For example, among the early Romans, adults who lived together for a year could declare themselves married and would be so in the eyes of the community. Today, in 13 states we still have common law marriages whereby a couple who live together and hold themselves out to the community as married, are married. While this is an example of old cultural patterns continuing in new times and places, there are times when old culture ends and new culture begins. These changes are due to structural changes, inventions, discoveries, and diffusion.

Structural Changes

As was pointed out in Chapter One, all social organizations have a social structure. As the structure changes there are changes in the culture. As examples, a population shift toward the more elderly will change the culture of the society. A family may begin with an intact husband and wife, but (due to divorce or death) it may become a single parent household. A community may be built around automotive production (e.g. Detroit) and then lose that industry. A society may begin the century with predictions that horse manure will be a major problem for cities to deal with and then experience the development of the automobile to eliminate the need for horses. All of these **structural changes** would produce different ways of thinking and acting within social organizations. In effect the culture of the population, family, community, and society would change.

Inventions

Culture also changes as new inventions arise. **Inventions** are new creations that are put together from pre-existing and known ideas. Inventions are usually created because of some existing need. For example, the grocery cart was developed because the inventor was tired of carrying purchases around the store. In the past 100 years we have experienced several dramatic inventions— electricity, cars, jets, iPods, spacecrafts, and laser surgery. All of these inventions are new creations of ideas and technologies that already existed.

Other examples of inventions include new concepts, machines, and toys. Some societies have developed the concepts of mediation and arbitration as ways of settling disputes. New machines are developed to get oil and gas out of the ground, to transmit sound and pictures (television) across thousands of miles, and to produce lifelike images on high definition Blue Ray discs. Toys include robots that serve breakfast, remote control cars that race each other, and holograms that produce lifelike images.

Discoveries

Sometimes culture changes because a previously unknown or undiscovered phenomenon is found. Each new exploration of space seems to discover new moons, galaxies, and planets which were previously unknown. At one time, Europeans had no knowledge of North America, and radical change occurred when it was discovered. The first person who discovered fire, the atom, the existence of germs, and gold made **discoveries** which would also change the culture of various social organizations.

Diffusion

Cultures also borrow from each other. The video recorder was originally developed by Sony in Japan. Other cultures, including Korea and the U.S., have imported this Japanese invention and developed their own variation. The VCR and video tapes have now been replaced by DVD technology which now must compete with Blue Ray or face extinction. The Wright brothers invented the airplane which has been borrowed by other cultures. Similarly, French wines have become a part of American cuisine. With the vast array of worldwide communication technology, diffusion occurs quickly. The fax machine is an example of a relatively recent invention that has become diffused throughout the world.

Culture and Social Organization

All social organizations include a cultural element. In this section we discuss the cultural element and how it affects members in each of the nine types of social organization.

Populations

We earlier described a population as being identified on the basis of one or more common characteristics (e.g. age, race). A population may also be identified on the basis of its unique culture such as its artifacts, dress, speech, beliefs, and food. The artifacts of the elderly include bed pans, hearing aids, and walkers. The dressing attire of the Amish is distinctive: the black coats without collars for men and the solid color long skirts and aprons for women (topped off by the black bonnet).

Word usage is a cultural element that varies among different populations. Sociologists emphasize that cultural characteristics are valued to the degree that they are or are not mainstream. White Anglo-Saxon Protestant English is valued more in America than black English. Blacks may value their own cultural heritage and language. However, black word usage (e.g. "she don't" rather than "she doesn't") is viewed as incorrect by the larger dominant culture.

Norms for populations may also be distinctive. Norms for the elderly involve regular visits to the doctor, talking with peers about grandchildren, and helping offspring with financial needs. Sanctions are sometimes economic. Children may be cut off financially if they do not invest some amount of time with their elderly parents.

Collective Behavior/Social Movements

An example of collective behavior culture includes Mardi Gras as celebrated in New Orleans. People dress in unusual costumes, beads are thrown to young women who flash their breasts, and elaborate floats are pulled down the center of the street. Another example of collective behavior culture is the crowd at a Saturday afternoon college football game. Students wear colors reflective of their school, sing the Alma Mater, wave spirit sticks, and participate in the "wave" when led by their cheerleaders.

Collective phenomena are cultural in nature. When first released, Xbox 360 electronic equipment to play video games resulted in hordes of people lining up for hours to be the first to buy the equipment. Video gamers gathered in each others' dorm rooms to show their skill in reaching the next level. A gaming culture has developed with its own norms, values, symbols, and styles. Indeed, playing video games is enormously popular among youth, both in the United States and the United Kingdom. Upwards of ten billion dollars is spent annually in the US (over two billion in the UK). In the UK, more is spent on gaming videos than on movie tickets (Martens and Jansz, 2005).

Social Classes

The upper, middle, and lower social classes develop distinct cultural patterns regarding language, dress, manners, customs, and material goods. Upper class people say, "I beg your pardon?" whereas lower class people say, "Huh?" Upper class people wear personally tailored clothes; lower class people sometimes get their clothes at the Salvation Army or thrift stores. Upper class people sit at a dinner table and are served food by servants while lower class people may sit on the floor and pass a bowl around. Upper class people buy a Lexus RX Hybrid; lower class people walk or ride the bus. The cultural differences between social classes are large and range from the deportment at religious services to differences between opera and pro-wrestling.

The members of each social class transmit the culture of their class to the next generation. Upper class children are channeled into boarding schools and prestigious colleges and are told that they are the best. Lower class children may learn that college is only for the wealthy and may be taught not to consider the possibility for themselves.

Groups

There are numerous types of groups in America—yoga groups, motorcycle clubs (Hell's Angels), and scuba diving clubs. An engaged couple is also a group which develops a unique culture of symbols, values, norms, and sanctions. Assuming that the engaged partners do not live together, their respective rooms will have symbols of the relationship—photographs of the beloved or of the couple, ticket stubs from a concert they attended, or an empty bottle of wine they shared one evening. These private symbols of the relationship are in addition to any public symbols such as an engagement ring or a newspaper announcement of the engagement.

The engaged couple will also have developed an agreement on certain values which allows for their relationship to continue. Such values may pertain to exclusivity, money, and in-law relationships. Most engaged couples have an implicit understanding that they will date only each other and that other love relationships are not being pursued or nurtured. The couple will also have an implicit agreement about who pays for what when they are together. The nature of the agreement is less important than the fact that there is an understanding about what the agreement is. Values in regard to the future in-laws also develop during engagement and usually result in the value that each partner will attempt to get along with the other set of parents.

Notice that the cultural values of an engaged couple are often unspoken, yet their relationship will not continue unless each acknowledges and agrees to their unique culture. If either partner dates someone else, or asks the other to pay for everything, or refuses to meet the other's parents, the differences in cultural understandings become evident and the couple's relationship is at risk.

In addition to symbols and values, couples also develop norms and sanctions. Courtship norms include the amount of time the couple spends together, their tolerance for each other spending time away from each other, and their sexual expectations. The norm for some couples is to spend most of their time together. For other couples, particularly those in long distance relationships, it may be normative that they be together only a few times each year. In this case, other norms will develop in regard to how often they will email, text message, or phone each other.

Norms also develop about how much time may be spent pursuing other interests. Some partners become very jealous of their partner spending time with friends, parents, work, sporting events or other hobbies. Other partners want the freedom for themselves and are glad the other person has other interests.

Sexual norms also develop for each engaged couple. How often the couple has sex, what kind of sex they have and who initiates the sex become mutually understood norms by the couple. While some couples discuss the sexual norms of their relationship, others drift into a set of behaviors and identify the norms (to themselves) in retrospect if there is an infraction.

To help protect their relationship from terminating, couples develop sanctions to punish negative behavior (departing from the cultural norms of the relationship) in each other. A partner who is openly hostile to the other partner's parents is asked "Why were you mean to my parents?" Unless there is an acceptable answer, the partner's behavior may be punished by criticism or withdrawal. Similarly, norms will develop about how late a partner can be, how much alcohol a partner can drink, and what level of contact with former lovers (usually none) is appropriate.

The central point is that an engaged couple, like all groups, develops values, norms, and sanctions that comprise their unique subculture. These factors guide their relationship so that the behaviors of each partner become predictable. One of the reasons that terminating an engagement (or any significant relationship) is so difficult is that the mutually understood culture becomes shattered since the other person no longer is there to share the familiar culture the couple created. The search for a new partner involves giving up the meaning and comfort attached to the old culture and becoming involved in creating a new culture with a new person.

Families

Families express their own cultural patterns which vary by society. The war in Iraq has resulted in increased awareness of the Muslim world. Indeed, Muslim families reflect a unique cultural pattern. When these families come to America, they bring these patterns with them (Dar, 2007). For example, courtship is tightly controlled in that intimate mixing of the sexes is against Islamic teaching. Mixed-sex gatherings of children, teens, and young adults do not occur unless in the presence of adults. At such gatherings there is "separate seating" next to one's same sex peers. "Dating" in the sense of being alone with a partner to explore romance and sex is prohibited and contrary to the Muslim idea since marriage is viewed as between two families (not two individuals).

Ethnocentrism also develops among families. The way "we" conduct "our" family life seems right and better than the way "they" conduct "their" family life. Some adults take their children to 'R' rated movies on the premise that they want to expose their children to the real world. Other adults would never consider taking their children to such movies and think parents who do so are being morally irresponsible. Ethnocentrism is operating in both families.

Associations

Due to the media attention given the war in Iraq, we are constantly reminded of the military, an association which has a unique culture of symbols, values, norms, and sanctions. Symbols include the uniforms worn by the soldiers (members of the association), flags denoting particular companies or battalions, and stripes/insignia on a soldier's uniform indicating rank. The values promoted and required in the military include discipline, obedience to authority, and courage. Regarding the latter, General Patton slapped a soldier during World War II because the soldier was viewed as feigning sickness to escape the fray of battle. In this instance, it turned out that generals slapping soldiers was a controversial reflection of the value.

Norms (and associated values) of the military include regimentation, racial equality, and the communication of messages through a chain of command. New recruits in boot camp rise at 5:00 a.m. and are processed through a regimented day of exercise, food, training, weapon cleaning, and inspection. Racial equality implies that blacks and whites are treated equally. (Although the norm of racial equality is no longer unique, the military was one of the first to integrate blacks and whites.) Finally, each soldier in a particular rank is obligated to get his or her orders from the rank above (the president has the highest rank as Commander-in-Chief and gives orders to the rank below which gives orders to the rank below etc.).

Because the military must be able to predict and control the behavior of the individuals in the organization, there are strong sanctions to ensure obedience. Depending on the offense, disobedient soldiers are given demerits, court-marshaled, and/or imprisoned. If they disobey an order during combat, they may be shot. Recruits who leave the base without permission are labeled as "AWOL" (Absent Without Official Leave) and may be restricted to the base indefinitely for such violations.

Military culture is transmitted systematically. New recruits are given a basic orientation lecture, a manual, and told what they are to do next (e.g. rise at 5:00 a.m.). The ensuing indoctrination is so thorough that the well-socialized recruit does not question the values of the association and behaves almost without thinking.

The college or university you attend is another example of an association with a unique culture of symbols, values, norms, and sanctions. When the president of your college or university gives a presentation, she or he does so from a podium which displays the emblem (symbol) of your academic institution. The stationery sent from the president's office also has the emblem embedded in the paper. The robes and tassels displayed by the faculty during graduation exercises reflect the respective universities from which they earned their degrees.

All colleges and universities have values in reference to academic excellence, fairness to students, and service to the community. The faculty is expected to promote academic excellence in their students, punish plagiarism and cheating, and give free talks in the community in their area of expertise.

Norms guide the behavior of faculty, students, and staff. The faculty is expected to lecture on relevant content, give tests, and assign grades. Students are expected to attend class, prepare for tests, and accept the grade they earn. Staff such as secretaries and janitors are responsible for typing tests and keeping the classrooms clean, respectively.

Breaking norms results in negative sanctions. Faculty who do not teach classes are dismissed, students who do not take tests are failed, and secretaries who do not prepare documents on time are replaced. Such sanctions make it clear to faculty, students, and staff that they are expected to behave in ways consistent with the goals and values (culture) of the organization.

Students graduating from an academic institution are expected to remember the uniqueness of their school culture and transmit it to others. Alumni clubs are formed to keep the cultural memories of graduating students alive and to raise money from those committed to the culture.

It is important to note that the values and norms of an association are sometimes in conflict. Faculty are told (structure) that it is important that they be a good teacher but they learn that regularly publishing research in peer-reviewed journals is more important in order to be granted tenure (a permanent position on the faculty). Students are expected to learn academic content, but a high grade point average will increase their chance of getting into graduate school.

Communities

Communities also have unique cultures. Mayberry, North Carolina, is the name of a fictional community featured on *The Andy Griffith Show*, a television situation comedy. From Floyd's barber shop to Sheriff Andy Taylor's police station to Andy's house, these physical structures were cultural symbols of a life of order and tranquility. Mayberry was also a law-abiding town (values). Other values evident in the town were family values, positive relationships between members of the community, and no drugs.

Norms of the Mayberry community included helping each other in a time of crisis, sticking together when threatened by an outsider, and being protective of each other's privacy. Community sanctions were applied by the townspeople and the sheriff. If Floyd raised his price too high for a haircut, the townspeople would boycott his store. If a person drove too fast through Mayberry, Barney Fife would issue a citation. Andy Taylor would lock up Otis for public drunkenness.

The small town atmosphere of the Mayberry community differs from New York City and its over eight million inhabitants. Known as the "city that never sleeps," New York City represents a pluralistic community of diversity with a wide tolerance for differences. The values, norms, and sanctions of the city depend on which part of the city (the Lower East Side, Greenwich Village, Upper Manhattan) a person lives.

Networks

Networks link formal organizations. Towns like Mayberry and New York are linked by a communication system whereby officials in one community interact with another. When natural disasters strike (wildfires in California, hurricanes along the coast) governors ask for federal assistance. Culture is operative in that it is normative for smaller towns to seek and be awarded disaster relief.

The Republican and Democratic parties, both national organizations, are linked by a network of regional, state, and local organizations. In order to be chosen as the presidential candidate for one of the parties, the networks must mobilize the individuals at each level to encourage others to vote for their candidate. Such a network has a culture which includes symbols (the emblem of the party), values (getting their person elected), norms (making phone calls, handing out brochures) and sanctions (stuffing the ballot box is not tolerated).

Societies

Every society has its unique culture reflected in its symbols, values, norms, and social sanctions. In America, the flag is a symbol of freedom and liberty. The values include those of individualism and opportunity. The norms include driving on the right side of the road, celebrating Washington's and Martin Luther King, Jr.'s birthdays, and fireworks on the Fourth of July. Sanctions include fines for speeding and imprisonment for not paying taxes.

England has its own cultural symbols such as Big Ben, Buckingham Palace, and Parliament. The values are similar to those of America with a greater reverence for tradition and royalty. The driving norms include driving on the left side of the road. Sanctions are applied for speeding and tax evasion.

The French have their own cultural symbols: The Eiffel Tower, the value of a 35-hour work week, and liberal leave policies for parents of newborns. French police also walk about to sanction traffic violations.

Popular Beliefs and Scientific Data:
Love Is Immune to Social Control

Every society and culture recognizes love as an emotional experience. However, societies differ in terms of the value assigned to love and its timing in the relationship sequence. Americans value romantic love and feel that it should precede marriage. Parents in Pakistan feel that love should not dictate who marries whom as such pairings should be more about the uniting of two families than two individuals. Love should follow rather than precede marriage.

The American popular belief about love is that it operates without direction or sanctions. Many believe that love is a mysterious feeling that is incapable of being understood. It is also believed that love cannot be controlled since people can fall in love and reject all forms of social control in the name of love.

Social scientists who study love have a different view. Love is too powerful a human emotion (because of its potential to link families) not to be controlled and directed. Individuals are not free to fall in love with whomever they choose. Grace Kelly was a movie star of the 1950s who married (with her parents' approval) Prince Rainier of Monaco. Previously, she had been in love with and wanted to marry various men. But, as her biographer expressed it:

> Her life, as it differed from family strictures, was simply not her own ... no matter how many important magazines ran profiles of her. It was a depressing realization. Her choice of a marriage partner, she feared, could not be based upon her own needs and desires, but rather on what was best for the Kelly family, what advanced their position in the eyes of their neighbors and the world. As Cassini (a lover) put it, 'Her family regarded her as a prize possession, a property, like a racehorse that must be handled, above all invested, wisely—not wasted" (Spada, 1987, 105).

Most social organizations exercise some degree of control over the love relationships of their members. Families have rules of **endogamy** (individuals are expected to marry someone within their own racial, religious, ethnic, educational category). Data on marriages where one spouse is black and the other is white provides concrete evidence that love relationships are under enormous social control. Of the 60 million marriages in the United States, less than one percent represents a black-white union. (*Statistical Abstract of the United States: 2008*, Table 59). Another family rule is **exogamy** (individuals are expected to marry someone outside their own family). Woody Allen violated the exogamy rule when he married his stepdaughter.

Endogamous and exogamous rules help to insure that, in most cases, love develops only with certain individuals—someone of the same race/ethnic origin who is not one's sibling or parent. Very tight social control of love is still maintained in parts of India, China, and Japan where marriages are viewed as alliances between families rather than between individuals. The parents arrange the marriage for their offspring which rarely gives primary consideration to the feelings between the partners. Spouses and lovers also exercise social control over each other to ensure that their partners do not fall in love with someone else. Grave disapproval awaits the spouse or lover who falls in love with someone else.

In the U.S. only certain segments of the population are allowed to consider each other as love objects. For example, same sex love relationships continue to have limited approval. Only Massachusetts legalizes same sex marriages and only state benefits are available to same sex "spouses." Once the couple leaves the state, the legal status of their marriage disappears, and there are no federal benefits in terms of social security payments to a surviving partner.

Associations formed at work also exercise social control over who can fall in love with whom. Persons who work on cruise ships are not allowed to "date" or "see" tourists after hours on board. Corporations frown on romantic entanglements between their senior level married executives and the secretaries. Religious groups encourage their members to marry someone of the same faith. Catholics are encouraged to marry Catholics, Jews are encouraged to marry Jews, and Protestants are encouraged to marry Protestants.

Upper class parents ensure that their offspring select others within their social class to marry. By living in elite neighborhoods, sending their children to private schools, and Ivy League universities, their offspring can only meet "proper" mates. Thus, upper class offspring are not "free" to fall in love with and marry anyone they choose. Rather, contrary to popular belief, love is socially controlled by the various social organizations of which an individual is a part.

References

Dar, Saeed. 2007. "Muslim family values." Prepared for this section by Dr. Dar, a Muslim and Professor of Pharmacology and Toxicology, East Carolina University School of Medicine.

Girion, L. 2008. "Health Net Ordered to Pay $9 Million after Canceling Cancer Patient's Policy." *Los Angeles Times*. Feb 23.

Jenkins, H. 1998. "Complete freedom of movement: Video games as gendered play spaces." In Cassell, J. & H. Jenkins. (eds) (1998) *From Barbie to Mortal Kombat: Gender and Computer Games*. Cambridge, Mass: MIT Press, 262–297.

Malinowski, Bronislaw. 1961. *Sex and Repression in Savage Society*. New York: Meridian Books.

Martens, L. and J. Jansz. 2005. "Gaming at a LAN Event: The Social Context of Playing Video Games." *New Media & Society*, 7:333–355.

Spada, J. 1987. *Grace*. Garden City, New York: Doubleday.

Statistical Abstract of the United States: 2008. 127th ed. Washington, D.C.: U.S. Bureau of the Census.

Sumner, W.G. 1906. *Folkways.* Boston: Ginn.

Toro, Paul. A. 2007. "Toward an International Understanding of Homelessness." *Journal of Social Issues,* 63: 461–481.

UCLA-American Council on Education Survey. 1988. "The American Freshman: National Norms for Fall, 1987." Los Angeles, California.

UCLA-American Council on Education Survey. 2006. "The American Freshman National Norms for Fall, 2006." Los Angeles, California.

Whorf, Benjamin Lee. 1941. "The Regulation of Habitual Thought and Behavior to Language." In Leslie Spier (ed.), *Language, Culture, and Personality.* Menasha, Wis: Sapir Memorial Education Fund.

Wilson, E. 1975. *Sociobiology: The New Synthesis.* Cambridge: Harvard University Press.

Chapter 3

Socialization

Always remember that you are absolutely unique. Just like everyone else.
Margaret Mead, anthropologist

As a first semester student you were encouraged to attend various "orientation" sessions with the goal of teaching you the rules of the university. To the degree that you internalized these norms (paid your fees, organized your time, attended class, prepared for exams, etc.) and learned the positions, statuses, and roles of the social organization, you earned a grade point average that allowed you to stay in school. In effect, your socialization to function as a college student was successful.

In the last chapter we examined how culture represents the shared ways of thinking, doing, and making things in our society and in all other social organizations. Culture is the blueprint of life which defines how we are to act out our lives in each context we enter. **Socialization** reflects how culture is transmitted to new members. It is the process whereby social organizations teach their members to fit in and to function appropriately in the organization.

Although more important in some areas than others, each of the nine areas of sociology involves socialization. A baby in America and in China has not yet been socialized into the different cultures. The child will learn about the respective social organizations and how to appropriately fit into them. The family and groups along with some associations, like schools, churches, and sports organizations will have significant impacts on the child.

We will return later in this chapter to view the importance of each type of social organization as they relate to socialization. First, we look at how socialization involves sociology, biology, and psychology. By viewing socialization from the perspective of these three disciplines, we may better understand the complex process we call "socialization."

Socialization in Perspective

There are three important factors involved in the socialization of a human being: sociological, biological, and psychological factors.

Sociology

Sociologists view the socialization process in terms of how social interaction contributes to the development of human beings. Studies of "feral" children and children reared in institutions demonstrate the critical importance of social interaction.

Ferals are children who have presumably been reared with limited or no parental interaction. While the existence of feral children is still questioned by social scientists, Newton (2002) detailed nine such children, the most famous of which was Peter the Wild Boy found in the Germanic woods at the age of 12 and brought to London in 1726. He could not speak; growling and howling were his modes of expression. He lived until the age of 70 and never learned to talk. The focus of these case studies has been the impact of the absence of social behaviors on the part of feral children. They cannot talk, walk upright, eat, or toilet as do children socialized by humans.

Children reared in institutions where they experience only limited human contact and nurturing also do not fare well. Spitz (1945) compared children who were reared by mothers who spent a lot of time with them to children who were housed in institutions. The latter were taken care of by overworked nurses who had very little time to interact with each child. The result was a "failure to thrive" on the part of the institutionalized infants. Not only were they developmentally delayed (they did not learn to walk and talk when other children their age did), they had more health problems, and they were more likely to be depressed.

Such studies emphasize that social interaction is a critical aspect of socialization. Infants deprived of interaction with others do not develop properly. It is also important that such interaction occur early so that infants may bond with their parents. Child development specialists emphasize the importance of early parent-infant bonding by encouraging parents to delay a return to work after the child is born in order to provide sufficient time for the infant to experience a secure emotional/interactive context with parents.

Socialization: Eight Sociological Facts

In addition to emphasizing early interaction and emotional bonding, there are eight additional aspects of socialization that are considered important factors to sociologists.

1. **Socialization is Goal Directed**. The infant is not allowed to develop as he or she wants but is quickly socialized into what is socially acceptable. Early childhood socialization is directed toward teaching the child social norms, the social roles for self and others, how to be good at fulfilling these roles, and the appropriate skills for functioning in society. Children reared in the United States learn to eat Corn Flakes, not ants. They learn that they are in the role of a child who interacts with other roles such as parents and siblings. Children are also taught how to be a "good child," a "good student," and a "good team player." Not only do children learn roles, they learn that their self-concept depends on performing these roles well. Parents tell children they are proud of them for telling the truth, teachers give students stars for doing their schoolwork, and coaches tell players they have "good hustle" and are "good sports" when they perform well on the field.

Children are also taught the skills necessary to function in society. They must know how to use the language, how to toilet, how to dress, and how to interact with strangers. Later they must develop job skills such as being on time, taking orders, typing, and using a computer.

2. **Earliest Socialization is Most Influential**. The first socialization a child experiences, usually from his or her parents, is often the most influential and durable. If a child develops a negative self-concept from his or her parents by being told that he or she is "no good," these negative feelings may stay with the child for life. Similarly, the child who is reared to feel a certain way about music, or neatness, or politeness may carry these same values throughout life.

3. **Socialization Varies by Culture**. Thirumurthy (2004) observed parents and children from over 27 countries who participated in a university preschool program. She noted that parents in Western cultures socialized their children to be individualistic and autonomous which translated into being assertive. Hence, the defiant child is seen as a child who is expressing his or her will. In contrast, Asian and Hispanic parents socialize their children to collaborate and to cooperate. Being assertive may be seen as being disobedient.

4. **Socialization Content Changes**. As societies move from rural to urban and from primitive to modern, individuals must be socialized for new roles in their changing society. A person reared on a farm to be a farmer may discover that the role has become obsolete as small farms are taken over by big business. A person taught to use Word Perfect as a software word processing program may discover it is out of date and learn Word as the newer software. To avoid becoming obsolete, the individual must anticipate new positions in the society and begin a socialization process for those positions. We will discuss this later under anticipatory socialization.

5. **Socialization Has Both Manifest and Latent Content**. What is intended in socialization (manifest content) and what actually occurs (latent content) may

be very different. Parents may intend to teach their children the value of family life by staying married no matter what. This is the manifest or intended function. However, they may inadvertently be teaching their child to stay in an empty, emotionally and physically abusive relationship—that may even become life threatening. Staying in a dead marriage is a latent and unintended function of the socialization to stay in a marriage "till death do us part." Similarly, formal education may teach students to be obedient (manifest function) but may dull their creativity (latent function).

6. **Socialization Involves Numerous Social Contexts.** Although parents often take the credit—and the blame—for the way their children turn out, they are only one among many socialization agents. Although parents are the first significant influence in the life of a child, peer influence becomes increasingly important during adolescence. Pinquart and Silbereisen (2002) studied 76 dyads of mothers and their 11 to 16-year-old adolescents and observed a decrease in connectedness between the children and their mothers and a movement on the part of the adolescent toward their peers.

Siblings also have an important and sometimes lasting effect on each other's development. Siblings are social mirrors and models (depending on the age) for each other. They may also be sources of competition and can incite jealousy in each other.

Teachers are also a significant influence in the socialization of a child's values. Some parents send their children to religious schools to ensure that they will have teachers with conservative religious values. This may continue into the child's college and university education (e.g. Bob Jones University, Liberty University).

Media in the form of television, replete with MTV and "parental discretion advised" movies, are a major source of socialization for language, lifestyles, and values. Aubrey (2007) studied the exposure of undergraduate females to soap operas, prime time dramas, etc. and found that the amount of television viewing was negatively related to having a positive sexual self concept. In other words, the more soap operas a female viewed, the lower her sexual self concept. In effect, these media sources served to socialize the undergraduate female that she was inadequate in regard to the presumed cultural norm of beauty and femininity.

Media may also transmit values to children that differ from those of their parents. Parents concerned about the socialization effects of media often monitor the exposure of their children to television. Some parents do not own a television and do not allow one in their house. The authors know of such a couple. The only time their children watched television was when they visited in the home of a friend. Both children ended up with full scholarships to Princeton.

Another social influence for children is the Internet. Though parents may encourage their children to conduct research and write term papers using the Internet, they may fear the accessing of pornography and related sex sites. Parental supervision of teens on the Internet and the right of the teen for privacy remain potential conflict issues.

7. **Socialization Experiences Affect Each Social Organization**. Social organizations are mutually interdependent and affect each other. The school depends on the parents to teach the child how to toilet, businesses depend on schools to teach employees how to read, the government depends on the media to educate the public about current political issues and candidates so that voters can make informed choices at the voting booth.

8. **Effective Socialization is Effective Role Functioning**. If socialization is successful, the individual is capable of fulfilling his or her roles effectively. Otherwise, socialization has failed. Students who don't learn how to organize their time or who don't develop good study habits flunk out of school. Employees who don't show up on time are fired. Marriage partners who don't communicate and compromise get divorced. Friends who don't reciprocate or provide support end up getting dropped.

Biology

The interactive socialization children experience is preceded by the biological heritage that infants receive from their parents. While some children have parents who transmit the basis for a healthy life, others are born with AIDS, hemophilia, or the predisposition for obesity. These biological beginnings will influence the total socialization experience of the child. Indeed, the AIDS child has a threatened life span. The hemophiliac will automatically be encouraged to avoid playing sports (with the consequent loss of some peer socialization experiences) where an injury could trigger unwanted bleeding. The obese child may be shunned and made fun of by peers. Persons born deaf, blind, or without legs will have a different socialization experience than those who can hear, see, and walk.

The biological heritage of an infant begins long before the infant is born. Whether the mother eats a nutritious diet, smokes, drinks alcohol, or uses other drugs will influence the biological makeup of her infant and the socialization experiences to follow. Some infants begin life with an addiction to drugs (e.g. heroin) because of the mother's addiction during pregnancy. This addiction will influence how others must interact with the child (as a sick infant). Although it is common in our culture to blame the "mother," it is important to recognize that mothers exist in a social context and that it is the context (from a purely sociological point of view) that contributes greatly to whether the mother overeats, smokes, or uses drugs.

After the infant is born, adequate nutrition continues to be necessary for healthy development. Inadequate amounts of iron, zinc, and copper in the diet predispose the infant to anemia, skin rashes, and severe diarrhea. An enduring vitamin A deficiency can lead to total blindness. This latter biological effect on the infant would have a dramatic effect on the subsequent socialization experiences of the child.

Populations (e.g. racial) differ in the degree to which they are born healthy. Low birth weight (less than 5 pounds, 8 ounces) is the most accurate predictor for future health problems. The percentage of low birth weight black infants is 13.4 compared to 7.1 percent of white infants (*Statistical Abstract of the United States: 2008*, Table 85). Black infants die (within 28 days) at the rate of 14.6 per 1,000 live births compared to 7.4 per 1,000 live births for white infants (Table 108). Blacks also have a shorter life (72.9 years) compared to whites (78.2 years) (Table 102). Part of this decreased life expectancy may be related to biologically inherited vulnerabilities to heart disease and diabetes.

As noted, sociologists believe that most of the above differences are due to context effects, in this case social class. Children whose parents are among the lower socioeconomic groups may not receive a sufficient variety of foods to get the vitamins and minerals that they need. Their parents lack not only the resources to purchase the important foods but the knowledge that it is important to do so. The important point is that the socialization an infant receives is dependent on the body of the infant which is influenced by his or her parents' biological heritage, access to nutritional information, and access to economic resources (social class) to provide the most desirable diet. Socialization experiences for children who do not have healthy bodies are different from those who do.

Psychology

In the same way that biology determines outcomes such as hearing, seeing, the color of one's skin, eyes and hair, it may also affect such characteristics as motivation, perception and emotional states. Indeed, there may be a biological link to being timid, sociable or motivated. And it is these psychological predispositions which will affect the socialization of the child. For example, people vary by motivation. Some individuals tend to be rigid and impatient, while others are more flexible and relaxed. Some have the motivation to be president, while others prefer to lie in a hammock and drink beer.

Motivation influences perception and perception influences behavior. When you are driving on the interstate and become very hungry, you look for signs identifying the availability of food and take the next exit. Persons deprived of sex look for potential partners.

Quick perceptual skills are also a prerequisite to fill certain social roles. Quarterbacks must be able to perceive various people in their visual field at the same time, to make quick decisions, and to act. The presence or absence of this cognitive ability may influence whether or not the individual will be exposed to the socialization experiences of an athlete.

Individuals also vary in the degree to which they experience emotion. Some laugh easily while others cry easily; some are prone to develop phobias while others seem fearless; some love deeply while others are detached. Although aspects of these emotions are learned, other aspects are embedded in the unique personality of the individual. Parents of two or more children will testify to the tremendous differences between the personalities of their offspring who have the same genetic background.

People develop as individuals. Their cognitive and emotional style will prevent or enhance the degree to which they will fit into various social organizations. Some people have great difficulty adapting to the regimentation of military life while others find great comfort in doing so. Likewise, some people enjoy the emotional security of a monogamous relationship while others feel trapped by it. Some who join a corporation are able to move up the ranks while others resist the structure and end up being demoted or fired. Some individuals may have "addictive" personalities which make them vulnerable to alcohol, cocaine, and nicotine, while others do not.

The interaction between one's social influences, biological inheritance and psychological makeup is unclear. It may be impossible to separate out which factor is responsible for a child being sociable—his or her parents, genetic makeup or personality predisposition.

Whatever the influences on psychological development, it is clear that the social context shapes, creates and accepts or rejects individual characteristics. For example, some personality types are required in certain organizations. Funeral homes are associations in the business of death. A person who is serious and solemn will function quite well in the role of mortician. A person who laughs a great deal would be more suitable in a circus as a clown but not as mortician.

Structure and Socialization

As you recall from Chapter One, four aspects of social structure include position, status, role, and norm. We may think of structure as the framework within which all interaction takes place. Next we look at how the four aspects of social structure relate to the process of socialization.

Position

A **position** is a place in the social structure. People are assigned a position in all social organizations. In a bar, there are the positions of bartender and customer; at a football game there are the positions of player and spectator; at a lecture, there are the positions of lecturer and listener. Families have positions of father, mother, and child. Churches have positions of minister and parishioner. Schools have positions of teacher and student. Knowledge of positions is important because socialization is always in reference to occupying a position. Parents who say, "I want my child to grow up and be a doctor" know the position toward which they will direct their socialization efforts.

Status

Status is the rank order from high to low of a given position. Many sociologists use the terms status and position interchangeably, but the word status refers more directly to a ranking given to a position title. Physician, psychologist, and judge are higher status positions than maid, waiter, and janitor.

People in a position are usually aware of their status in reference to other positions. Employees are aware of their lower status with regard to their employer. Children are usually aware that they have a lower status than their parents. Individuals of high status are also knowledgeable of rank order differences. Couples who have been married over fifty years have more status than a divorced couple. Part of socialization involves teaching the child his or her status. A child who calls a teacher names is oblivious to the importance of status differentials and the attendant requisite behavior.

Role

Role specifies the behavior a person is to engage in for a given position and status. A judge is to wear a black robe and listen attentively to what attorneys, defendants, and plaintiffs say in court. It is not appropriate for a judge to wear a white suit, swear at defendants, or text message a fishing buddy during a court hearing. Children are quickly socialized into appropriate role behavior—brush you teeth before bed, say your prayers, and don't talk back.

Norm

Norms are role expectations. They are expectations of behavior of people in a certain role. While a role identifies the actions for the individual who occupies a particular position and status, norms are the expectations others have of one who occupies the role.

Although sociologists do not regard it a social science law, all positions, statuses, roles, and norms exist in complementary relationships. There is no husband without a wife, no mother without a child, no teacher without a student and no doctor without the complementary patient. In most societies, a husband ranks higher than his wife and believes his role is to be a provider.

The value accorded a role is in reference to who is evaluating the role and what yardstick is being used. A husband may make $150,000 a year, but his wife may regard him an inadequate provider if the husbands of her friends make $500,000 a year. On the other hand, a woman whose husband earns $16,000 may consider her husband a good provider if those of her friends make considerably less. Norms or expectations are critical to determine the success in organizations.

All social organizations require that individuals who enter their system be aware of the positions, statuses, roles, and norms of the organization and fit in appropriately. An eating establishment is an association whose function is to provide food for customers. In order for a child to learn how to eat in a restaurant, the child must be aware of positions (the child is a customer), of statuses (the child has lower status than the owner of the restaurant), of roles (to order/eat food) and norms (use spoon to consume soup rather than drink from the bowl). All norms are expectations that come from other positions. Parents socialize their children to fit into the organization by insuring that they know their position, status, role, and that they behave consistently with the norms. Children must be taught that talking loudly and getting up and running around the table is not normative in a restaurant.

Process and Socialization

Process refers to the manner in which socialization actually occurs. All members of all social organizations are taught how to function. For example, in our society, the infant is socialized how to be a child, the child is socialized how to be a teenager, the teenager a young adult, the young adult an employee and a spouse, and socialization continues until death.

Primary Socialization

Primary socialization is the first exposure an individual has in reference to functioning in a social organization. Parents provide a primary socialization experience for their children and expect them to learn their position, status, role, and norms within the family. The child is taught how to walk, talk, toilet, and interact with others. He or she is also taught the values of the family. Evangelical parents value "abstinence till marriage." Muslim parents do not drink alcohol and socialize their children to avoid it. Parents also believe in teaching their children to "just say no" to drugs.

Anticipatory Socialization

Anticipatory socialization focuses on future positions, statuses, roles, and norms. Parents anticipate what their four-year-old needs to know when he or she goes to kindergarten and attempt to socialize him or her to enter the social organization of the school. Knowing their position (student), status (lower than teacher), role (be obedient) and normative expectations from teachers (be polite, do what teacher says) will provide an effective anticipatory socialization experience for the child before he or she enters school.

Resocialization

Resocialization involves unlearning what one has previously learned and relearning new ways of thinking and behaving. Resocialization often occurs when people make a role transition or the move from one status to a new one. Young girls are taught to smile and be friendly to others. As they grow into early adolescence they are taught not to be too friendly and not to sit on the laps of strangers. Similarly, a child may be encouraged to play house and to anticipate the positions of wife/mother or husband/father. But the person may not get married and may never enter these positions or roles. Hence, he or she will occupy the position of a never married adult and must be resocialized to learn the norms of this role. Another example is the person who learns how to be a spouse but gets divorced. He or she must learn how to date as a divorced 35-year-old (which is different from when one was single at 19).

When Enron filed for bankruptcy, 21,000 workers lost their jobs, health, and medical benefits. These former employees went through a period of resocialization in their new work roles—finding a new job, adapting to a new employer, etc. Similarly, most people are socialized to navigate in the world on the assumption that they will have the use of their legs. Individuals who have motorcycle or car accidents and become paralyzed must be resocialized to move about and to care for themselves. Soldiers who return from Iraq with missing limbs undergo a period of resocialization. Some suffer post traumatic stress disorder (PTSD). The difficulty in their resocialization is manifested in higher rates of chemical abuse, chronic unemployment, and difficulty in maintaining close personal relationships (divorce).

Resocialization is the task of cults who seek new members for their organizations. The section on Popular Beliefs and Scientific Data at the end of the chapter demonstrates how resocialization may be achieved through a process of brainwashing.

The ray gun is a new weapon the Pentagon is unwilling to resocialize US troops to use. The gun is really an antenna which shoots out this very high-frequency radio beam that penetrates the skin to a depth of 1/64 of an inch, which is just deep enough to hit the nerves. The beam creates an instantaneous sensation of heat which makes anyone who is hit with it try to get out of the way as fast as possible.

Reverse Socialization

Sometimes changes occur so fast in a society that what an individual learns is no longer useful in the new technological society. Some parents who were born in the 1950s were socialized to type on a typewriter and to cook in an oven. Their children, products of the new technological society, teach them how to use word processing on computers/text message and how to cook using a microwave. **Reverse socialization** involves the younger generation teaching the older generation.

Corporations today must also learn how to adapt to the work ethic norms held by **millenials**, the 80 million workers born between 1980 and 1995 (Textor, 2007). Having been told that they are special, that performance is not required for praise, and that fun and lifestyle come before giving one's life to a job or career, these millenials are socializing their bosses to be more flexible or to find someone else to work for them. Indeed, corporations today are hiring consultants to socialize them how to cope with a work force that wants a job on their own terms. They are told that they must be not just a boss but a life coach and a shrink, and that they must motivate rather than demand. These millenials don't need the money as one half of college seniors will live with their parents after graduation.

Socialization and Social Organization

Socialization is an important concept in each of the nine areas of sociology. We now examine how the nine types of social organization relate to the concept of socialization.

Populations

Over four million babies (4.2 million by 2010) are added to the United States population annually. Each individual in the population may be differentiated on the basis of such variables as sex, race, relationship status (unmarried, married, divorced, and widowed), which in turn will be associated with different positions, statuses, norms, and roles. While there is no one socialization experience for all people, there are socialization experiences that are specific to each subpopulation. For example, females are socialized to be more affectionate and to be more expressive of their emotions than males. Not only may they hug longer and hold hands in the mall, they are free to cry without condemnation. Conversely, males are socialized to be very reserved in the display of their physical affection (particularly to same-sex individuals) and to keep their emotions under control. In addition, males are socialized to devote more time and attention to their career. Indeed, a national study on work habits revealed that men were much less likely than women to take vacation time offered by their job (Maume, 2006).

Blacks, Hispanics, and Asian Americans are socialized in the context of being a minority amid a white majority. Such socialization may have implications in reference to their self concept and hope for the future. Those who are never-married, married, and divorced will also be exposed to a different socialization experience. Each of these population segments will spend most of their time with others in the respective population categories: singles with singles, marrieds with marrieds, and the divorced with the divorced. The strategies for coping with each lifestyle will be part of the socialization for the respective members by those in the same population.

From another perspective, the entire population born in 2008 will be socialized to replace the 2 million plus who will die that year. These populations are 80 years apart and will be products of different socialization experiences. Most of the 80-year-olds will have never operated a computer (or have limited skills in doing so). All of the infants born in 2008 will likely have some exposure to a computer before they die.

Each generation also has a different historical socialization. Only individuals who were alive during World War II, the Kennedy/Martin Luther

King, Jr. assassinations, and the Vietnam War have these historical backdrops as part of their socialization. Similarly, the current generation will have the Iraq war, Hurricane Katrina, and global warming as part of their historical experience.

Collective Behavior/Social Movements

Social movements represent a concerted effort on the part of a group to change an aspect of society. The civil rights movement has had a dramatic influence on the way in which people are socialized in our society. In the 1950s, whites and blacks were socialized to drink from different water fountains, sit in different sections of the bus, and attend separate colleges and universities. As a result of the civil rights movement in the 1960s, blacks and whites began to drink from the same fountain, sit next to each other on the bus, and attend the same educational institutions. By 2008 American society was moving toward electing a black president.

The terms colored, Negro, black and African American represent different time frames in the United States (fifties, sixties, seventies, and eighties). These terms reflect changes brought about by minority mass movements which change the socialization content of each generation. Mass movements by women, gays/lesbians/bisexuals/transsexuals, pro-choice, and pro-life groups have also influenced the socialization content of each new generation.

Social Classes

Parents in lower socioeconomic classes are more likely to discuss personal and financial problems with their children than parents in higher socioeconomic groups. The former feel that the sooner their children become aware of the harsh realities of life, the better. Middle class parents, on the other hand, believe that they should protect their children from the realities that lie ahead.

The type of discipline a child experiences as part of his or her socialization is different based on that child's social class. Working class families are more likely to use corporal punishment whereas middle class families are more likely to use talking and "time out" as methods of discipline. Similarly, blue-collar families are more likely to provide rigid sex role socialization for their children than white-collar families. For example, blue-collar children would more likely feel that only males should mow the grass and that only females should take care of the kitchen.

High status children continue their socialization in carefully selected educational institutions. In the United States, middle class parents send their children to state colleges and universities. Upper class parents send their children to elite private schools—Duke, Harvard, Brown. In Great Britain, upper class teenage children go to exclusive private boarding schools. The most exclusive of them, Eton, has socialized eighteen prime ministers. Following high school, most upper class graduates attend Oxford or Cambridge universities. Lower class children often drop out of school and work in factories.

Groups

Groups provide direct socialization experiences for their members. For adolescents, the peer group becomes primary and teaches its members sexual norms, alcohol/drug use, health norms, dress codes, and homophobia. Regarding the latter, Poteat (2007) confirmed the effect of one's peer group on the development of homophobic attitudes and behaviors during adolescence. Teenagers thrive on spending time together during which they socialize each other. Parents may be, literally, shut out from their teenager's life.

Buote et al (2007) studied new friendships with peers among first year university students at six Canadian universities and found that making new friends was associated with adjustment to the new social environment. In effect the students socialized each other into learning ways of adapting to college life. The effect was stronger for residence students than commuters.

Peer groups use entrance to and maintenance of membership in the group to socialize the behavior of new recruits. Individuals who do not conform to group norms are ostracized. Teenagers who shoplift, drink alcohol, take drugs, and race cars may do so for peer approval. When one's peers scatter after graduation, these behaviors often stop and new behaviors begin in reference to the new groups formed (e.g. with a lover or spouse).

In a study on "what I did for love," college students reported that "driving drunk," "dropping out of school to be with my partner," and "having sex without protection" were among the more dubious choices they had made while involved in a love relationship with their partner (Knox et al., 1998). Similarly, a team of researchers used data from the National Longitudinal Study of Adolescent Health to examine the relationship between having a romantic love partner and engaging in minor acts of delinquency (smoking cigarettes, getting drunk, skipping school). They found that females were particularly influenced by their "delinquent" boyfriends (Haynie et al., 2005). Furthermore, researchers have found that women who are "romantically in love" with their partners are less likely to use a condom with their partner. Doing so isn't regarded as very romantic, and they elect not to inject realism into a love context (East et al., 2007).

Further evidence of how lovers provide influential socialization experiences for each other comes from one of our students. One woman noticed that after living with her boyfriend for three months that her music preference changed from rock-and-roll to jazz, her sandwich preference changed from peanut butter and jelly to sprouts and tomatoes on pita bread, and her television preference changed from watching news to watching old movies.

Finally, DeMunck and Korotayev (2007) studied spousal intimacy cross-culturally. They defined intimacy as sleeping together, eating together, spending leisure time together, and the husband attending the birth of his child. They found that spouses in different societies are socialized to expect different levels of intimacy and that the more equal the partners, the greater their intimacy.

Families

Parents represent the most important agent of socialization for most people. The gender role socialization parents provide for their children is both obvious and subtle. The names parents assign to their children, the clothes they dress them in, and the toys they buy them all reflect socialization in regard to one's gender. Parents may also be more strict on female children, especially regarding the age they are allowed to be out of the house at night, curfew, and the expectation to "call your mamma when you get to the party."

Panayiotou and Papageorgiou (2007) noted that depression among women is twice as common as among men and may relate to differences in socialization that result in different emotions (women are taught to be more attentive to their emotions and to "feel" deeper), cognitions (they may feel mastery is elusive), and coping reactions (get depressed rather than "snap out of it"). The authors acknowledged that other factors contributing to higher rates of depression could be less decision-making power and having limited access to resources (which may lead to feelings of helplessness and low self-esteem).

Siblings are also important socialization influences. Indeed, the relationship with one's sibling (particularly in sister-sister relationships) is likely to be the most enduring of all relationships (Meinhold et al., 2006). Growing up in a family of all sisters or all brothers intensifies social learning experiences toward femininity or masculinity. A male reared with five sisters and a single-parent mother is likely to reflect more feminine characteristics than a male reared in a home with six brothers and a stay-at-home dad.

The socialization a child experiences in a family is also influenced by whether the child is a first, second, or third child. Sulloway (1996) examined how a child's birth order influences the development of various personality characteristics. His thesis is that children with siblings live in different social contexts and develop different strategies to maximize parental investment in them. Some personality characteristics that have their basis in a child's position in the family include the following:

1. Conforming/traditional—Firstborns are the first on the scene with parents and always have the "inside track." They want to stay that way so they are traditional and conforming to their parent's expectations.

2. Experimental/adventurous—Later born children learn quickly that they enter an existing family constellation where everyone is bigger and stronger. They cannot depend on having established territory so must excel in ways different from the first born. They are open to experience, adventurousness, and trying new things since their status is not already assured.

3. Neurotic/emotional unstable—Since firstborns are "dethroned" by younger children to whom parents have had to divert their attention, they tend to be more jealous, anxious, and fearful. Later born children were never number one to begin with so they did not likely experience this trauma.

As support for his ideas, Sulloway (1996) cited 196 controlled birth order studies and contended that, while there are exceptions, one's position in the family is a social context factor influencing personality outcomes. Nevertheless, he acknowledged that researchers disagree on the effects of birth order on the personalities of children and that birth order research is incomplete in that it does not consider the position of each child in families which vary in size, gender, and number.

Associations

Associations such as churches, schools, and businesses are also influential in socializing individuals. Religion remains a potentially important influence in the lives of college students. Only 8.4 percent of a sample of 1,319 undergraduates at a large southeastern university viewed themselves as "not religious at all" (Knox and Zusman, 2008). Because women (particularly white women) are "socialized to be submissive, passive, and nurturing," they may be predisposed to greater levels of religion and religious influence (Miller and Stark, 2002). Such exposure includes a traditional framing of gender roles. Male dominance is indisputable in the hierarchy of religious organizations, where power and status have been accorded mostly to men. Mormons, particularly, adhere to traditional roles in marriage where men are regarded as the undisputed head of the household. Hence, the greater one's exposure to religion, the greater religion's potential to be a socializing influence.

The educational institution serves as an additional socialization agent for gender role ideology. But such an effect must be considered in the context of the society/culture in which the "school" exists and of the school itself. An "all girl's" school may socialize their students differently than a coed school.

Businesses also socialize their employees. McDonald's has a film strip they show each new employee which details how they are to greet customers, take an order, and return change. The well-socialized McDonald's' employee has learned to always smile, be courteous, and be helpful.

Communities

Small rural communities characterized by informal and personal interactions between people who know each other on a first name basis result in a different socialization experience than urban communities replete with secondary group relationships, formal interactions, and anonymity. Hence, a person reared in a small rural community (e.g. Mayberry) is more likely to feel connected to others, to feel a part of a cohesive group, and to feel as though he or she matters. In contrast, a person from a large urban community (e.g. New York City) is more likely to feel distant from others and to feel immune to the approval of others.

Networks

Mass media in the form of television ties the socialization experience of people in American society together. While individuals are reared in different families, social classes, and communities, almost all homes have television sets which are capable of bringing in music television, the news, *20/20* and *Sixty Minutes*. Nielson (2006) noted that there are more televisions in the typical household than people (2.73 TV sets to 2.55 people) and that, in the typical home, television is on more than a third of the day (8 hours and 14 minutes). The sheer amount of this socializing agent is daunting.

Social networks also function to socialize people within the network. The explosion of computer technology with iPods and text messaging allows individuals to communicate and socialize with each other relentlessly. Computers are also hooked together so that computer networking throughout the U.S. socializes computer users on how to use various hardware and software.

Societies

Nolan and Lenski (2006) identified various types of human societies as hunting and gathering, horticultural, agrarian, industrial, fishing, maritime, and herding societies. Each society will socialize their young differently to meet the needs of the society. Maritime societies teach their children how to throw nets and "read" the tides, wind and water temperature to maximize fishing success. In industrial societies, children (particularly middle class children) are encouraged to play and avoid work roles. They also have limited opportunity to assess work roles (listening to parents talk about work, watching television).

The society in which a person is socialized will influence the outcome of the personality of that individual. Individuals socialized in Ireland, Australia, Iraq, the United States, and India are socialized to have different languages, food preferences, and political perspectives.

Popular Beliefs and Scientific Data: You Can't Be Brainwashed

In the section on resocialization, we noted that we would discuss brainwashing at the end of the chapter. Brainwashing commonly refers to having one's thoughts, feelings, and behaviors taken over by another individual or group against the person's will. **Brainwashing** from a sociological perspective is any tightly controlled socialization process which excludes competing influences. Regardless of how it is defined, popular wisdom says that most individuals are "too strong" for this to happen and that saying one was "brainwashed" is an excuse for doing what one wanted to do anyway.

Research studies on cults suggest that brainwashing can and does occur. There are an estimated 5,000 cults in the United States (Lottick, 2005). When brainwashing is viewed as resocialization, we need only look at the way in which the socialization is tightly organized and controlled to understand that, indeed, "brainwashing" is a reality. Otherwise, how might we explain the willingness of suicide bombers to strap an explosive belt on and ignite it or drive a car loaded with a bomb into a building or group of people?

The mechanism cults use for socializing new recruits follows:

1. Selection. Rarely are children under 10 or middle aged married individuals recruited into cults. Children and middle aged married individuals are firmly entrenched into their own social organization (e.g. the family) and accept the values, roles, and norms of that organization. Rather, individuals who are recruited into cults are between the ages of 18 and 25 who are breaking away from one social organization (the family in which they were reared) but are not yet established in a new social organization (the new family they create by getting married and having children). Hence, they are "between" social organizations and vulnerable to any alternative socialization experience to provide structure for their life and philosophical answers to questions they may be asking. Individuals vulnerable to joining a commune are likely to be depressed

or experiencing a transition in their life (between high school and college, between romances, between marriages). They may also have a religious motive such as Jihad in the Cause of Allah. In effect a person sees himself as a martyr who sacrifices his own life for the Cause of Allah (restoring the land and preserving one's dignity).

2. New Role Models. Socializing an individual into a cult necessitates getting the individual to believe that if he or she will adopt the values and behaviors of the identified leader, all of life's problems will disappear.

3. Isolation and Indoctrination. Removing an individual from competing sources of information is crucial. Once the person is isolated, he or she is indoctrinated with the new propaganda. Being totally resocialized by a new organization is understandable as long as the new social organization duplicates the process of the initial socialization. Hence, we are all capable of being socialized and resocialized as long as we are psychologically vulnerable, isolated from our primary socialization units, and immersed in the socialization process of a new social organization.

Jesus Camp is a documentary about the "Kids On Fire School of Ministry," a pentecostal summer camp located just outside Devils Lake, North Dakota, and run by Becky Fischer and her ministry, Kids in Ministry International. The film was nominated in 2007 for an Academy Award for Best Documentary Feature. The documentary depicts the essence of brainwashing where children are immersed in a social context of content espoused by authority figures and peers (while isolated from competing influences). The extent of the socialization is revealed in the film which shows members of the *Jesus Camp* going up to strangers at a bowling alley and asking them about their faith in Jesus. The camp has subsequently been discontinued since the owners of the property used for the camp in the film were concerned about vandalism to the premises following the film's release.

References

Aubrey, Jennifer Stevens. 2007. "Does Television Exposure Influence College-Aged Women's Sexual Self-Concept?" *Media Psychology*, 10: 157–181.

Buote, Vanessa M., Panceer, M. S., Pratt, M. W., Adams, G. et al. 2007. "The Importance of Friends: Friendship and Adjustment Among 1st Year University Students." *Journal of Adolescent Research*, 22: 665–673.

De Munck, Victor and Korotayev, Andrey. 2007. "Wife-Husband Intimacy and Female Status in Cross-Cultural Perspective." *Cross Cultural Research*, 41: 307–328.

East, L., D. Jackson, O'Brien L. and Peters, K. 2007. "Use of the Male Condom by Heterosexual Adolescents and Young People: Literature Review." *Journal of Advanced Nursing,* 59: 103–110.

Haynie, D. L., Giordano, P. C., Manning, W. D. and Longmore, M. A. 2005. "Adolescent Romantic Relationships and Delinquency Involvement." *Criminology,* 43: 177–210.

Knox, D. and M. E. Zusman. 2008. "Relationship and Sexual Behaviors of a Sample of 1319 University Students." Unpublished data. Department of Sociology, East Carolina University, Greenville, NC.

Knox, D., M. Zusman, and Nieves, W. 1998. "What I Did for Love: Risky Behavior of College Students in Love." *College Student Journal,* 32: 203–05.

Lottick, E. A. 2005. "Prevalence of Cults? A Review of Empirical Research in the U.S.A." Paper, International Cultic Studies Association, Universidad Autonoma de Madrid, July 14.

Maume, D. J. 2006. "Gender Differences in Taking Vacation Time." *Work and Occupations,* 33: 161–190.

Meinhold, J. L., Acock, A. and Walker, A. 2006. "The Influence of Life Transition Statuses on Sibling Intimacy and Contact in Early Adulthood." Previously presented at the National Council on Family Relations Annual meeting in Orlando in 2005 and submitted for publication.

Newton, N. 2002. *Savage Girls and Wild Boys: A History of Feral Children.* New York: Thomas Dunne Books/St. Martin's.

Nielson Ratings 2006. "More TV Sets than People in U.S. Homes." http://www.showbuzz.cbsnews.com/stories/2006/09/21/tv/main2032136.shtml.

Nolan P. and Lenski, G. 2006. *Human Societies: An Introduction to Macrosociology.* Boulder, Co.: Paradigm.

Miller, A. S., and Stark, R. 2002. "Gender and Religiousness: Can Socialization Explanations be Saved?" *American Journal of Sociology,* 107, 1399–1423.

Panayiotou, Georgia and Papageorgiou, M. 2007. "Depressed Mood: The Role of Negative Thoughts, Self-consciousness, and Sex Role Stereotypes." *International Journal of Psychology,* 42: 289–296.

Pinquart, M., and Silbereisen, R. K. 2002. "Changes in Adolescents' and Mothers' Autonomy and Connectedness in Conflict Discussions: An Observation Study." *Journal of Adolescence,* 25: 509–22.

Poteat, Paul V. 2007. "Peer Group Socialization of Homophobic Attitudes and Behavior During Adolescence." *Child Development,* 78: 1830–1842.

Spitz, Rene A. 1945. "Hospitalism: An Inquiry into the Genesis of Psychiatric Conditions in Early Childhood." *The Psychoanalytic Study of the Child,* 1: 53–74.

Statistical Abstract of the United States: 2008. 127th ed. Washington, D.C.: U.S. Bureau of the Census.

Sulloway, F. J. 1996. *Born to Rebel: Birth Order, Family Dynamics, and Creative Lives.* New York: Vintage Books.

Textor, K. 2007. "The Millennials are Coming." *Sixty Minutes,* November 11. CBS Television.

Thirumurthy, Vidya. 2004. "Kaleidoscope of Parenting Cultures." *Childhood Education,* 81: 94–50.

Chapter 4

Social Order and Deviance

You cannot kill two people and get away with it, no matter how much money
you have, no matter how many lies you tell.

Daniel Petrocelli, *Triumph of Justice*

The opening quote by the lead attorney in the civil case *Fred Goldman vs.*
O.J. Simpson reflects the importance of social control in a society. The judicial
system provides a network of police, jailers, and attorneys cooperating to ap-
prehend, secure, and prosecute violators. The goal is to ensure social control
so that murder is severely punished.

Social control occurs in every society at all levels. Over three hundred million individuals live in the United States. With this many people, we might expect utter chaos—people scrambling for food, bumping into each other on
city streets, and crashing into each others' cars on roadways. Instead, people
go to the refrigerator for cold milk, walk on one side or the other of the street,
and drive according to traffic rules. Random and individual action has become
patterned and predictable by the social organizations of which the individuals
are a part. The roles of farmer and grocer have developed in society to insure
that someone produces and someone sells milk. The family has assigned someone responsibility to buy the milk and put it in the refrigerator. In this chapter we identify how individuals are molded to fit the social organizations of
which he or she becomes a part and how social order results from this process.
Our central point is that social organizations influence the behavior of those
who become a part of them.

Social Organizations versus the Individual

Psychologists suggest that individuals have free will and create the world in
which they live while sociologists suggest that individuals are born into a world

or social context that largely creates them. For example, the psychologist might say that you will drink alcohol if you want to, due to motivation and self discipline, which lies within you. In contrast, the sociologist would point out that the use of alcohol is more often the result of the importance of social context, family, group or society—that you will drink alcohol if your society considers it proper and depending on whether you are with your parents or peers, in church or at a bar. Being with your parents in church is a social context which predicts that you will not consume alcohol just as being with your peers at a bar suggests otherwise. Neighbors et al. (2007) studied a sample of 818 first year college students and confirmed that their alcohol consumption was specific to the pro social alcohol norms of the college context, rather than individual choice or free will.

Although individuals differ in their personalities and behaviors, they share in common the fact that they are all members of various social organizations. Most social organizations predate the individual, demand their own behaviors, and continue long after the individual is deceased.

Social Organizations Precede the Individual

Social organizations already exist, and it is the individual that must adapt to them, not vice versa. Populations consisting of blacks, whites, men, women and other categories are already in existence with meanings attached to them when the individual is born and becomes a member. The families into which we are born, the audience (collective behavior) we join when we see a movie, the place we work (association), the schools we attend, and the community and society in which we live all existed before we joined. There are exceptions to this, especially in the area of groups and associations. For instance, a marital dyad (group) cannot exist prior to each marital partner joining the unit. Also, many individuals do not join preexisting associations, but rather start their own associations, e.g. a business. Yet they do so within a context that regulates the limits of their actions.

Social Organizations Demand Conformity to Their Expectations

The fact that most social organizations predate the entry of the individual suggests that various ways of thinking and behaving are already established in those organizations which individuals are expected to fit into. Families, communities, and societies already have established positions, roles, norms, and sanctions. For example, in the family, the positions (e.g. husband, wife, child), roles (e.g. in egalitarian families each spouse expected to earn an income and participate in child care), norms (e.g. children are expected to be respectful and not talk back), and sanctions (e.g. child who talks back can't watch TV) are established.

All social organizations do not allow individuals to behave as they wish, but rather socialize them to engage in behavior required by the organization. Children cannot go to bed when they please but are expected to conform to the bedtime set by their parents (family). Military (association) personnel are not assigned to the places they want to go (e.g. Key West) but rather are sent to the places the organization needs them to be (e.g. Iraq). U.S. citizens cannot keep all of the money they earn but must pay taxes to the society of which they are a part. Since you have become a member of the college or university (association) you attend, this social organization has required that you register (e.g. provide evidence of high school graduation), pay fees, and attend class. You cannot be a member of an organization and do what you want; rather your individual desires are channeled so that, to a large degree, you do what the organization wants you to do.

Tyler et al.(2007) studied police departments and noted that organizational control of police officers and their strict adherence to rules was more clearly followed when police officers viewed their superiors as legitimate. When they viewed their superiors positively, the officers considered the rules they were expected to follow as acceptable. Given these views, officers were more likely to self regulate and to minimize misconduct. In fact, the context determined what the individual did.

Social Organizations Endure

By getting individuals to do what the organization wants, the organization endures. Universities, societies, families, and militaries will continue long after the individuals who have been members are gone. The existence of these organizations gives continuity to society. The historical perspective of a university becomes evident when a football game is telecast and the announcer says, "This is the 112th time these two teams have played each other."

Getting Individuals to Fit into Social Organizations

We have seen that individuals will both conform and be obedient in group contexts. Let's examine the factors involved in getting individuals to do as social organizations wish.

Initial Group Membership

All organizations hold the carrot of entry into membership to induce behavioral compliance. Fraternities and sororities (associations) require their pledges to learn the history of the organization, to do the grunt work (e.g. cleaning, making homecoming floats), and to go through "hell week" before they are initiated. The United States (society) requires immigrants to pass a test on knowledge of the political system. Graduate schools (associations) require an undergraduate degree and an acceptable score on the Graduate Record Examination. Failure to meet the requirements for membership means no entry.

Maintenance of Group Membership

All social organizations require a modicum of behaviors to continue membership. The U.S. deports traitors, fraternities/sororities expel members who don't pay their dues, and spouses (group) divorce each other for chronic infidelity.

Knowing that poor grades result in their children losing membership in their age appropriate classes at school, parents are motivated to monitor and control the study behavior of their children. Qian et al. (2007) studied 806 American and Chinese seventh graders (mean age = 12.73 years) in a 6-month longitudinal study and found that parental behavioral control predicted positive academic functioning in their children.

The Old Order Amish (societal counterculture) practice **shunning** which means a member who "strays" from exhibiting the norms of the community (e.g. drinks alcohol, commits adultery) discovers that other members of the community will not talk to or interact with him or her. In effect the member is cut off from all social ties with members who will, thereafter, have nothing to do with the shunnee. This method of social control is particularly effective since the individual may have no other social links or group alternatives with which to associate.

Interpersonal Approval

In addition to providing entry into a social organization and allowing one to continue to be a member, interpersonal approval is another mechanism of social control. Spouses (groups) attempt to engage in behavior consistent with each other's expectation so as to continue the partner talking with them, doing things with them socially, and having sex. A spouse who disregards the behavioral expectations of the partner may get the "silent treatment," the partner going away for a weekend without them, and the partner no longer being interested in sex.

Bradley (2007) interviewed strippers who revealed that maintaining their deviant role was facilitated by finding a partner who accepted (e.g. provided social approval) their dancing. These partners were difficult to find unless they were from the "inside" (e.g. bouncers, deejays) whom the girls often regarded as lower quality partners (e.g. they had limited employment and limited potential for upward social mobility).

Mutual Interdependence

Individuals are also motivated to behave according to the social organizations' expectations out of mutual interdependence. Students, teachers, staff, and administrators need each other in order to exist. If students do not attend class, take tests, and pass courses, they will fail and eventually be dropped from school. Without students, teachers have no classes to teach, secretaries have no tests to type, and administrators have no budgets to prepare. Doctors and nurses are dependent on each other to insure the proper medical care of their patients. It is the team which results in a successful surgery, not individuals. The patient is sometimes a part of the team and may be kept awake so that he or she can give feedback to the team during surgery. Each person is not acting as an individual but as a social actor in a particular position, status, and role which involves specific norms. These positions interact with complementary positions out of mutual interdependence.

Coercion

Individuals who do not readily comply with the expected norms of a social organization may be coerced to do so. **Coercion** involves forcing an individual to behave in a certain manner through the use of threat, pressure, or intimidation. Students who make bomb threats on campus are expelled, physicians who conduct surgery while drunk are barred from the hospital, and nurses who steal/sell drugs lose their license. Conformity and obedience are expected, but force is used if necessary.

Our society imposes an income tax on us. Individuals are not allowed to do with their money as they wish. It is hoped that members of our society will recognize the common goal of national defense, the ethics of paying what is due the government, and the recognition that we can best function as a society if all members do their respective parts (mutual interdependence). However, if these sources of encouragement fail, the government is prepared to send Internal Revenue representatives to your bank to seize the money you have in your account and to put you in prison for acting as an individual who decides he or she does not want to pay taxes.

Rewards/Punishments

Rewards are positive sanctions for doing what the social organization wants. **Punishments** are negative sanctions for noncompliance. All social organizations offer compensations for compliance and threaten to take these away for noncompliance. New faculty members are rewarded with higher income, promotion, and tenure for publishing articles in peer-reviewed journals. New faculty who sit around and drink coffee and don't meet their classes are fired. Whether to use punishment to control a deviant behavior is exemplified by the social response to prostitution. Scoular and O'Neill (2007) noted that some societies use punishment (e.g. put prostitutes in jail) while others regulate the profession.

Students are also compensated for doing what their college or university wants through grades. In exchange for attending class, taking tests, and making good grades the student may continue to receive financial aid, live in a college or university environment, have access to one's friends, earn a degree, learn new information, and have a flexible sleep and recreation schedule. Not bending one's desires to the social organization is to risk being deprived of the compensations—failing in coursework, losing financial aid, living at home under the supervision of one's parents, being separated from one's friends, and getting a job with standard working hours.

Survival

We have discussed several ways in which social organizations mold individuals to behave in ways which are consistent with the goals of those organizations. An overriding reason individuals give up their individuality to the will of the group is the awareness that their own survival in that social organization is at stake. If they do not play by the rules of the social organization of which they are a part, they will no longer be allowed to be a member of that organization. When two individuals meet, date, and fall in love, they may give up their own individuality to some degree because they want their relationship to continue. If he likes country western music and she doesn't, she may listen to country western records as though she enjoys it too. If she likes roller skating and he doesn't, he may go skating because he wants to be with her. Each will do what is necessary to maintain their dyad, (the social organization, the group) as neither wants it to dissolve (e.g. the relationship to end and to be left alone).

Theory and Social Order

The fact that there is social order doesn't account for why it exists or explain its meaning. Functionalists, conflict theorists and symbolic interactionists have different views of social order.

Functionalist Theory

Functionalists view social control as a mechanism that contributes to social stability. It is important to note that "functional" does not necessarily mean "good". Social order is functional in that it maintains stability in a social organization; whether that is good or bad is not a scientific but a public issue. Societies benefit when there is social order and stability in families and take a hit when there is disorder and instability. For example, Hipp (2007) noted that divorced households are associated with increased crime. In contrast, children typically benefit when there is social order in families. Fomby and Cherlin (2007) studied the well-being of children who live in different family structures and found that children who experience multiple transitions (e.g. divorce of parents, remarriage of parents) in family structure may face worse developmental outcomes than children raised in stable, two-parent families.

However, stability in social order in a society may not be "good". For example, Saddam Hussein was quite effective in maintaining social order in Iraq. But from the point of view of most Americans, the stability of the Saddam regime was not considered to be "good."

Conflict Theory

The conflict perspective views social order as the outcome of a struggle between competing interests. It views conflict as natural to social organizations. Those who win the struggle create what is "normal," and those who lose the struggle are controlled through both informal and formal means in order to maintain the social order. For example, the rich perpetuate the belief that anyone can succeed if they try hard enough (facts show this is unrealistic.) This belief supports their position that the failure of the poor should be sanctioned with few benefits from welfare. If the poor rise up to demand benefits, the law will be "used" to keep order.

Conflict theorists do not believe that social order arises from the smooth functioning of a system that represents the wishes of the masses. Rather, social order results from the elite protecting their interests by passing laws. For example, there are "rules" against the homeless sleeping overnight on park benches.

Symbolic Interactionist Theory

This perspective views social order as a creation of social actors within social organizations. It is created using "symbols" and "language." These have meaning only for those participants in a social organization. The meaning of social order is defined and redefined by members of each group, family or other social organization. The social actor can redefine social order by redefining the symbols of that order, such as the American flag, giving someone the finger, or going on strike. At one time the word "strike" was viewed as unpatriotic and unprofessional. Today the term is defined as looking out for one's own interests. The writer's strike in 2007–2008 which shut down new programs on TV and resulted in an avalanche of reruns was regarded as writers seeking their fair share of the profit earned from their work.

The power of a symbol was again illustrated when the noose became the focus of a large civil rights demonstration in Jena, Louisiana, in the fall of 2007. Earlier, a black student at Jena High School had asked permission from a school administrator to sit under a tree only to find that three white students hung nooses from the tree. In effect, the whites were attempting to control the blacks with the symbol of the noose. Capeci (2007) noted that modern scholars have failed to understand the meaning of the word lynching and to recognize its many politically rhetorical uses including certain forms of vigilantism: repression of white horse thieves in the West and social control of Hispanics in the Southwest.

Deviance

Social order includes the control of deviance. In this section we define deviance and the three central theories. It is important to remember, that a deviant also lacks free will and that his or her behavior is not random, but predictable by understanding the context in which he/she finds himself/herself.

Definition of Deviance

Deviance is any behavior which breaks socially accepted norms. In Chapter 2 we discussed minor violations as "folkways" and major violations as "mores." Picking your nose in public, humming "The Star Spangled Banner" during class, and not answering when spoken to are examples of minor deviance, or folkways. All deviance is a departure from social norms created by social organizations. Obesity may be unhealthy but becomes deviant when a social organization labels it negatively. In the Marine Corps, being five pounds overweight is deviant. For the cheerleaders of a professional football team, deviance may be three pounds. Some police and fire departments also have weight limits, but any social organization can create a norm or define an action as deviant.

What is important to remember is that deviance is a violation of norms accepted by the members of a social organization. Divorce is deviant only to the degree that the family, community, association, or society views it as deviant. In the 1950s, divorce was very deviant, a "more". By mid 2000, friends would throw a party to celebrate the divorce of a co-worker. In the 1950s, smoking was not viewed as deviant. Today smoking is banned in most public places and is being considered in some social organizations as sufficient reason to avoid hiring or actually firing current employees.

Deviance is not inborn or inherent in the person but is a social creation that changes with time. All behavior, attitudes, and appearance can be considered deviant by some social organizations at some historical time. Homosexuality, jaywalking, drinking alcohol, coloring ones lips, eating horse meat, and being too thin are all defined as deviant acts within some social organizations. To understand the deviant, it is important to understand the explanations of how deviance is the product of the context, not the individual.

Theoretical Views of Deviance

As we indicated in Chapter One, functionalists view deviance in terms of the function performed for social organizations. Deviance is controlled so that social organizations can achieve their goals. It also creates clear social bonds for group membership by dividing the world into two groups—'we' and 'they.' "We" do it right while "they" do it wrong. The "saints" exist because there are "sinners". Pro choice exists because of pro life. Mainstream America can identify itself since they are different from those into punk rock and Goth. Every deviant structure that comes into existence remains in existence because it performs some function, and to these theorists the goal is to determine what the function may be.

Conflict theorists emphasize that competing groups try to control each other. The group in power (capitalists) can make the rules and control those who stray from the rules. Capitalists who own the means of production can define the stealing of property as deviant and criminal and control those who steal by incarceration. Because of the disparity of access, various groups have the desired material goods in our society. Other groups create a subculture (e.g. organized crime) which uses illegitimate ways to gain access to the desired material goods. For example, a person deprived of fashionable cars may become a member of other social groups (professional criminals) who specialize in getting such cars illegally—thus legitimate among criminals. To conflict theorists there will always be conflict and deviance which reflects the normal outcome of competition for the material things people want.

Symbolic interactionists emphasize that deviance is a label. Individuals become deviants because they are labeled as deviants, begin to believe the labels, and act in ways which are consistent with the labels. Smoking a cigarette only becomes deviant behavior when a social organization is able to put the deviant label on the behavior of an individual and make it stick. So, smoking in 1980 might be seen as healthy and normal but in 2010 as unhealthy and deviant. The focus here is the label and the labeler. A person who is labeled as a "smoker" may begin to see himself/herself as a deviant.

Social Organizations:
Maintenance of Order and Control of Deviance

Social organizations not only maintain social order but control deviance. An examination of how this works in the various social organizations follows.

Population

While population is not a social organization in the sense that it is not organized, we use various elements of population (e.g. age, sex, race) to show how these characteristics affect order and relate to deviance. If we are studying marijuana use, we note differences in age, sex, race and other population characteristics as marital status, religion or nationality. We would not be surprised by some characteristics of use, such as more males or singles, but would be by others. For example, it would be odd to find large numbers of the elderly smoking joints or stealing cars.

Social Control and Age. Every 15-year-old knows that it is illegal for him or her to drive a car, buy a gun, or drink alcohol. Because the lives of those who make the laws are at stake, legislation has been passed to carefully control when a young person drives a car (age 16), the entry into that status (only after successfully completing a driving test), and the consequences for drinking and driving (license taken away). Fifteen-year-olds also know it is against the law to purchase, use or possess (PUP laws) tobacco (Jason et al. 2007).

College students represent another population that illustrates the need for social control. Imagine the potential deviant behavior on your campus with no social control (e.g. alcohol, vandalism, sexual assault). Payne and Salotti (2007) studied crime among college students and found that the absence of both social control mechanisms and peers as deviant models was related to both crime and drug abuse.

Social Control and Sex of the Individual. Women in our population are more likely than men to die from breast cancer. A portion of public health media is used to alert women to the need for a periodic mammogram. If women do not take care of their health, we will have a society without mothers and spouses. Inducing fear of death through media coverage of breast cancer is a form of indirect social control.

Deviance and Age. Deviance does not exist apart from its social context. Deviance depends on social organizations (e.g. society) identifying norms to break, a group (e.g. youth gang) socializing someone to break the norms, and a network (e.g. juvenile justice system) to levy sanctions against offenders. In regard to deviance and age, most of the arrests for crime are among young people. Forty percent of the 1.7 million arrests for crime are of people under the age of 25 (Crime in the United States, 2005a). Sociologists can predict the amount and type of crime in a society by looking at population characteristics such as age. When the society is composed of large numbers of young people, the crime rate will be higher. Societies with large numbers of older people will have lower crime rates.

Among the many sociological explanations for a higher proportion of crime among youth, two will be instructive. First, young people (particularly those between the ages of 18 and 24) have the least amount of social control. Two major social control agents in our society are the family of orientation and the family of procreation. The **family of orientation** is the family into which an individual is born consisting of the individual and his/her parents. The **family of procreation** is the family an individual begins himself/herself with a marriage partner. Parents and spouses exercise a great deal of social control over their children and their mate respectively. The predictable questions of every spouse who observes a mate leaving the house are, "Where are you going?" and "When are you coming back?"

Individuals in late adolescence/young adulthood are usually between these two social control groups. The control of their parents is weakening yet the control of a mate does not yet exist because the individual is still unmarried.

As adolescents move into adulthood and get married (move into a new social control context), their deviant and criminal behavior radically decreases.

The second explanation for more crime among youth focuses on economics. Young people are less likely to have legitimate means to obtain the things that they want. Many do not have jobs or a legitimate source of income. Hence, they may shoplift, steal and rob to obtain the things that they want. The peak age for stealing a car is age 16, an age when a car has high value and the adolescent is without economic means to obtain the car (Crime in the United States, 2005b).

As a person moves out of adolescence and into the mainstream of life, they are likely to become both married and employed. Marriage provides social control and employment provides income (a legitimate mechanism) to buy the desired material goods. The older they become, the less likely deviance and crime occur. In fact, less than one percent of persons age 65 and older are arrested for stealing a car (Crime in the United States, 2005b).

Deviance and Sex of the Individual. With the exception of prostitution, males are arrested for a larger percentage of crimes than females (76.2% vs. 23.8%) (Crime in the United States, 2005c). Explanations for a higher crime rate among males include aggression, risk taking, and socialization. It is important to remember that these are not simply psychological but sociological characteristics. That is, aggression is learned behavior in social context, and some women are now learning to be as aggressive as men. Since most crimes (e.g. robbery) require an element of aggression, and since most males are socialized to be more aggressive than females, it is not surprising that males are arrested for committing more crimes than females.

Males are also more likely to take risks than females. Men teach their sons to climb trees, jump off of swings and slide into second base just before the ball arrives; boys learn to take risks that their sisters are not taught to take. Crime involves taking risks, so the association is not surprising. Finally, males typically get more socialization from peers to engage in deviant behavior. Males are less attached to social institutions (e.g. church, family) than females and, therefore, under less social control. Males are also more likely to continue criminal behavior and to end up in prison. Over 85 percent of all people in jail are male (*Statistical Abstract of the United States, 2008*, Table 339).

Deviance and Race. Although whites are arrested for committing a larger percentage of crimes than blacks (70% vs 28%), the latter are arrested for committing proportionately more crimes (*Statistical Abstract of the United States, 2008*, Table 318). Blacks comprise only 13 percent of the population (Table 9).

Explanations for higher crime rates among blacks must focus on context. It is in the community, family and groups that there are more violent models among blacks, greater frustrations as a result of living in a discriminated, prej-udiced, economically deprived social context, and a greater tendency to han-dle personal grievances through personal attack than through legal means. Blacks are less likely to have the money to hire an attorney and proceed against another through the legal system than whites.

When blacks are arrested for violent crimes, they are also more likely to go to prison than whites. Again, while race is a population characteristic, it is best understood by the other social organizations identifying race as rele-vant. In some societies, being old carries a high status or being female is ranked higher than being a male. In this same way, black is a color of no meaning until a context gives it meaning. In our society, arrest statistics by race may be a function of black defendants being more likely than white defen-dants to have chronic histories of criminal behavior and hence, to be pun-ished more severely for crimes. Alternatively, the explanation may be due to structural factors. Blacks are more likely than whites to be imprisoned in states where the black population is a small percentage of the total population and is predominately urban.

Collective Behavior/Social Movements

Collective behavior such as demonstrations, mobs, and theater audiences must be controlled. If crowds form and get out of control, revolutions can occur. In fact, in the winter of 2008, China saw several hundred thousand people try to get home for the Chinese New Year and become stranded with no toilet fa-cilities, food or comfort in train stations. The government was concerned that these crowds could get out of control and called out over 500,000 soldiers.

Social Control and Collective Behavior. In the United States, demonstrators must get a permit to conduct a march down city streets (police are assigned to escort the demonstrators), and the length of time they are allowed to demon-strate is restricted. Demonstrators who refuse to leave when the time is up are handcuffed and arrested for disturbing the peace and disorderly conduct.

Social control of mobs is more difficult. In September 2007, thousands of Burmese Buddhist monks and other protesters marched in Rangoon. Myan-mar (formerly Burma) officials imposed a dusk-to-dawn curfew in the coun-try's two main cities after pouring security forces into Rangoon to try to end the biggest protests against military rule in 20 years.

In late 2007, in Islamabad, Pakistan, President General Pervez Musharraf used the police to control riots and lock up dissidents. He did this in the name of "emergency rule" to maintain democracy in the country. His goal was to main-tain power for another five years.

It is important that social control be exercised over all forms of collective behavior, as such behavior can undermine the social organization. Societies can lose control when millions violate norms.

Deviance and Collective Behavior/Social Movements. Some collective behavior and social movements are outside the norms. The pro-life movement sometimes organizes picketing and non-sanctioned splinter groups may bomb abortion clinics. Although members of the movement are breaking societal laws, the individual members of the group are engaging in behavior that is approved of by the group. Indeed, all behavior is purposeful in the sense that members are conforming to specific norms, but such behavior may be deviant or criminal from a societal view.

Social Classes

Members of the respective social classes are engaged in the social control of their members.

Social Control and Social Class. Upper classes attempt to control the dating and mating behavior of their offspring by both indirect and direct controls. The hope of upper class parents in socializing their offspring is to get them to internalize (indirect control) upper class values, norms, and behaviors. Attending the right church (Episcopalian), going to the right Ivy League college (Yale), wearing name brand or tailored clothes, and knowing what a finger bowl is help to insure that only those with similar values and behaviors will be acceptable as a date or mate. The upper class individual is likely to feel little in common with someone who attends a Pentecostal church, drops out of high school, wears clothes from the thrift store, and licks his or her fingers at the dinner table while eating ribs.

Occasionally, a person reared in the upper class rebels against his or her socialization and crosses class lines to date and to marry. The upper class male announcing his intention to marry an uneducated female socialized in the lower class may be disinherited (direct social control) by his upper class parents. Similarly, one's throne may be taken away for noncompliance. Such happened to Edward VIII (1894–1972), the oldest son of King George V and Queen Mary of Great Britain. On January 20, 1936, he became king upon his father's death. But he had fallen in love with Wallis Warfield Simpson, an American divorcee, and was informed that his government was opposed to his marrying a divorcee. In effect, he could not be king and be married to this woman. His reaction to this form of social control was to abdicate his throne and leave England.

Deviance and Social Class. People in different social classes engage in different types of deviant and criminal behavior. People in the lower class are more likely to rob a gas station while people in the upper class are more likely to rob investors through the use of insider information. The Enron collapse revealed upper class CEOs (Ken Lay and Jeffery Skilling) encouraging employees and investors to buy more stock (it hit a high of $90 a share) while they were privately selling their own company stock. In the end the stock sold for pennies, and thousands of employees lost their jobs and pensions.

Reiman (1979) observed that the upper classes have been successful in getting society as a whole to focus on lower class criminal activities as the major crime threat. By focusing attention on the fear of being robbed, assaulted, or murdered (all of which are very low probabilities), attention is diverted from a concern about and prosecution of corporate crime, environmental pollution, and income redistribution. The middle and lower classes are so concerned that someone will break into their house that they do not question the system that makes the rules which determine the quality of water they drink, the air they breathe, or the interest rates/taxes they are expected to pay. In essence, they are being plundered from above by those who make the rules in society. When Dick Cheney makes an announcement supporting the war in Iraq, one wonders the degree to which he profits from the war through private contracts with companies (Halliburton) with whom he has had an association (see Halliburton Watch http://www.halliburtonwatch.org/).

Poor people are more likely to be arrested for crime than persons with high incomes. Not only are the poor under greater surveillance, the behavior they engage in is more likely to be defined by the ruling classes as deviant (being homeless) or criminal. A lower class person who uses crack cocaine may be sentenced to prison whereas an upper class corporate executive who authorizes the dumping of thousands of pounds of toxic chemicals in a river is likely to get a letter from the Environmental Protection Agency and may end up paying a fine. Or, if he uses powdered cocaine, he or she will get a different (lower) sentence.

Capitalism in our society assumes that the possession of material goods is important. Although people in all classes are socialized to want objects (iPod, high definition television, Lexus), the opportunities for obtaining them are real for only the educated and the employed. Since educational values and economic support to attend school are less evident in lower class homes, such children end up with limited education and low paying jobs. Crime becomes one alternative for obtaining the socially desired objects which result in criminal penalties from the rule makers. Again, the focus is typically on the individual criminal (the young adult who steals) not on the system (inadequate schools, parents who never discussed college with their children) which produced the criminal. Furthermore, the upper classes do not want to eliminate crime because they need crime in the form of drugs, larceny, and robbery to divert attention from their more pervasive crimes and insignificant penalties. If a high enough ranking official is caught, the "penalty" is resignation from office and public disgrace tempered with a $60,000 a year pension from the government.

Groups

All groups are small and consist of very few members. These two, three or four member groups may be smaller close-knit parts of larger families, associations or communities. They might include close friends who are members of rock groups, peer groups, religious associations or fraternities and sororities (associations). All groups attempt to exercise control over their members. They also provide negative sanctions for deviance.

Social Control and Groups. In the case of a fraternity, there are always smaller peer groups within them that talk and discuss what needs to be done. Social control begins by only admitting pledges who, in the opinion of small close-knit groups is worthy of being considered for membership. Small peer groups present their desires to the entire fraternity (association). With no initial opposition, the pledge enters a six week period of probation in which he is required to attend "pledge class" where he is carefully socialized into the history, norms, and values of the fraternity. He must also learn the name and major of each fraternity brother and demonstrate that knowledge at an evening meal (by standing up and naming all 60 brothers). Failure to "fit in" to the values and norms of the fraternity results in the pledge not being initiated. One male at a prestigious university observed that snorting cocaine was a common practice among the "brothers" and that anybody who did not join in on occasion was "blackballed" (a black rather than a white ball was put in the small voting box passed around the room). Once initiated, the fraternity continues to control the behavior of the new member. Dues must be paid on time, work must be performed (painting the house, making the homecoming float) and new members must be recruited. Social approval from one's "brothers" is the primary mechanism of indirect control. Groups are often at the core of social organizations from married couples to networks. These close-knit contexts of two or three "friends" initiate and regulate overall conduct.

Deviance and Groups. Fraternity members who don't pay their dues, who get embarrassingly drunk at parties, and who bring bad publicity to the fraternity (e.g. caught stealing on campus) are engaging in deviant behavior and are put on probation or expelled. Even though it is the association that finally rules against them, their behavior is identified as unacceptable by small groups within the association that are offended and powerful.

Crime is another area where deviance and groups can be illustrated. Almost all crime is committed in groups of two or more people. Sutherland and Cressey (1974) emphasized that delinquent and criminal behavior are learned while interacting with others in small groups. The degree to which a person associates with delinquents and criminals rather than law abiding citizens will directly influence whether that person engages in crime. Consistent with Sutherland's **differential association theory** (Sutherland, 1939), a person's behaviors and values will be in reference to the groups with whom he/she identifies. The interaction of lower class children with peers who engage in delinquent behavior increases the likelihood that they, too, will engage in delinquent behavior and adopt such behavior as normative.

Delinquents, when compared to non delinquents, tend to have other delinquents as friends and to have parents who are criminals. In a classic study, Hazani (1986) studied a group of eight boys (ages 4 to 9) during summer vacation. Over a period of several months, the boys spent less time at home (where they were under adult supervision) and more time in a cafe in their neighborhood (where they met four petty criminals ages 21–27). Soon they were serving as lookouts for the criminals, stealing, and sneaking into stores for criminals (group behavior). When summer was over, most of the boys stopped spending their time with the petty criminals and reverted back to their conventional behavior. The power of the group in influencing the behavior of individuals has been a consistent theme throughout this text.

While gangs (groups) are commonplace in large ghetto areas (communities) where gangs often fight over turf to sell drugs and use guns, not all criminal behavior is in the form of gangs. A dramatic example of group criminal behavior occurred during the 1919 World Series between the Chicago White Sox and the Cincinnati Reds. Eight players (group) on the White Sox team (association) agreed to lose the game in exchange for $100,000 from gamblers. The Sox won only three games; the Reds won five games of the nine game series (the first team to win five games won the series). The event brought shame on the history of baseball and changed the name of the White Sox to the "Black Sox."

Families

Family members use both indirect and direct means to control the behavior of each other. Deviance is always linked to the social organization, as adultery is specific to families. Deviance is also addressed with negative sanctions.

Social Control and Families. Parents attempt to control the behavior of their children indirectly through socialization. It is the parents' hope that their children will want to eat vegetables, brush their teeth, and clean their rooms. If they do not, parents resort to more direct control by such methods as withholding television and inflicting pain (spanking). Parents try to directly control their college age children with money. One couple told their daughter that if she did not stop living with her boyfriend (deviance) that she would have to pay her own tuition (direct sanction).

Children attempt to control the behavior of their parents by being nice to them when the parents do what they want. The child who throws a temper tantrum at the check out counter at K-Mart because his or her parent will not buy some candy is teaching the parent that it is easier to buy the candy than to deal with a screaming child.

Deviance and Families. Parents discourage deviant behavior in their off-spring by providing both direct and indirect control. Direct control is in the form of requiring compliance with manipulation or sanctions for violations of curfews, choice of companions and failing to clean rooms. If they fail to comply with parental social control, they lose access to the car, allowance or rights to date. Indirect social control of offspring occurs when parents have only one television or phone and thereby make it difficult for their children to stay on the phone for a long time or to watch a lot of television outside their supervision.

The state also has an interest in controlling deviant behavior in families— 411 children were taken by Child Protective Services from the families at the Yearning for Zion Ranch in San Angelo, Texas, in 2008 in response to a call from what they understood was a 16-year-old girl that her 50-year-old husband had beaten and raped her. The renegade Mormom sect (Fundamentalist Church of Jesus Christ of Latter Day Saints) was alleged to encourage girls under 18 (some at 13) to enter a "spiritual marriage" and to have as many children as possible.

Associations

All associations (eg. work, religious, educational) exercise social control of their members, and they punish deviance.

Social Control and Associations. Sixty-five percent of the U.S. work force is employed. The fact that people join work associations (McDonald's, IBM, military) and schedule their time in reference to the demands of an employer is yet another example of social control. While some people work for prestige and interaction with colleagues, most work for the money. Industry pays their employees to do as they are told and is prepared to hire someone else if they do not comply. Associations often try to control each other. In late 2007, the Writers Guild of America went on strike against the Alliance of Motion Picture and Television Producers. In effect, the writers stopped work as a way of pressuring the various producers on TV to pay them a share of the residual profits including DVD revenues.

Deviance and Associations. Deviance in the form of crime also occurs in associations such as hospitals (charging Medicare and Medicaid for services not performed), churches (televangelism collecting money from the poor and elderly that may not go to those specified), universities (Richard Roberts resigned as Oral Roberts University president, amidst charges that he misspent school funds to support a lavish lifestyle and ordered an accountant to help hide improper and illegal financial maneuvering), and corporations (Enron scandal). Regarding the latter, the government vigorously prosecuted the CEO and other high ranking officials. However, physicians in medical associations or clergy in religious associations may be quietly dealt with or ignored.

Southwest Airlines knowingly flew 46 jets that had not received required inspections for cracks in the fuselage. When such inspections were finally completed, mechanics found cracks on six of the jets. Similar cracks caused a fatal crash on a previous jet in Hawaii. The airline was fined $10.2 million for violations and congressional hearings followed about the safety of airlines. Social control of associations which serve the public is critical (Levin, 2008).

A subcategory of corporate crime is **corporate violence** where corporations actually harm or risk harm to consumers. The harm occurs as a result of decisions by corporate executives, corporate negligence, and willful violations of health and safety. Merck pharmaceuticals pulled the widely used painkiller Vioxx from the market in September 2004 because it was tied to a higher risk of heart attack and stroke. Thousands of lawsuits ensued, and after three years, Merck and the lead plaintiffs' lawyers negotiated a $4.85 billion settlement in late 2007.

Arguments for the plaintiffs included that Merck & Co. conducted a clinical study involving 2,600 patients to determine whether Vioxx was effective in preventing colon cancer and halted the study before its conclusion after it became clear that Vioxx increased the risk of heart attacks and other serious cardiovascular problems. Even with this data, on August 26, 2004, just one month prior to the withdrawal, Merck stated publicly that the drug was safe. The company said it stood behind the "overall safety and cardiovascular safety" of Vioxx. Merck attacked studies from other research groups that found a link between Vioxx and heart attacks, strokes, blood clots, and other serious side effects.

What is it about the structure of corporate decisions which lends itself to making decisions which have extraordinarily inhumane consequences? Some explanations include: 1) Profit Priority. The context within which corporate executives make decisions that jeopardize human life is one in which profits and production schedules take priority. 2) Denial of Responsibility. Because occupational tasks are segmented, corporations can pass along the responsibility if something goes wrong. "We didn't know the part we received was defective" is the mantra. 3) Denial of Injury. Rarely does any corporate decision maker come face to face with victims who die. Tobacco companies have known for 40 years that their product was addictive and caused lung cancer but denied any real negative outcome to consumers.

The future for controlling corporate violence is bleak. Giant corporations escape severe sanctions by helping to shape the laws and the kinds of legal settings in which their socially injurious behavior is handled. Corporate offenders are often tried in civil (rather than criminal) court and are monitored by agencies such as the Food and Drug Administration (which is understaffed). Whatever fines are levied are passed on to consumers through increased prices. When laws are passed that industry does not like, they sue. When the government tried to force McDonald's, KFC, and Burger King to post the nutrition information for the item a customer was about to purchase (there are 576 calories in a Big Mac), the giants filed a lawsuit saying that they had been unfairly targeted to institute this practice. They contended that the calories for their food items were posted on the Internet and available for all interested consumers.

Communities

New York, Chicago, and Los Angeles, as well as the smallest communities in America, maintain social order. They also respond to deviance.

Social Control and Communities. An example of community social control is that individuals are not always allowed to live where they want. Housing ordinances "zone" what land is allocated for housing, parks, and commercial buildings. Each community has rules about when the garbage will be picked up, when people can burn leaves, and how far from the road a house must be built. What may initially appear as "individuals doing their own thing" turns out to be a carefully constructed set of norms with both informal and formal levels of control operating. These dual sets of controls are common in communities. Shanhe, Lambert, and Wang (2007) noted that while there are both informal (family, peers) and formal (police, courts) forms of social control in China, there has been movement in recent decades from informal to more formal social control.

Deviance and Communities. Shaw and McKay (1942) found that high socioeconomic status neighborhoods were associated with low crime rates and that low socioeconomic status neighborhoods were associated with high crime rates. Children in the higher status neighborhoods had consistent exposure to conventional values in peer groups, schools, and churches. Children in the lower status neighborhoods had greater exposure to unconventional values and were far more likely to commit deviant acts.

The community has various ways to punish an offender. In addition to locking up an offender, the person may be put under house arrest (where the offender wears a bracelet that sets off alarms if he or she leaves the house), in a half-way house and/or on probation. All of these mechanisms accomplish the same goal—keeping the person away from negative, criminal models where more "crime skills" can be learned. In addition, traditional institutions have been ineffective in reducing recidivism. They have been regarded as inhumane by civil liberty groups, have encouraged stigmatization by isolating and segregating deviants, and have been very costly.

While the debate about "community" as the best solution to the crime problem continues, crime remains in both large and small communities. In general, social disorder varies by the degree of urbanization. Violent crime and theft increases with population density for two reasons. First, there is greater anonymity in urban areas than rural because people are less likely to recognize strangers and to engage in guardianship activities for their neighbors. Second, hundreds of tenants in high rise buildings make it impossible for adequate police surveillance, and so motivated offenders have an abundance of victims.

Networks

Networks provide an example of how social control is implemented in a community. Networks tie together numerous social organizations through their concern with the deviant activity.

Social Control and Networks. Neighborhoods establish "community watch" programs whereby families meet with other families and pledge to watch out for strangers in the neighborhood who may be potential robbers. Networks tie together numerous families, schools and organizations to control deviant behavior. Signs are posted in the neighborhood, schools, and local churches with plastic stickers placed just above front door handles indicating that the neighborhood is being protected by "community watch." The purpose of such networks is to increase the fear on the part of potential criminals that they are under surveillance and are likely to get caught.

Networks also exist between states in apprehending and returning criminals to the place where they committed the crime. A criminal who flees across state borders soon discovers that the police in the next state have been notified and are cooperating with the law enforcement officers to capture and extradite him or her.

Deviance and Networks. Organized crime depends on networks to carry out their business. For example, a member of organized crime might arrange with a construction contractor to have his heavy equipment such as bulldozers and lift trucks "stolen" and loaded onto a ship (with collusion of government/shipping officials) and sold in South America. The contractor would receive a commission in addition to collecting from his insurance company. Without a network of individuals in construction, shipping, and South America, the scam could not operate. The HBO hit *The Sopranos* depicted the various schemes of the mafia in bilking the public via bogus contracts—made possible by networks within the criminal system.

After a person is detected and arrested for criminal behavior, he/she enters a new network of the judicial system including prosecutors, judges, and lawyers in a variety of courts (trial courts, courts of appeal, and supreme courts) at both the state and federal level. Sentencing involves applying sanctions which include retribution (a person who steals a car would return it with a fresh paint job), rehabilitation (emphasis is on treatment—e.g. DWI offender is required to attend "traffic" school), incapacitation (imprisonment), or deterrence (execution).

A prevailing philosophy operating in the judicial network is to derail the offender from the network as soon as possible. Davis (2007) noted that families informally try to control their adolescents but when this fails, more formal mechanisms such as calling the police are sometimes used. However, doing so may result in the adolescents becoming engaged in the juvenile justice system with its attendant labels. Avoiding entry into the network of police, courts, and detention centers is desirable since the longer a person stays in the judicial system the greater the probability that he/she will return to society with more criminal skills. **Labeling theory** suggests that a person who is labeled by the judicial system as a criminal begins to think and act like one. By not arresting, or not jailing, or not taking the offender to court, negative labeling is avoided. In some cases, police officers cannot overlook criminal acts (robbing a bank). In other cases they can let the offender off with a warning (speeding).

Societies

Societies differ in their manner and ability to control the behavior of their members.

Social Control and Societies. Large, industrial societies characterized by impersonal, **gesellschaft** relationships depend more on formal mechanisms of control than smaller, less technologically developed societies characterized by personal, **gemeinschaft**, intimate face-to-face interactions. Formal mechanisms of social control may not be as effective in the control of large numbers of behaviors as the more pervasive mechanisms of positive and negative sanctions from one's intimates and peers.

In an effort to limit population growth, China has a one child policy that restricts couples to only having one child. Begun in 1979 as a "temporary measure" and restricted to the Chinese living in urban areas (not citizens living in rural areas), the policy has been extended through 2010. Formal sanctions include fines, pressures to abort a pregnancy, and forced sterilization accompanying a second or subsequent pregnancy.

Deviance and Societies. Societies differ in terms of what behaviors they define as criminal. Crime and criminals are socially created. The Puritans of New England had numerous laws regulating public displays of affection. Public kissing resulted in being lodged in the stocks. Sanctions against premarital intercourse were even more severe and could include being whipped and branded on the cheek.

Capitalist societies develop numerous laws defining and protecting property rights. Where property is not central to the functioning of a society, little attention is given to burglary and larceny. Capitalists also define what recreational behaviors are legal and illegal. Capitalists in the tobacco industry have been successful in defining the smoking of tobacco as legal. Although tobacco has been demonstrated to be as addictive as cocaine and a cause of lung cancer, the government continues to run the stabilization program of price supports for tobacco. Marijuana is defined as illegal because the tobacco capitalists do not want their product associated with marijuana.

Popular Beliefs and Scientific Data: Capital Punishment Deters Crime

There is a cultural belief in America that individuals can be stopped from committing crime if the sanction attached to the crime is severe enough. Popular wisdom says, "Tell a person that he or she will receive a fine for armed robbery and he or she is likely to pay no attention. But tell that person that he or she will be executed and he or she is not likely to commit an armed robbery."

Scientific data has revealed that the connection between sanctions and crime deterrence is much more complex. First, in general, the threat of negative sanctions for criminal behavior has only a limited effect in deterring crime. In order for punishment to be effective in keeping behavior under control, it must occur immediately (in animal studies this means within five seconds) after the behavior occurs. Furthermore, when the threat of punishment is removed, the suppressed behavior due to the threat of punishment will re-emerge. Hence, giving the death penalty for a crime is not likely to reduce the frequency of that crime because there is too great a delay in the time from when the crime occurs and the execution. The appeal process allows a convicted criminal to remain on death row for decades. Haapanen et al.(2007) noted that while there is formal social control for criminal behavior, there is considerable variation in types of criminal behavior from murder to safe-cracking (e.g. career criminals).

Second, the effectiveness of deterrence also depends on the certainty of being punished. The death penalty may not be an effective deterrence because people who commit crimes punishable by death may either not get caught or may receive lighter sentences. Peterson and Bailey (1988) collected specific data on the issue of capital punishment and deterrence. Based on their research, they concluded that:

1. Average rates for murder are higher in those states which have retained the death penalty than in those states which have abolished it.

2. When the actual number of death sentences is used as an indicator of the certainty of capital punishment, the findings are uniformly contrary to the deterrence argument. The data indicate that the more people executed, the higher the murder rate.

Two additional variables relating to the effectiveness of deterrence are the type of offender (career vs. non-career) and the type of offense (expressive vs. instrumental). Deterrence is more effective for non-career criminals who engage in isolated criminal acts than for career criminals who repeatedly engage in criminal behavior. **Expressive criminal acts** refer to acts that are intrinsically or emotionally rewarding to the offender. Vandalism, rape, and "passion killings" are expressive acts. **Instrumental criminal acts** are those that achieve a goal or are a means to an end. Committing arson in order to collect insurance and shoplifting food in a grocery store to obtain food for the next meal are examples of instrumental acts. In general, instrumental criminal acts are easier to deter than expressive criminal acts.

Pasternoster and Iovanni (1986) found that the severity and certainty of formal sanctions is insignificant in controlling delinquent behavior. What controls such behavior is parental supervision (parents know where their offspring are and who they are with when the offspring are away from home), moral beliefs (vandalism, drinking alcohol under age and smoking marijuana are regarded as "wrong"), and informal social sanctions (good friends who would be hurt if they knew the person had been arrested).

In summary, while it is widely assumed that the knowledge of capital punishment deters crime, scientific data show that this may not be so. First, criminals or potential criminals may feel confident that they will not get caught.

Second, even if they get caught, they feel that they will get off or get a light sentence. Third, if the crime is an expressive one, the thought of the death penalty will have little influence on the decision to commit an expressive crime such as rape.

References

Bradley, Mindy S. 2007. "Girlfriends, Wives, and Strippers: Managing Stigma in Exotic Dancer Romantic Relationships." *Deviant Behavior*, 28: 379–406.

Capeci, Jr. Dominic J. 2007. "Lynching in America: A History in Documents." *The Journal of Southern History*, 73: 769–771.

Crime in the United States. 2005a. "Age of Persons Arrested in Metropolitan Areas." http://www.fbi.gov/ucr/05cius/data/table_53.html.

Crime in the United States. 2005b. "Age of Persons Arrested in Metropolitan Areas Who Stole an Auto." http://www.fbi.gov/ucr/05cius/data/table_39.html.

Crime in the United States. 2005c. "Gender of Persons Arrested in Metropolitan Areas." http://www.fbi.gov/ucr/05cius/data/table_33.html.

Davis, Carla P. 2007. "At Risk Girls and Delinquency: Career Pathways." *Crime & Delinquency*, 53: 408–435.

Fomby, Paula and Andrew J. Cherlin. 2007. "Family Instability and Child Well-Being." *American Sociological Review*, 72: 181–204.

Haapanen, Rudy, Lee Britton, and Tim Croisdale. 2007. "Persistent Criminality and Career Length." *Crime and Delinquency*, 53: 133–153.

Hazani, Moshe. 1986. "A Path to Deviance: Multi-Stage Process." *Deviant Behavior*, 7: 159–174.

Hipp, J. R. 2007. "Block, Tract, and Levels of Aggregation: Neighborhood Structure and Crime and Disorder as a Case in Point." *American Sociological Review*, 72: 659–681.

Jason, Leonard A., Steven B. Pokorny, Monica Adams, Yvonne Hunt, Gadiraju Praveena, Morello Taylor, Michael Schoeny, and Crystal Dinwiddie. 2007. "Youth Caught in Violation of Tobacco Purchase, Use, and Possession Laws." *Behavior Modification*, 31: 713–731.

Lefin, A. 2008. "Revenge, Threats, Coddling Alleged: Whistle-blowers Tell of Ills Regarding Southwest" *USA Today* April 4–6. p. A1.

Neighbors, Clayton, Christine Lee, Melissa A. Lewis, Nicole Fossos, and Mary E. Larimer. 2007. "Are Social Norms the Best Predictor of Outcomes Among Heavy-Drinking College Students?" *Journal of Studies on Alcohol & Drugs*; 68: 556–565.

Paternoster, Raymond and Leann Iovanni. 1986. "The Deterrent Effect of Perceived Severity: A Reexamination." *Social Forces,* 64: 751–777.

Payne, Allison A. and Steven Salotti. 2007. "A Comparative Analysis of Social Learning and Social Control Theories in the Prediction of College Crime." *Deviant Behavior,* 28: 553–573.

Peterson, Ruth D. and William C. Bailey. 1988. "Murder and Capital Punishment in the Evolving Context of the Post-Furman Era." *Social Forces,* 66: 774–807.

Qian,Wang, Eva Pomerantz, and Chen Huichang. 2007. "The Role of Parents' Control in Early Adolescents' Psychological Functioning: A Longitudinal Investigation in the United States and China." *Child Development,* 78: 1592–1610.

Reiman, Jeffrey H. 1979. *The Rich Get Richer and the Poor Get Prison.* New York: MacMillan.

Rothwell, Gary R. and J. Norman Baldwin. 2007. "Whistle-Blowing and the Code of Silence in Police Agencies." *Crime & Delinquency,* 53: 605–632.

Scoular, Jane and Maggie O'Neill. 2007. "Regulating Prostitution: Social Inclusion, Responsibilization and the Politics of Prostitution Reform." *British Journal of Criminology,* 47: 764–778.

Shaw, Clifford R. and Henry D. McKay. 1942. *Juvenile Delinquency.* Chicago: University of Chicago Press.

Shanhe, Jiang, Eric Lambert, and Jin Wang. 2007. "Correlates of Formal and Informal Social/Crime Control in China: An Exploratory Study." *Journal of Criminal Justice,* 35: 261–273.

Sutherland, E. H. and D. R. Cressey. 1974. *Criminology.* Philadelphia: Lippincott.

Sutherland, E. H. 1939. *Principles of Criminology.* Philadelphia: Lippincott.

Statistical Abstract of the United States: 2008. 127th ed. Washington, D.C.: U.S. Bureau of the Census.

Tyler, Tom, Patrick E. Callahan, and Jeffrey Frost. 2007. "Armed, and Dangerous (?): Motivating Rule Adherence Among Agents of Social Control." *Law & Society Review,* 41: 457–492.

Part III

Less Organized Contexts

Chapter 5

Population and Human Ecology

We all worry about the population explosion, but we don't worry about it at the right time.

Art Hoppe, American columnist

All social organizations are populated. Universities, libraries, communities, families and societies are formed by people. While this is obvious, what is not so obvious is that these same organizations would look and function differently if the characteristics of the people that made them up changed. If universities educated the elderly, if libraries were used mostly by Hispanic Americans, if the communities were made up largely of single unmarrieds and if families and societies were made up of mostly women, these social organizations would be different. Our focus in this chapter is to look at the characteristics of various populations and the changes that occur as populations take different forms. As noted earlier, **population** is the study of characteristics which can be identified on the basis of how they impact the development of social organizations. Although, from a strictly definitional sense, populations are not social organizations, because they have no organization, populations form the core of all other organizations and are a central focus of sociology.

The Study of Population

The study of population is probably one of the oldest areas of human investigation. The ancient Chinese emperors (as did the Greeks and Romans) took a census of their inhabitants for tax and military purposes. Even before sociology became a discipline, population was recognized as a fundamental aspect of social organization. Through the years the study of population has developed into two sub disciplines, demography and human ecology.

Demography

Demography is the scientific study of population. A demographer is one who studies population in terms of its births, deaths, size, distribution, migration and change. Demography is concerned with how population characteristics affect social life. Specific characteristics such as race, religion, age, national origin and sex have profound and far reaching effects on social organizations. Demographic changes also influence social organization. For example, an increase in population may affect associations like education by producing more people than can effectively be educated by the existing schools, thereby creating a great deal of illiteracy. In much the same way growth may come so fast that the occupational workforce is flooded with new entrants who cannot be absorbed, creating unemployment and lower wages for greater numbers of people. With too many people the society may not be able to produce the housing and food necessary to keep its people sheltered and fed. In fact, society must continue to maintain control over ever increasing numbers of people and the problems that may arise with increased numbers. It has been argued that with increasing numbers of people, social order can only be maintained if rules and laws are passed, and social control is exercised over individual freedoms (e.g., China and its one child policy)

Although we have identified the problems of overpopulation, growth is only one example of demographic change. The loss of population is also problematic. Countries with a small population cannot defend themselves and repopulating the population is difficult if the birthrate is low and migration to other societies is high. Other population problem changes involve the growth or decline of specific populations such as women or men, the elderly, or Mexican-Americans. A society with significant increases in women or the elderly or Chicanos changes the whole nature of the entire social organization.

Some of the factors that account for demographic change are births, deaths, and migration. Next, we look at these factors and how they influence social organizations.

Births. The birth of a baby has an impact on existing social organizations. The family structure of a couple changes immediately. When the couple has their first child, instead of just one relationship (between father and mother) suddenly there are four (mother-child, father-child, father-mother, and father-mother-child). In a family of four, 11 relationships are possible; in a family of five, 26; in a family of six, 57. These structural changes are important since they change the potential power alignment in the relationship. When a couple has a baby, the mother and the baby can split off and become a unit in conflict with the father (or vice versa). The fact that there is now a baby in the marital unit decreases the chance that the couple will get a divorce. Beyond the impact on the marital dyad, births impact communities which must now provide more water, sewage treatment, paved streets and electricity, as well as the creation of associations such as day-care for working mothers, education for school-age children, and hospitals for medical problems.

Birth is a biological phenomenon and not everyone is capable of having a child. The biological ability to reproduce is known as **fecundity**. People are either **fecund** (able to reproduce) or **in fecund** (sterile). Demographers study fecundity to determine the potential birth rate of a population. **Fertility** is the actual number of children produced by a woman in her lifetime.

In all societies, people have fewer children (fertility) than they are biologically capable of producing (fecundity). Biologists argue that we need fewer men than women to reproduce a population as one man could impregnate many women if the norms permitted such behavior. On average, women can start reproducing at approximately age 12 and continue having children into their forties. An average woman is biologically capable of producing about twenty-five children in her lifetime. The world population in 2007 was 6.6 billion; in 2050, it is expected to be over 9 billion.

Cultural variables that influence fertility rates include the attitudes, laws, and technology regarding birth control and abortion. To sociologists, individual behavior is not as important as aggregate behavior which determines social patterns. The important focus is the behavior of entire categories of people. If current fertility rates continue, American women will have an average of 2.0 children compared to 1.5 in Canada and Europe and 1.3 in Japan. Higher numbers of children by U.S. women are due to greater ease in combining career and family, higher incomes, and more egalitarian husbands (Population Bulletin, 2007). More recently, women have begun to have their children before becoming established in a career since they are less certain than their mothers that they can "have it all" (baby, husband, career) (Vere, 2007).

Fertility rates are determined, in part, by the social control mechanisms of a society's culture. The mores, folkways and laws tell men and women in each society at what age they may begin to have children. It is the already existing social organization that affects just how many children a woman will have. That organization defines when sexual behavior may begin, with whom, and at what age marriage is allowed. For example, Muslim families carefully restrict the access female children have to males so that they are not allowed to be in the presence of the other sex unless an adult is there to supervise. "Dating" in the American sense of going out alone is not permitted. Indeed, touching and kissing a male is only appropriate once married. Marriage is to occur in one's late teens or early 20s, and having children is expected. Factors such as social class, differences in housing, diet, and healthcare are also operative in terms of whether the woman will have a healthy child.

Birth rates are important because they affect all social contexts. The fewer the number of children a couple has, the happier their marriage, the higher the self esteem of the children, and the more likely the children will go to college, etc. The larger the family, the less happy the marriage (but a lower chance of divorce), the lower the self esteem of the children, and the less likely all of the children will attend college.

The more children the society has the more it must find room for them. The greater the number of children the more resources it must locate and secure, even if that results in war. The lack of resources for a society means that its people will be hungry and have a lower standard of living. Some societies have the problem of too few births. In some parts of Italy, males do not marry and have children until their mid forties. A "tax" on unmarried singles has been considered. If there are no new children being born in a town, and immigration is low, the town can literally cease to exist. The birth rate of a population gives sociologists an important background factor to predict and understand other changes occurring in each of the other eight areas of social organization (discussed later in the chapter).

Deaths. A population changes not only by births but deaths. Just as biological and sociological factors influence births, these same factors also influence deaths. We measure death in both biological and sociological terms. Biologically, **lifespan** refers to the length of life or how old a person could live to, if the person did not die by an accident or disease. The longest unambiguously documented lifespan of a person is that of Jeanne Calment of France (1875–1997), who lived 122 years. The oldest verified American was Sarah Knauss who was 119 when she died in 1999.

The actual (not potential) years that a person lives is called **length of life or longevity**. The longevity experienced by an individual is not the proper subject matter of sociology. If you personally live to be 50 or 100, that may be due to your own motivation (psychology) or genetics. Sociologists are interested in the fact that entire categories of people experience different longevity (see Table 5.1).

In addition to life expectancy by sex and race, there is also variation by categories such as social class, including education, income, and occupation. The higher your social class, the greater your access to health care, your socialization to take care of your health, and your ability to afford it.

Table 5.1
Life Expectancy by Sex and Race, 2010 Projections

Race	Sex		Difference
	Female	Male	between Sexes …
Blacks	77.8	70.9	6.9 years
Whites	81.8	76.1	5.7 years
Difference between all Whites (79.0) and all Blacks (74.5) is 4.5 years			

Source: *Statistical Abstract of the United States, 2008.* 127th edition. U.S. Bureau of the Census, Washington, D.C., Table 98.

Married people are also healthier and live longer than single people. One explanation for better health is that healthy people may be more often selected as a marriage partner. Another explanation is that a spouse often nudges the partner to "go see the doctor for that cough" or other malady so that symptoms are treated earlier. In addition, married people get more sleep, drink less alcohol, and take fewer drugs than single people.

Migration. In addition to births and deaths, demographers study migration. Persons who enter a new country with the thought of making the new country their permanent home are known as **immigrants**. The United States is a nation of immigrants. We sometimes forget that the first settlers to this country were immigrants (our forbearers). In 1776, this country had around 3 and one-half million people who had immigrated to the new shore. From 1900 to 1930, nearly 20 million immigrants came to America.

For the first 100 years of U.S. history, all immigrants were allowed to enter and become permanent residents. The continuing influx of immigrants, especially those coming from nonwhite, non-European countries, created fear and resentment among native-born Americans who competed with these immigrants for jobs. Increasing pressures from U.S. citizens to restrict or halt entirely the immigration of various national groups led to legislation. America's open door policy on immigration ended in 1882 with the Chinese Exclusion Act, which suspended for 10 years the entrance of the Chinese to the United States and declared Chinese ineligible for U.S. citizenship. The Immigration Act of 1917 required all immigrants to pass a literacy test before entering the United States. And in 1921 the Johnson Act introduced a limit on the number of immigrants who could enter the country in a single year, with stricter limitations for certain countries (including those in Africa and the Near East).

The United States is currently debating the immigration issue in response to the estimated 12 million unauthorized migrants in the U.S. The Pew Research Center (2006) estimates that 57% of this population are from Mexico;

24% from Central America and to a lesser extent, South America; 9% from Asia; 6% from Europe; and the remaining 4% from elsewhere. Americans divide about evenly among three main approaches for dealing with people who are in this country illegally: 32% think it should be possible for them to stay permanently; 32% believe some should be allowed to stay under a temporary worker program under the condition that they leave eventually; and 27% think that all illegal immigrants should be required to go home (Pew Research Center, 2006).

There are three primary effects of wave after wave of immigrants (not just Mexicans but Spaniards, Nigerians, Poles, Jews, Irish, Puerto Ricans, Germans, Cubans, and Japanese to name but a few). The first effect is cultural. Americans have been confronted with cultural patterns such as dress, food, values and beliefs that are different from their own.

A second effect involves intergroup relations whereby the composition of neighborhoods, schools, religious institutions and society are changed. New questions arise: What language should be spoken? What food should be served in public schools? What holidays and rituals (e.g. Ramadan of the Muslims) should be observed? Who should be promoted and on what basis? How should people who dress differently and who have different values be treated? There has always been resentment and strife toward immigrants.

Third, compared with the native-born U.S. population, illegal immigrants are more likely to be unemployed and to live in poverty (Larsen 2004). Almost 43 percent of immigrants work at jobs that pay less than $7.50 an hour, compared with 28 percent of all workers (National Immigration Law Center 2007). The states bear the cost of social services, education, and medical services for the immigrant population. However, research suggests that the economic benefits that immigrants provide for the states outweigh the costs associated with supporting them. For example, a study of immigrants in North Carolina found that over the prior 10 years, Latino immigrants had cost the state $61 million in a variety of benefits—but were responsible for more than $9 billion in state economic growth (Beirich 2007).

Sociologists also study **emigration** which is the rate or number of individuals who leave their native country. Emigration may have either beneficial or negative effects upon the country being left behind. On the positive side, people emigrate for more food, shelter, jobs and resources, and for them, the effect may be positive. If large numbers of political dissenters emigrate from a country, it can relieve political stress upon a government. On the negative side, if those who leave are the most educated or belong to segments of the society which are necessary for the society's survival it may cause serious disruption. For example, out of fear for their lives considerable numbers of physicians have left Iraq leaving the country's health care at risk. This **brain drain** of those with advanced medical knowledge can leave behind a country without adequate medical expertise.

Births, deaths and migration are three demographic factors that help us to understand how social contexts exist and change. In addition to demography, population specialists study human ecology.

Human Ecology

To understand the growth and decline of population it is important to keep in mind the fundamental necessities of human life. Air, food, and water are necessary for populations to sustain themselves. As far as we know, Earth is the only planet that has all of the properties necessary to sustain human life. These properties are together called the **biosphere**. We develop our social contexts within this biosphere. Families and communities not only exist within a biosphere but also interact with it. We produce garbage, carbon dioxide, and chemicals which are fed back into the biosphere. This system of interaction between living organisms and the earth's biosphere is called the **ecosystem**. The study of the ecosystem that focuses on how humans interact with the biosphere is called **human ecology**.

Ecologists are concerned with how social actors interact with one another within their existing ecosystem. There are many different ecosystems in America, let alone the world. Some Americans live in very cold climates such as Alaska and some live in the deserts of the Southwest. Some live in cities of several million people while others live in small towns of a few hundred. Each ecosystem is different and requires a different adaptation. Ecologists are concerned not only with how we organize life within our environment but how we affect that environment.

Relationship of Demography to Ecology. Demography is very much linked to the ecological conditions. Births, deaths, and migration are fundamentally tied to ecological factors. For a woman to have a successful birth, she must have reasonably good nutrition and be free of disease. If she lives in an environment in which there is a scarcity of food or a diseased water supply she may be unable to get pregnant or to have healthy children. In a few countries in Africa, more than fifty percent of women are unable to conceive children due to untreated diseases. In some areas of the United States, the death rate for such diseases as childhood leukemia has been abnormally high, as have been childhood birth defects. At the Love Canal area of New York (in the early 1980s) where waste was discovered seeping into basements on 99th Street, four of 39 babies developed birth defects. As birth and death rates vary depending upon ecological factors, so does migration. At Love Canal, 1,030 families migrated out of the area when it could no longer be denied that the air, groundwater and soil were contaminated and probably caused increased dizziness, respiratory problems, and breast cancer rates.

The Environment. Ecologists focus on several aspects of the environment that affect life. They are concerned with the land, atmosphere, food, water and how these elements interact. Ecology raises serious questions for sociologists. The agricultural land of the world is being buried under cities and highways as well as being overused to the point where it is no longer capable of producing an efficient crop yield. The Amazon jungle, one of the world's most important sources of oxygen, is being cut down at an alarming rate. The atmosphere is being polluted with toxins from chemical plants, steel mills and automobiles. The last section of this chapter is devoted to coping with issues of air, water, and food quality.

Population and Social Organization

There are numerous ways that population affects all levels of social organization. In the next section we specify how population affects collective behavior, social classes, groups, families, communities, associations, networks, and societies.

Collective Behavior

An example of how population affects collective behavior is in terms of crowd density. Black Friday is the day after Thanksgiving—one of the busiest shopping days of the year. The term Black Friday refers to the heavy traffic, stress and confusion of the day and gets its name from the infamous Black Tuesday of the 1929 stock market crash. On Black Friday, stores may open at 7:00 A.M. and stay open for 24 hours. Cities with a high population density have enormous crowds, and parking lots are jammed.

Inside the stores, the crowds are so large that movement may grind to a near halt as shoppers slowly nudge their way to merchandise and registers. Individual shopping personality styles are sublimated to the ebb and flow of the mass. From a sociological point of view the interaction between positions such as sales clerk and shopper may change as the characteristics of the crowd change. Conversations at the checkout counter become shorter and specific to the purchase. Social actors who at any other time of the year would wait patiently may exhibit various crowd behaviors which appear rude, impolite, and even hostile. One of the authors observed two women who grabbed the same dress at the same time. They both pulled on the dress so that the whole rack of dresses came down, and both women fell to the floor. They continued their struggle over the dress after they hit the floor. This behavior was in specific reference to population density that changes crowd behavior.

Social Classes

There is a clear relationship between social class and demographic differences in terms of health and life expectancy. Although life expectancy is influenced by biological factors, it is also a social outcome. For example, birth rates are highest among some minority groups and the poor. The lower one's social class, the less food, shelter, fuel (for heat), and health care the individual gets. The result is poorer health and lower life expectancy.

As populations grow, they limit the numbers of individuals who can attain higher social class status. More and more people end up with occupations that provide few benefits. The overall population is often poorer and fewer people find positions in society that will provide power, privilege or prestige. When birth rates are high and large numbers of a population are under thirty and have yet to begin a family, the population as a whole has greater inequality and larger numbers of the poor. When populations change, those changes have direct impacts on the size and growth of lower, middle or upper class ranks.

Groups

Changes in population characteristics affect the formation of groups. Throughout our society, new groups are forming to deal with population changes. Where once (in small towns in rural areas) children's play groups formed spontaneously, mothers of today (in large urban areas) advertise in newspapers and over the Internet for play groups so that they will have someone to talk to and their children will have someone to play with. Where once individuals found partners through their friends and at church and school, increasingly the Internet has become the new place to find a partner. Support groups for singles, nursing mothers, and people with every type of disease are formed through the Internet. These changes are in direct reference to the increase in population where people move away from their hometown and become disconnected from others who share similar characteristics.

Families

Family composition also reflects population changes. An increasing number of elderly need care. About 6.1 percent of the U.S. adult population over the age of 65 are defined as being severely disabled and are not living in nursing homes. Since most do not have long term health insurance, the bulk of their care falls to their children. These 14 million adults not only provide family care giving to their elderly parents but to their own children simultaneously. In effect they are known as the **sandwich generation** since they are in the middle of taking care of the needs of both parents and children. This dual role is in direct reference to population characteristics.

The caregiving for an elderly parent has two meanings. One, caregiving refers to providing personal help with the basics of daily living such as helping the parent get in or out of bed, bathing, toileting, and eating. A second form of caregiving refers to instrumental activities such as grocery shopping, money management (including paying bills), and driving the parent to the doctor. The typical caregiver is a middle-aged married woman who works outside the home. High levels of stress and fatigue may accompany caring for one's elders. Martire and Stephens (2003) noted even higher levels of fatigue and competing demands among women who were both employed and caring for an aging parent. Fifty-five percent of a sample of women at midlife (most of whom had children) reported that they were providing care to their mothers; 34 percent were caring for their fathers (Peterson, 2002).

Population predictions estimate that the number of individuals in the sandwich generation will increase for the following reasons:

1. Longevity. The over-85 age group, the segment of the population most in need of care, is the fastest-growing segment of our population.

2. Chronic disease. In the past, diseases took the elderly quickly. Today, diseases such as arthritis and Alzheimer's are associated not with an immediate death sentence but a lifetime of managing the illness and being cared for by others. Family caregivers of parents with Alzheimer's note the difficulty of the role. "He's not the man I married," lamented one wife.

3. Fewer siblings to help. The current generation of elderly had fewer children than the elderly in previous generations. Hence, the number of adult siblings to help look after parents is more limited. Only children are more likely to feel the weight of caring for elderly parents alone.

Caring for a dependent, aging parent requires a great deal of effort, sacrifice, and decision-making on the part of these adults who are challenged with this situation. The emotional toll on the caregiver may be heavy. Guilt (over not doing enough), resentment (over feeling burdened), and exhaustion (over the relentless care demands) are common feelings that are sometimes mixed. One caregiver adult child said, "I must be an awful person to begrudge taking my mother supper, but I feel that my life is consumed by the demands she makes on me, and I have no time for myself, my children, or my husband."

Communities

Changes in population also have dramatic effects on communities. Population growth and urbanization have left cities with problems of flight. In some areas schools are closed because parents with young children no longer live there. In contrast, large suburban growth has created the need to build new schools (with increased taxes) to accommodate the large influx of students. Some communities also find that they have a large number of elderly. To meet those demographic changes communities have developed programs for the elderly, such as buses to take them to appointments and Meals on Wheels.

Similarly, the influx of Mexicans into border cities of the U.S. has caused an increased need to meet the needs of these individuals. Emergency clinics, food, and housing shelters sometimes find the needs greater than their resources.

Associations

Demographic changes have affected our educational systems at both the high school and college levels. Many high schools have been left with a burgeoning population of poor students with high flunk out and drop out rates. Many colleges and universities have adapted to students who must work full time. Online and evening classes cater to these as well as nontraditional students who have spouses and children.

As the population increases or changes in its basic characteristics, all associations change. If we add another twenty million children, we must build more schools, hospitals, and police stations and produce more jobs. As populations age, the types of occupations change. The need for pediatricians or geriatric specialists is always associated with changes in population. As populations decline, societies need fewer schools, hospitals, and religious associations.

Networks

The rapidly increasing elderly population has led to the development of networks to care for the needs of the elderly. Members of the elderly population may find themselves at the end of their lives with no children living near them and in nursing homes without primary relationships. Networks have developed to provide these elderly with physical (Meals on Wheels), financial (reverse mortgages), emotional (social workers), and medical support (hospice end of life teams). These networks work to identify elderly who have needs and to reach them with the appropriate and necessary help.

Organ donors' networks have developed which identify the person who has died and the part he/she has donated. They also identify the person in America who matches the organ donated and coordinate getting the organ anywhere in America. These networks help not only the elderly but others in need.

Societies

Changes in births, deaths, migration, and the environment alter the structure and process of the society. People are also mobile so that they change their place of residence as their characteristics change. While the young move anywhere the jobs are, the elderly move to warmer climates (Florida and Arizona). These internal migrations change the political composition of those states and the country as a whole.

Population, Social Organizations, and Social Control

Population growth must be controlled. Too many births (uncontrolled fertility), too many deaths (disease and war can decimate a society), and too many immigrants (unwanted expansion) can create problems which must be dealt with by sociologists, politicians, and the public at large. For example, due to loss of life in the war in Iraq, the U.S. is now re-evaluating how many wars it can fight at one time. As the war in Iraq (and Afghanistan) has dragged on, there has been a decrease in the aggressiveness of politicians (both Barack Obama and Hillary Clinton in their bid for the Democratic nomination pledged to end the war) toward war rhetoric as they consider what to do about the nuclear weapon threats of Iran, North Korea, and Pakistan. In the following section we look at how demographers view population control via births, deaths, and migration.

Birth Control Strategies

Some amount of fertility is necessary for a society to reproduce itself. Some societies have enough economic resources to handle a large birthrate. Other societies are already so poor that they must control the birthrate in their nation. There are many forms of birth control which would reduce fertility and allow a society to use its resources for its already existing population. While an average female is capable of producing a child at age 12, the longer she waits before engaging in sexual intercourse, the lower the birth rate and the lower the risk of complications in childbirth. To accomplish the goal of postponing pregnancy, women can abstain from intercourse, reduce the frequency of intercourse, or use one of several methods of birth control. However, the availability of birth control methods has little impact on the birth rate unless the society is organized in such a way as to promote use of birth control. The actions of individuals must be controlled for any society to effectively control its birth rate. One society which has been seriously concerned with its birth rate and has worked hard to control it is China.

With just over 1.3 billion people, China is the world's largest and most populated country. China has one fifth of the world's entire population. By the late 2010s, China's population is expected to reach 1.4 billion. All of these individuals must be fed, clothed, sheltered and cared for medically, educationally, and economically.

China has organized to reduce its population and has the most ambitious program ever created on earth with a goal of zero population growth. China is the poster child for how social organizations (e.g. society) control individual behavior (e.g. number of children). The orchestration of the entire society via various networks is designed to ensure the elimination of large families. Family planning began in the early seventies, and the **one child family campaign** was initiated in 1979. In China, all women are monitored as to when their periods are due and are given a state indoctrination as to the benefits of having only one child.

The benefits for having only one child and the punishments for having more than one child are different depending upon where one lives in China (e.g. urban areas are more strict). Those who have only one child receive free education, medical aid and other services for the child. In addition, the state gives a housing preference and a cash award each year annually until the child is age 14. The child will also get preference when he/she applies for advanced education or a future job. Aging parents who have a certificate from the state showing that they had only one child will receive a larger retirement pension.

Those who choose sterilization after the birth of the first child receive a bonus. One child families in China are also given the same housing space as larger families. However, should a woman have a second child, there are a number of penalties. The couple will be given no bonuses at work. They will be given neither additional housing nor preference for housing. There are also examples of the government shutting off the water and electricity to the home and confiscation of family assets such as televisions for those who have more than one child. In addition, since each Chinese citizen receives a plot of land to grow food, no increased plot will be provided for any additional child born. Parents must pay a tax to the state for the additional child. All of the costs of maternity, birth, education, and health care must be paid by the parents.

In addition to controlling pregnancy, abortion is a commonly used technique to control population. In China, a network of government workers exists to identify those who are pregnant and to keep close watch over each woman's period. Each month women must report when their period has occurred and if it is late; consultations with the woman assure that she understands the norms.

While these sanctions may seem very intrusive and harsh, they are effective in achieving the goal of slowing China's population growth. The birth rate in China has fallen dramatically. While in the early 1960's the birth rate was 47 per 1,000 population, in 2007 it was 13 per 1,000 population or about 1.7 children per woman (total fertility rate) (*World Factbook, China*, 2007). Social control of reproduction in the form of laws and their enforcement (such as a prohibition on early marriage) as well as surveillance, rewards, and punishments have China's number of births under control.

Along with the slowing of the population growth in China, related changes have been that girls are now required to take care of their parents in old age. Previously only males had this responsibility but since a family may have only one child and that child may be a girl, accommodations were made. This reflects that changes in the demographic characteristics of a population will affect all levels of social organization in a society.

Death Control Strategies

In addition to controlling births, societies must develop strategies to increase the length of life. These strategies include (1) better care throughout pregnancy and for the newborn, (2) the use of medicines and, in particular, preventative medicines and (3) increased emphasis on public health and sanitation. The latter two factors are important death control strategies for the elderly and will become even more important in the future. The use of inoculations, particularly against influenza, will keep extending the length of life for most Americans. Increasingly, the elderly will be cared for by public health networks. These networks are replacing the family networks which have been reduced by the high mobility of family members who move from their communities to seek better jobs in other geographic areas. In addition, increasing numbers of women have a full time job which removes them as free labor that is readily available for elder care.

Societies struggle with elder care. It will work to keep the elderly alive with food, shelter, and the necessities of life. In the heat of summer, fire departments send out teams to "make sure the elderly are OK" (don't die of heat exhaustion). Indeed, caring for the elderly involves changes at multiple levels. For example, communities will need more facilities and housing for the aged, and associations will need to cater their goods and services to the elderly. Also, as Social Security continues to be inadequate, the tax structure and governmental expenditures of our society will change. The young will be taxed at higher rates so that the government can spend more money on the elderly.

Although some social actors in all populations wish to die, few societies have given them the opportunity to do so. **Euthanasia** is from the Greek words meaning "good death," or dying without suffering. It is the act of putting an end to a person's life painlessly with the goal of ending their suffering. Euthanasia may be passive, where medical treatment is withdrawn and nothing is done to prolong the life of the patient, or active, which involves deliberate actions to end a person's life.

Active euthanasia received nationwide attention through the actions of Dr. Jack Kevorkian who was involved in over 130 physician-assisted suicides (PAS) at the patients' request. He was sent to prison but paroled in 2007 (which included his agreement to not be involved in subsequent PAS). The Supreme Court has ruled that state law will apply in regard to physician-assisted suicide. In January 2006, the Supreme Court ruled that Oregon has a right to physician-assisted suicide. It's Death with Dignity Act requires that two physicians must agree that the patient is terminally ill and is expected to die within six months, the patient must ask three times for death both orally and in writing, and the patient must swallow the barbiturates themselves rather than be injected with a drug by the physician.

Migration Control Strategies

Any society can only take care of a limited number of people. If the society continues to experience a large influx of foreign immigrants, it will have a serious problem. America as a nation began with open arms to everyone, everywhere. On the Statue of Liberty is the phrase "Give me your tired, your poor, your huddled masses yearning to breathe free …" Well, the masses came to the point that America has said "enough." About 1.5 million legal immigrants are admitted to the United States annually. This number is in addition to the illegal immigrants, estimated to be close to another million. Already, there are estimated to be over 8 million illegal household members from Mexico alone.

Coping with Environmental Destruction

In addition to developing strategies to control birth, death, and migration changes in the population, each society must contend with the environment to ensure that it provides the basics for human survival. The earth can sustain only so many people. Biologists refer to **carrying capacity,** or the ability of the ecosystem to sustain life. Sometimes the population interacts with the ecosystem in a way that results in its destruction. We have reached a point when our social organization must change for life to continue. Some of the problems we consider are air and water pollution as well as food contamination.

Air Pollution

Hold your breath, and you will soon be reminded of the value of air to maintain human life. Stop holding your breath, and fill your lungs with air. What goes without notice is that the quality of the air now in your lungs is being contaminated on a daily basis. The fumes from transportation vehicles and industrial processes (such as the burning of coal and the processing of minerals from mining) contribute to the toxic levels of air pollutants, including carbon monoxide, sulfur dioxide, nitrogen dioxide, mercury, and lead. Air pollution levels are highest in areas with both heavy industry and traffic congestion, such as Los Angeles, New Delhi, Jakarta, Bangkok, Tehran, Beijing, and Mexico City.

Air pollution kills about three million people annually (Pimentel et al. 2007). Air pollution is linked to heart disease, lung cancer, and respiratory ailments, such as emphysema, chronic bronchitis, and asthma. In Western and Central Europe, air pollution shortens average life expectancy by almost one year (European Environment Agency 2007). In all regions of Europe, the estimated annual loss of life due to air pollution is significantly greater than that due to car accidents.

In the United States, nearly half (46 percent) of the population lives in counties that have either short-term or year-round unhealthy levels of either smog or particulate air pollution. Nearly one in five U.S. residents lives in an area with unhealthful levels of particulate pollution (American Lung Association 2007). Indoor air pollution from burning wood and biomass for heating and cooking, which we discuss next, is a significant cause of respiratory illness, lung cancer, and blindness in developing countries.

1. *Indoor Air Pollution.* When we hear the phrase *air pollution,* we typically think of industrial smokestacks and vehicle exhausts emitting gray streams of chemical matter into the air. But indoor air pollution is also a major problem, especially in poor countries. Indeed, more than half of the world's population cook food in their home and generate heat by burning dung, wood, crop waste, or coal on open fires or stoves without chimneys (World Health Organization 2005). The resulting indoor smoke contains health-damaging pollutants including small soot or dust particles that are able to penetrate deeply into the

lungs. Exposure is particularly high among women and children, who spend the most time near the domestic hearth or stove. Every year, indoor air pollution is responsible for the death of 1.6 million people. Exposure to indoor air pollution increases the risk of pneumonia, chronic respiratory disease, asthma, cataracts, tuberculosis, and lung cancer.

Even in affluent countries much air pollution is invisible to the eye and exists where we least expect it—in our homes, schools, workplaces, and public buildings. Sources of indoor air pollution include lead dust (from old lead-based paint); secondhand tobacco smoke; by-products of combustion (e.g., carbon monoxide) from stoves, furnaces, fireplaces, heaters, and dryers; and other common household, personal, and commercial products (American Lung Association 2005). Some of the most common indoor pollutants include carpeting (which emits more than a dozen toxic chemicals); mattresses, sofas, and pillows (which emit formaldehyde and fire retardants); pressed wood found in kitchen cabinets and furniture (which emits formaldehyde); and wool blankets and dry-cleaned clothing (which emit trichloroethylene). Air fresheners, deodorizers, and disinfectants emit the pesticide Para dichlorobenzene. Potentially harmful organic solvents are present in numerous office supplies, including glue, correction fluid, printing ink, carbonless paper, and felt-tip markers. Many homes today contain a cocktail of toxic chemicals (Rogers 2002). In reference to population, more people equal more toxic products.

2. *Destruction of the Ozone Layer.* The **ozone layer** of the earth's atmosphere protects life on earth from the sun's harmful ultraviolet rays. Yet the ozone layer has been weakened by the use of certain chemicals, particularly chlorofluorocarbons (CFCs), used in refrigerators, air conditioners, spray cans, and other applications. The depletion of the ozone layer allows hazardous levels of ultraviolet rays to reach the earth's surface and is linked to increases in skin cancer and cataracts, weakened immune systems, reduced crop yields, damage to ocean ecosystems including reduced fishing yields, and adverse effects on animals.

Satellite data reveal that the ozone hole in 2007 was 9.7 million square miles—just larger than the size of North America (NASA 2007). The ozone hole was largest in 2006 when it reached a record-breaking area of 11.4 million square miles. Despite measures that have ended production of CFCs, the ozone hole is not expected to shrink significantly for about another decade. This is because CFCs already in the atmosphere remain for 40 to 100 years. Full recovery of the ozone layer is expected in about 2070 (NASA 2007).

3. *Acid Rain.* Air pollutants, such as sulfur dioxide and nitrogen oxide, mix with precipitation to form **acid rain.** Polluted rain, snow, and fog contaminate crops, forests, lakes, and rivers. As a result of the effects of acid rain, all the fish have died in a third of the lakes in New York's Adirondack Mountains

(Blatt 2005). Because pollutants in the air are carried by winds, industrial pollution in the Midwest falls back to earth as acid rain on southeast Canada and the northeast New England states.

Acid rain is not just a problem in North America; it decimates plant and animal species around the globe. In China, most of the electricity comes from burning coal, which creates sulfur dioxide pollution and acid rain that falls on one-third of China, damaging lakes, forests, and crops (Woodward 2007). Acid rain also deteriorates the surfaces of buildings and statues. "The Parthenon, Taj Mahal, and Michelangelo's statues are dissolving under the onslaught of the acid pouring out of the skies" (Blatt 2005, p. 161).

4. *Global Warming and Climate Change.* Former Vice President Al Gore's bestselling book and award-winning film *An Inconvenient Truth* are widely credited for raising public awareness of global warming and climate change. The seriousness of global warming was underscored in 2007 when the Nobel Peace Prize was awarded to Al Gore and the Intergovernmental Panel on Climate Change for their work to raise awareness of global warming.

Global warming refers to the increasing average global air temperature, caused mainly by the accumulation of various "greenhouse gases" (carbon dioxide (CO_2), methane, and nitrous oxide) that collect in the atmosphere. While there are skeptics that global warming exists, the Intergovernmental Panel on Climate Change (IPCC)—a team of more than 1,000 scientists from 113 countries concluded that "Warming of the climate system is unequivocal, as is now evident from observations of increases in global average air and ocean temperatures, widespread melting of snow and ice, and rising global average sea level" (2007a, p. 5). Eleven of the 12 years spanning 1995 to 2006 ranked among the 12 warmest years in global surface temperature since 1850. Average global surface temperatures have increased by about 0.74° C over the past century (1906–2005) (Intergovernmental Panel on Climate Change 2007a). If current greenhouse gas emissions trends continue (in part related to an expanding population), average global temperatures may rise another 2° C by 2035. Although 2° C may not seem significant, average temperatures during the last Ice Age were only 5° C lower than they are today (Woodward 2007).

Deforestation also contributes to increasing levels of carbon dioxide in the atmosphere. Trees and other plant life use carbon dioxide and release oxygen into the air. As forests are cut down or are burned, fewer trees are available to absorb the carbon dioxide. Total world carbon dioxide emissions were 9.9 billion tons in 2006, 35 percent above emissions in 1990 (Global Carbon Project 2007). The growth of emissions is strongest in developing countries, particularly China.

Even if greenhouse gases are stabilized, global air temperature and sea level are expected to continue to rise for hundreds of years. That is because global warming that has already occurred contributes to further warming of the planet—a process known as a *positive feedback loop*. For example, the melting of Siberia's frozen peat bog—a result of global warming—could release billions of tons of methane, a potent greenhouse gas, into the atmosphere (Pearce 2005). And the melting of ice and snow—another result of global warming— exposes more land and ocean area, which absorbs more heat than ice and snow, further warming the planet.

Droughts are also expected to increase with rising temperatures. Globally, the proportion of land surface in extreme drought is predicted to increase from 1 to 3 percent (present day) to 30 percent by 2090 (Intergovernmental Panel on Climate Change 2007). Drought threatens agricultural production and food security in areas of the world where hunger is already epidemic (United Nations Development Program 2007). In summer 2003, more than 52,000 Europeans died from heat-related causes (Larsen 2006). In the summer of 2006, more than 140 Californians died in a triple-digit heat wave that lasted for nearly two weeks.

Another effect of global warming is an increase in the number and size of forest fires. In the Western region of the United States, wildfire activity increased suddenly and markedly in the mid-1980s, with higher large-wildfire frequency, longer wildfire durations, and longer wildfire seasons (Westerling et al. 2006). Warmer temperatures dry out brush and trees, creating ideal conditions for fires to spread. Global warming also means that spring comes earlier, making the fire season longer. In 1988, a massive fire burned a third of Yellowstone National Park. Since then, fires have broken records in nine states (CBS 2007).

Water Pollution

Our water is being polluted by a number of harmful substances, including pesticides, vehicle exhaust, acid rain, oil spills, and industrial, military, and agricultural waste. Fertilizer runoff from agricultural lands in the Mississippi River Basin is the main cause of the annual "Dead Zone"—a seasonal phenomenon in which oxygen depletion causes an area of the Gulf of Mexico the size of Massachusetts to become uninhabitable to marine organisms.

Water pollution is most severe in developing countries, where more than 1 billion people lack access to clean water. In developing nations as much as 95 percent of untreated sewage is dumped directly into rivers, lakes, and seas that are also used for drinking and bathing (Pimentel et al. 1998). Mining operations, located primarily in developing countries are notoriously damaging to the environment. Modern gold-mining techniques use cyanide to extract gold from low-grade ore. Cyanide is extremely toxic: One teaspoon of a two percent cyanide solution can kill an adult (cyanide was used to kill Jews in Hitler's gas chambers). In 2000, a dam holding cyanide-laced waste at a Romanian gold mine broke, dumping 22 million gallons of cyanide-laced waste into the Tisza River, which flowed into Hungary and Serbia. Some have called this event the worst environmental disaster since the 1986 Chernobyl nuclear explosion. Most gold is used to make jewelry, hardly a necessity warranting the environmental degradation that results from gold mining. To make matters worse, about 300,000 tons of waste are generated for every ton of marketable gold—which translates into roughly 3 tons of waste per gold wedding ring (Sampat 2003).

In the United States one indicator of water pollution is the number of fish advisories issued; these advisories warn against the consumption of certain fish caught in local waters because of contamination with pollutants such as mercury and dioxin. In 2006, there were 3,851 state-issued fish advisories in effect covering more than one third (38 percent) of total U.S. lake acreage (excluding the Great Lakes) and about one-fourth (26 percent) of river miles (EPA 2007a). The U.S. Environmental Protection Agency (EPA) advises women who may become pregnant, pregnant women, nursing mothers, and young children to avoid eating certain fish altogether (swordfish, shark, king mackerel, and tilefish) because of the high levels of mercury (EPA 2004).

Pollutants also find their way into the water we drink. At Camp Lejeune—a Marine Corps base in Onslow County, North Carolina—as many as 1 million people were exposed to water contaminated with trichloroethylene (TCE), an industrial degreasing solvent, and tetrachloroethylene (PCE), a dry-cleaning agent from 1957 until 1987. The Agency for Toxic Substances and Disease Registry found levels of PCE in Camp Lejeune's drinking water system during the affected years as high as 200 parts per billion, compared with 5 parts per billion, the amount that federal regulators set in 1992 as the maximum allowable level (Sinks 2007). Exposure to TCE may cause nervous system defects, kidney, liver and lung damage, abnormal heartbeat, coma, and possibly death. Exposure to TCE has been associated with adult cancers (such as kidney and liver cancer), and non-Hodgkin's lymphoma, as well as childhood leukemia and birth defects. Exposure to PCE can cause dizziness, headaches, sleepiness, confusion, nausea, difficulty in speaking and walking, unconsciousness, and death. Exposure to PCE-contaminated drinking water has been linked with non-Hodgkin's lymphoma, leukemia, bladder cancer, and breast cancer (Sinks 2007).

Food Contamination

In developing countries, food contamination, largely caused by poor sanitation, is a major public health problem causing millions of deaths each year.

Although food and water in the United States and other wealthy countries are far safer than in poor countries, there are still significant concerns about food safety in the industrialized world, where up to 30 percent of the population suffers from food-borne diseases each year (World Health Organization 2007). In the United States, there are about 76 million cases of food-borne illness each year, resulting in 325,000 hospitalizations and 5,000 deaths annually.

Public health food safety campaigns often stress how consumers can protect against food-borne illness by following recommendations for safe handling, storage, and preparation of food. However, most contamination of food occurs early in the production process, rather than just before consumption (U.S. Department of Agriculture 2001). For example, increasingly, food animals are not raised in expansive meadows or pastures. Rather, they are raised in concentrated animal feeding operations (CAFOs): giant corporate-controlled livestock farms where large numbers (sometimes tens or hundreds of thousands) of animals—typically cows, hogs, turkeys, or chickens—are "produced" in factory-like settings, often indoors, to maximize production and profits. Also referred to as "factory farms," CAFOs account for 74 percent of the world's poultry products, 68 percent of eggs, 50 percent of all pork, and 43 percent of beef (Nierenberg 2006). In the United States, there are 18,900 CAFOs.

The diet of factory-farmed animals consists largely of corn, which is cheap, plentiful, and efficient in fattening the animals. Corn-fed beef is less healthy than grass-fed beef, as it contains more saturated fat, which contributes to heart disease (Pollan 2006). In addition, the digestive system of cows is designed for grass; corn makes cows sick and susceptible to a variety of diseases. Other factory-farmed animals, including chickens, turkeys, and hogs, and farm-raised fish are also susceptible to disease because of the crowded and unsanitary living conditions. To prevent the spread of disease in CAFOs or fish farms, food animals are fed steady diets of antibiotics. Indeed, most antibiotics sold in the United States end up in animal feed. This overuse of antibiotics in food animals affects consumers by contributing to the emergence of super-resistant bacteria that cause infections that will not respond to treatment.

Another problem is cow milk. About a third of U.S. dairy cows are given recombinant bovine growth hormone (rBGH), manufactured by Monsanto and sold under the trade name Posilac, to increase milk production by about 10 percent. Although the Food and Drug Administration (FDA) approved Posilac in 1993 and has supported Monsanto's claims that milk containing rBGH is safe for consumers, some experts warn that the level of insulin-like growth factor found in rBGH raises the risk of breast, colon, and prostate cancer (Epstein 2006). Other countries, including **all** of Europe, Canada, Australia, New Zealand, and Japan, have banned milk containing rBGH.

The best-selling book, *Fast Food Nation*, and 2006 movie of the same title succinctly explained a major health problem related to modern slaughterhouse and meatpacking production techniques: "There is shit in the meat" (Schlosser 2002, p. 197). Schlosser cited a 1996 nationwide U.S. Department of Agriculture study showing that more than three-quarters of the ground beef sampled contained several microbes, which are spread primarily by fecal material. Schlosser explained that in the slaughterhouse, if the animal's hide has not been adequately cleaned, chunks of manure may fall from it onto the meat. When the cow's stomach and intestines are removed, the fecal matter in the digestive system may spill out and contaminate the meat as well. Schlosser (2002) explained that "the increased speed of today's production lines makes the task much more difficult. A single worker at a 'gut table' may eviscerate sixty cattle an hour" (p. 203). At least three or four cattle infected with the microbe *Escherichia coli* O157:H7, which can cause serious illness and death in humans, are processed at a large slaughterhouse every hour. Because of the mass production techniques of modern meat processing, a single cow infected with *E. coli* O157:H7 can contaminate 32,000 pounds of ground beef (Schlosser 2002). A single fast food hamburger contains meat from dozens or even hundreds of different cattle.

Finally, a number of health problems result from the massive quantities of animal waste that are produced and stored around factory farms. A single dairy cow produces more than 20 tons of manure annually, and a hog can produce more than two tons (Weeks 2007). In North Carolina, the amount of waste produced by the state's 7 million factory-raised hogs is four times the amount of waste produced by the entire human population of North Carolina (Robbins 2001). Manure is often stored in lagoons, but these lagoons leak, break, or are washed away by big storms, contaminating river and ground water. Sometimes manure is stored in large lagoons until it can be sprayed on fields as fertilizer.

Public awareness of health problems associated with modern animal food production methods has increased in recent years, leading many consumers to make different food choices. For example, many consumers are buying dairy products that are organic or otherwise labeled as rBGH-free (organic milk cannot contain rBGH) and organic meats and wild-caught fish that are not fed antibiotics. Communities are calling for safer methods of animal waste management, and residents are protesting the building of new factory farms. Some consumers are buying meat that is irradiated to kill pathogens; others are choosing to avoid undercooked meat or to avoid eating meat altogether.

The ecological state of the world is in crisis. This nation, as well as the world, must do more to maintain its biosphere. Given that we have destroyed so much, it is a wonder that we have not yet destroyed ourselves. From a sociological viewpoint, the solution to demographic and ecological problems will be found in new forms of social organizations.

Popular Beliefs and Scientific Data: Overpopulation and Societal Destruction

World population is projected to grow from 6.7 billion in 2007 to 9.2 billion in 2050 (United Nations 2007). Although China is the most populated country in the world today, India will become the most populated country by 2050.

It is commonly believed that overpopulation is occurring and that this has negative consequences for the planet. The data show that increases in population, per se, is not a problem but the effect of increased population on resource depletion. Also, not all societies are experiencing overpopulation.

Environmental Problems and Resource Scarcity

It is not the number of people that puts a society at risk but the demand these people make on natural resources and the pollution they leave behind. As Hunter (2001) explained:

> Global population size is inherently connected to land, air, and water environments because each and every individual uses environmental resources and contributes to environmental pollution. While the scale of resource use and the level of wastes produced vary across individuals and across cultural contexts, the fact remains that land, water, and air are necessary for human survival (p. 12).

Population growth places increased demands on natural resources, such as forests, water, cropland, and oil and results in increased waste and pollution. Over the past 50 years Earth's ecosystems have been degraded more rapidly and extensively than in any other comparable period of time in human history (Millennium Ecosystem Assessment 2005).

The countries that suffer most from shortages of water, farmland, and food are developing countries with the highest population growth rates. For example, about one-third of the developing world's population (1.7 billion people) lives in countries with severe water stress (Weiland 2005). However, countries with the largest populations do not necessarily have the largest impact on the environment. This is because the impact that each person makes on the environment—each person's **environmental footprint**—is determined by the patterns of production and consumption in that person's culture. The environmental footprint of an average person in a high-income country is about six times bigger than that of someone in a low-income country and many more times bigger than that in the least developed nations (United Nations Population Fund 2004). For example, even though the U.S. population is only one-fourth the size of India's, its environmental footprint is about three times bigger—the United States releases about three times as much carbon into the atmosphere each year as does India. Hence, although population growth is a contributing factor in environmental problems, patterns of production and consumption are at least as important in influencing the effects of population on the environment.

Humans have used more of the earth's natural resources since 1950 than in the million years preceding 1950 (Lamm 2006). Population growth, combined with consumption patterns, is depleting natural resources such as forests, water, minerals, and fossil fuels. For example, freshwater resources are being consumed by agriculture, by industry, and for domestic use. More than 1 billion people lack access to clean water (Fornos 2005).

Problems Associated with Below-Replacement Fertility

Although some predict that population will stabilize around the middle of the 21st century, no one knows for sure. There has been a significant reduction in fertility rates around the world, from a global average of 5 children per woman in the 1950s to 2.55 children in 2007 (United Nations 2007). To reach population stabilization, fertility rates throughout the world would need to achieve what is called "replacement level," whereby births would replace, but not outnumber, deaths. **Replacement-level fertility** is 2.1 births per woman, that is, slightly more than 2 because not all female children will live long enough to reach their reproductive years. More than 50 countries have already achieved below-replacement fertility rates, and by 2050 the average fertility rate worldwide is projected to be below replacement level.

In more than one-third of the world's countries—including China, Japan, and all European countries—fertility rates have fallen well below the 2.1 children replacement level (Butz 2005). Because these low fertility rates will eventually lead to population decline, some reports have sounded an alarm about the possibility of a "birth dearth." Low fertility rates lead not only to a decline in population size but also to an increasing proportion of the population comprising elderly members. A birth dearth eventually results in fewer workers to support the pension, social security, and health care systems for the elderly. Below-replacement fertility rates also raise concern about the ability of a country to maintain a productive economy, because there may not be enough future workers to replace current workers as they age and retire.

References

American Lung Association. 2005. "*Lung Disease Data in Culturally Diverse Communities: 2005*." Available at http://www.lungusa.org.

American Lung Association. 2007. "*State of the Air: 2007*." Available at http://lungaction.org.

Beirich, Heidi. 2007. "Getting immigration facts straight." *Intelligence Report* (Summer). Available at http://www.splcenter.org.

Blatt, Harvey. 2005. *America's Environmental Report Card: Are We Making the Grade?* Cambridge, Mass: MIT Press.

Butz, Bill. 2005. "The World's Next "*Population Problem*." *Population Reference Bureau*." Available at http://www.prb.org.

CBS. 2007 (October 21). "*Expert: Warming Climate Fuels Mega-Fires*." *60 Minutes*. Available at http://www.cbsnews.com.

EPA (U.S. Environmental Protection Agency). 2004. "*What You Need to Know About Mercury in Fish and Shellfish*." Available at http://www.epa.gov.

EPA. 2006. "*Municipal Solid Waste in the United States: 2005 Facts and Figures*." Available at http://www.epa.gov.

EPA. 2007a (July). "*National Listing of Fish Advisories*." Available at http://www.epa.gov.

EPA. 2007b. "*NPL Site Totals by Status and Milestone*." Available at http://www.epa.gov/superfund/sites.

Epstein, Samuel S. 2006. *What's in Your Milk?* Victoria, BC, Canada: Trafford.

European Environment Agency. 2007. "*Europe's Environment: The Fourth Assessment*." Copenhagen: European Environment Agency.

Fornos, Werner. 2005. "Homo Sapiens: An Endangered Species?" *Popline*, 27:4.

Global Carbon Project. 2007 (Oct. 20). "*Recent Carbon Trends and the Global Carbon Budget*." Available at http://www.globalcarbonproject.org.

Hunter, Lori M. 2001. "*The Environmental Implications of Population Dynamics*." Santa Monica: Rand Corporation.

Intergovernmental Panel on Climate Change. 2007a. "*Climate Change 2007: The Physical Science Basis*." United Nations Environmental Programme and the World Meteorological Organization. Available at http://www.ipcc.org.

Intergovernmental Panel on Climate Change. 2007. "*Climate Change 2007: Impacts, Adaptation and Vulnerability*." Available at http://www.ipcc.ch.

Lamm, Richard. 2006. "The Culture of Growth and the Culture of Limits." *Conservation Biology,* 20(2): 269–271.

Larsen, Luke J. 2004 (August). "The Foreign-Born Population in the United States: 2003." Current Population Reports P20-551. U.S. Census Bureau. Available at http://www.census.gov.

Martire, L. M., and M. A. P. Stephens. 2003. "Juggling Parent Care and Employment Responsibilities: The Dilemmas of Adult Daughter Caregivers in the Workforce." *Sex Roles: A Journal of Research,* 48:167–74.

Millennium Ecosystem Assessment. 2005. *Ecosystems and Human Well-Being: Synthesis.* Washington, D.C.: Island Press.

National Immigration Law Center. 2007. Facts about Immigrant Workers. Available at http://www.nilc.org.

NASA. 2007 (October 18). "*NASA Data Reveals 'Average' Ozone Hole in 2007.*" Available at http://www.nasa.gov.

Niemeier, H. M., H. A. Raynor, El E. Lloyd-Richardson, M. L. Rogers, and R. R. Wing. 2006. "Fast Food Consumption and Breakfast Skipping: Predictors of Weight-Gain from Adolescence to Adulthood in a Nationally Representative Sample." *Journal of Adolescent Health,* 39(6):842–849.

Pearce, Fred. 2005. "Climate Warming as Siberia Melts." *New Scientist,* August 11. Available at http://www.NewScientist.com.

Peterson, B. E. 2002. "Longitudinal Analysis of Midlife Generativity, Intergenerational Roles, and Care Giving." *Psychology and Aging,* 17:161–68.

Pimentel, David, Maria Tort, Linda D'Anna, Anne Krawic, Joshua Berger, Jessica Rossman, Fridah Mugo, Nancy Don, Michael Shriberg, Erica Howard, Susan Lee, and Jonathan Talbot. 1998. "Ecology of Increasing Diseases: Population Growth and Environmental Degradation." *BioScience,* 48: 817–827.

Pew Research Center. 2006. "America's Immigration Quandary." Retrieved December 2, 2007, http://people-press.org/reports/display.php3?PageID=1045.

Pollan, Michael. 2006. *The Omnivore's Dilemma.* New York: Penguin.

Population Bulletin: 2007 World Population Highlights. Vol. 63, No. 3 September. http://www.prb.org/pdf07/62.3Highlights.pdf.

Robbins, John. 2001. *The Food Revolution.* San Francisco: Conari Press.

Rogers, Sherry A. 2002. *Detoxify or Die.* Sarasota, FL: Sand Key.

Sampat, Payal. 2003. "Scrapping Mining Dependence." In *State of the World 2003,* Linda Starke, ed. (pp. 110–129). New York: W. W. Norton.

Schlosser, Eric. 2002. *Fast Food Nation.* New York: HarperCollins.

Sinks, Thomas. 2007 (June 12). *Statement by Thomas Sinks, Ph.D., Deputy Director, Agency for Toxic Substances and Disease Registry on ATSDR's Activities at U.S. Marine Corps Base Camp Lejeune before Committee on Energy and Commerce Subcommittee on Oversight and Investigations United States House of Representatives.* Available at http://www.hhs.gov.

United Nations Development Programme. 2007. *Human Development Report 2007/2008: Fighting Climate Change: Human Solidarity in a Divided World.* New York: Palgrave Macmillan.

United Nations Population Fund. 2004. *The State of World Population 2004.* New York: United Nations.

U.S. Department of Agriculture. 2001. Economics of Food borne Disease: Food and Pathogens. Available at http://www.ers.usda.gov.

Vere, James P. 2007. "'Having it All' No Longer: Fertility, Female Labor Supply, and the New Life Choices of Generation X." *Demography,* 44: 821–828.

Weeks, Jennifer. 2007 (January 12). "Factory Farms." *The CQ Researcher,* 17(2).

Westerling, A. L., H. G. Hidalgo, D. R. Cayan, and T. W. Swetnam. 2006. *Science,* 313 (5789): 940–943.

Woodward, Colin. 2007. Curbing Climate Change. *CQ Global Researcher,* 1(2):27–50. Available at http://www.globalresearcher.com.

World Health Organization. 2005. *Indoor Air Pollution and Health.* Fact Sheet. Available at http://www.who.org.

World Health Organization. 2007. *World Health Report 2007: A Safer Future: Global Public Health Security in the 21st Century.* Available at http://www.who.int.

World Factbook, China. 2007. https://www.cia.gov/library/publications/the-world-factbook/print/ch.html.

Chapter 6

Collective Behavior and Social Movements

Major social movements eventually fade into the landscape not because they have diminished but because they have become a permanent part of our perceptions and experience.

Freda Adler, author

Prior to the taping of the Jay Leno and David Letterman nighttime shows, someone comes onstage to greet the audience and "warm them up." They are told that the success of the show will depend on their clapping and laughing. Indeed, large signs light up with the word APPLAUSE so that there will be no mistake what is expected. Initially, it all seems so staged but soon the group norms take hold, everyone laughs at everything. In effect individuals change in the context of an audience. They have become an **aggregation**—a minimally ordered, more or less spontaneous collective that lasts for only a brief time.

Individuals routinely become an aggregation—when they are on a subway or plane; when they attend a concert, when they eat in a restaurant, or when they watch a movie in a theater. An aggregate becomes a **collective** when the individuals act in unison. An example of **collective behavior** is students gathering on the student mall protesting a proposed increase in student fees. Other examples of aggregations and collectives studied by sociologists include fads (tattoos, piercings), crazes (latest video game), panics (stampede at concert when gates open), riots (Jena 6) and revolutions (against dictatorships).

In contrast to aggregations or collectives are **social movements.** These are usually planned and structured and involve widespread social action unifying large numbers of a segment of the population who believe in a political or social cause not yet accepted as "normal." Social movements are about making or undoing social change. Tilly (2004) defined social movements as a series of contentious performances, displays and campaigns by which ordinary people make collective claims on others. Examples of social movements include the anti-Iraq war movement which seeks an end to the war, the women's movement which seeks the elimination of oppression and inequality, the civil rights movement which has the goal of eliminating racism and the gay rights movement which seeks an end to discrimination against gays including the legalization of same-sex marriage. Still other social movements include the pro-choice movement, the environmental movement, and the free software movement. Social movements often have specific behavioral goals such as the environmental movement which exhorts individuals to participate in a range of behaviors to ameliorate the negative impact of their lifestyles (Barr and Gilg, 2007). Other social movements may focus on moral issues, such as the anti-sweatshop movement which has its basis in the idea of moral rights (absence of harm) (Meyers, 2007). In this chapter we discuss both collective behavior and social movements in detail.

Collective Behavior

Aggregations may engage in collective behavior, and this behavior may affect all levels of social organization. The important point is that when aggregations form, the individual no longer acts with free will—no longer behaves as an individual.

Aggregations and Collective Behavior

As noted, examples of aggregations include crowds, audiences, and mobs. In effect these are spontaneous groups of people that begin to act in unison—an audience for Leno or Letterman to cheer them on, a crowd gathering on the street to look at an accident, or a mob out to taunt O.J. Simpson as he leaves the courtroom and gets in a van on the way back to his cell. These collectives reflect a common culture and socialization to act in predictable ways. No one is going to throw a frisbee at Leno or Letterman, the accident gawkers will look and leave, and the Simpson mob will disband in disgust when he enters the van and is driven away.

The Effects of Collective Behavior on Established Social Organizations

Collective behavior comes into existence almost without warning, doesn't last very long and doesn't begin as a well organized reaction. Collective behavior is sometimes the result of the inability of social actors to realize their goals in existing social organizations. The Writers Guild of America strike in 2007–2008 was a result of 12,000 writers of film, television and radio being ignored through formal channels. The members stopped work to get recognition for their demands from eight corporations including CBS, Metro-Goldwyn-Mayer, NBC, and Paramount Pictures. At issue was money to the writers for sales from reruns, DVDs and secondary markets.

Crowds

A **crowd** is a large gathering of individuals who share a common concern. This common focus often changes the individuals into adopting new crowd roles and behaviors. These changes are due, in part, because the crowd context produces anonymity, contagion, and suggestibility. *Anonymity* allows the actions of the individuals to occur without the usual fear that they would be held accountable. In a mass of hundreds or thousands, the actions of any one person are lost in the totality of the crowd. An individual feels less constrained to follow the usual norms. *Contagion* occurs as the emotions of the crowd spread and each feels influenced by its impact. Each social actor becomes excited by the overall effect and is *suggestible* to new forms of action (Le Bon, 2002).

Gustave Le Bon viewed crowds as having their own mind, reducing individuals to an automaton that follows the crowd. All individuals become a part of a crowd at some time every day, and they act in reference to the aggregation rather than as an individual. For example, assume that you are in a line of 12 cars on a busy street. Ahead, you can see that the cars are not moving. Suddenly one individual in one car beeps, then two. Before long there is a cacophony of beeps. The individuals in each of the cars have become an aggregation acting in unison. In the next section, we examine the different types of crowds. Indeed, the nature and type of crowds we belong to will have a different affect upon our behaviors.

Crowds as Social Organizations

A large number of individuals are simply numbers to be counted. One hundred different people in a public park may be doing 100 different things. But when each individual perceives a common focus of the group, they become a crowd. When a terrorist bomb is heard and someone yells "run," the population of individuals becomes a crowd on the run. Or, someone on a plane may spot a passenger who looks suspicious (e.g. the shoe bomber) and yell "that person has a bomb" and thereby create a unified focus of fellow passengers on that individual person.

Types of Crowds

There are different types of crowds—casual, conventional, expressive, protest and acting crowds (Blumer, 1951; McPhail and Wohlstein, 1983).

Casual crowds consist of a group of individuals engaging in routine activities. These aggregations come together largely by accident and display little interaction but are centered upon the same activity. Examples include a group of observers of a street musician or of an ambulance team at an accident. The observers mull around, observe the event, and move away from the crowd to return to their organizational jobs. These casual groups or aggregations are unplanned, transitory, informal, and have minimal organization.

Conventional crowds consist of people who plan to see a specific organized event where norms will dictate their behaviors. Attending an opera involves dressing up and bringing special binoculars. Attending a funeral also means dressing up but one's facial expression is expected to be somber and laughing and telling jokes is unacceptable. Attending a university lecture means casual dress and raising one's hand to ask a question. In each case, the crowd forms in reference to a formal, organized activity where the norms will dictate the behavior of the individuals. The social differences that exist between the individual members in terms of class, race, and religion will be of no importance.

Expressive crowds focus on activities designed for emotional expression. Wedding receptions, New Year's Eve parties, bachelor and bachelorette parties all have the same goal—to be expressive. In some aggregations you may have fun and in others take the event more seriously, but in all cases the release of energy is shared. The nature of expressive crowds may vary from a women's mud wrestling competition to a religious evangelical revival, but the norms of all expressive crowds are the same—to allow members of the crowd to release emotion.

Protest crowds exist to protest an action and to register disapproval with whatever the group members find unacceptable. Protest crowds are usually organized and associated with ongoing desired social change. These crowds may protest U.S. involvement in the war in Iraq, immigration issues (e.g. giving or protesting legal status to illegal immigrants), or legalizing same-sex marriage (e.g. gay pride march). Some protest crowds may be orderly and march peacefully through the center of a city while others may engage in sit-ins, walkouts, picketing, strikes or boycotts. Protest crowds marching on our nation's capital are routine.

Action crowds are hostile and members may throw rocks or turn cars over. These crowds are much more disorderly by intent, but they remain focused on accomplishing a given action. Often, the police may counterattack with mace, rubber bullets, and tear gas in an attempt to contain the crowd.

A **mob** is a type of group that is out of control. The collective behavior of the mob is disorderly, lawless, emotionally charged, and intent on violence. Mobs feature task leaders who direct the focus of the crowd, and soci-emotional leaders who urge the crowd to action (e.g. "Let's lynch him"). They do not start and stop on any schedule and cannot sustain the heightened emotion for long. When the goal is achieved, the mob dissipates. An example is an impatient group outside a concert stadium waiting for the gates to open. Finally the restlessness of the members reaches a boiling point, and they storm the gates, trampling those in their wake.

It is important to note that mobs develop from crowds. A crowd may develop casually but turn into an action crowd or mob. For example, a crowd gathering to hear news of a slain leader could turn into a mob. In January 2008, it was revealed that a teenager was involved in the assassination of former Pakistani Prime Minister Benazir Bhutto in December 2007, and that he was part of a five-man squad deployed that day in the city of Rawalpindi, where Bhutto was killed. Dangerous crowds formed, but fortunately no mob violence was reported. The context can change at any time from a crowd to a mob.

Dispersed Groups

Dispersed groups or **dispersed social activities** may take place within an aggregation of people that is separated and spread over a wide geographic area. The after-Thanksgiving sales on "Black Friday" are examples of dispersed groups, as thousands of shoppers spread out across the country to find bargains. They often line up outside stores the night before and sleep on the pavement to be the first in line the next morning to get the best deals. This same phenomenon occurs when new video game equipment (e.g. Xbox 360 Core Console Video Game System) is released, and gamers wait overnight outside Target to be the first to own the new technology.

All of the gamers involved are not collectively concentrated in any one location. They were not a collective, people interacting together to pursue the same course of action. Nevertheless, when large numbers of people having no interaction with each other all engage in uncoordinated but like behavior or engage in the same general activity it is called **mass behavior**. Three forms of mass behavior are (1) crazes, fads and fashions, (2) panics and (3) mass hysteria.

Crazes, Fads, and Fashions

Crazes are dispersed social activities further characterized by a strong commitment to either a fad or fashion. Crazes are typically short term. They come into existence and may dissipate just as quickly. Beanie Babies are stuffed animals made by Ty Inc. First made in 1993, they were a craze reflected in the fact that people were paying hundreds of dollars for specific beanie babies which are now worth very little.

Fads are widely adopted new forms of activity. Throughout the country widely dispersed social actors may decide that something is the "in thing" or "fad." Much of the impetus may be based upon the mass media and marketing strategies. The iPod (for music) and iPod nano (for video) are examples of fads—the "in thing."

Fads exist at all levels of social organization. There are community fads, family fads, educational fads, business fads as well as mass societal fads. A community fad occurred in the city of South Bend, Indiana, when one woman painted her fire hydrant as a human form and before long the whole city did the same thing. In family socialization, it was the fad to use small appliances to create single hot dogs, hamburgers, and soups. In education, it is sometimes the fad to use the latest statistical technique to investigate the newest concept. In the youth culture in the late 70s Steve Martin's phrase, "Wild and crazy guy" was widely used. Video business associations struggle to create the latest fad to cash in. The war over Blu-ray versus HD DVD is over who can create and cash in on the fad. There will be other fads to follow.

Fads may also be deadly such as steroids (used by hip hop rappers, baseball players, and other athletes) or the "choking game." Eighty-two youths ages 6 to 19 died between 1995 and 2007 from the "choking" game (also called "space monkey" and "pass out game") (Korblum, 2008). Individuals cut off their air supply or have someone else do it to obtain a brief euphoric state or high. When the strangulation is prolonged, death or serious injury can result.

Fashions are the current styles of dress, appearance, conduct and manner. Again, it is important to remember that these are dispersed social activities. It was a fashion for men to wear Mohawk hairstyles and for women to put streaks of blue, green, pink, and yellow in their hair. It continues to be a fashion for some male high school students to wear very baggy pants.

In much the same way the culture has evolved a fashion of display for the human body. At one time in America, women could not display their necks, arms or legs. They wore hoops and corsets so that their figures were not apparent. In 1868, a girl could wear her dress just below the knee showing some of her leg at age 4, but had to progressively lower it until her leg was not seen at age 16. When women first went into the factories in World War II, they had to wear pants to avoid catching dresses in machines. Prior to 1940, it was not proper fashion for a woman to wear anything but a dress.

Fashions also exist for conduct. In the Middle Ages, men held their hands out to show that their hands were not on their swords. Thus, hands held out became a sign of friendship. Men now shake hands, and it is fashionable for a woman to initiate shaking hands with a man. There are also fashionable ways to serve meals or entertain—serving the latest drink or cheese before dinner reflects the "in" thing.

Fashions are pushed by the media and industries. Expressing the current fashion helps to give people social status. Wearing the latest fashion indicates that the individual is "in the know." Fashion also helps to define the progress of a society. Those societies that do not follow the latest fashion are defined as backward. Crazes, fads and fashions are dispersed social activities that vary by social organization. They differ by population characteristics, social class, community and all other social organizations.

Panics and Mass Hysteria

Other types of collective behavior that are considered to have a greater effect on social organizations include panics and mass hysteria. **Panics** are defined as a state of alarm and the spread of uncontrollable fear as a crowd perceives danger and reacts. The danger they perceive may be real or imagined, but in the words of W.I. Thomas "if people perceive something as real, it is real in its consequences" (Thomas and Swaine, 1928). In early 2008 there was fear that people would regard the U.S. economy as being in a recession (and the Dow dropped almost 2,000 points in two months). Such a panic results in less spending which can have the effect of plunging the country into a recession.

Panics occur in different social contexts. Panic may emerge in reference to a fire in a theater, a plane that has lost an engine, and a ground shaking earthquake. There was widespread panic after the terrorists attack on the Twin Towers in New York. Panic may become contagious and spread rapidly.

Panics are rare in social life but important to study and understand. Panics differ from mass hysteria, in that panics are generally concentrated social activities, while mass hysteria is a geographically dispersed social activity.

Mass hysteria is a widespread, dispersed social activity characterized by uncontrollable fear and reaction from a perceived threat. It differs from a panic in that it is a more widespread geographical fear reaction to whatever is being communicated. Mass communication involves rumor. The identification of witches in Salem, Massachusetts, was an example of mass hysteria. Earlier in the U.S., there were fears bordering on mass hysteria over the kidnapping of children. Newspapers, television, radio, and magazines focused the public's attention on child stealing for sexual reasons. Milk cartons, trucks, and billboards displayed pictures designed to teach children not to talk to strangers. Families across the U.S. fingerprinted and video recorded their children for identification purposes. Some parents insisted that their children carry cell phones and installed GPS chips in their shoes. While the number of children actually abducted is low, this fear and its reaction significantly changed the culture, socialization and structure of America.

Public Opinion in Mass Society

When the mass (of people) share a similar opinion and make it known as a shared view of the people as a whole it is considered public opinion. It is only a public opinion when there is a shared view held by a dispersed collectivity expressed collectively to influence some action. The polls of political candidates reflect public opinion since the mass of people, although dispersed, make known their preference.

The Nature of Public Opinion

Public opinion is centered on issues—the war in Iraq, the economy, out of control health costs, obesity, and extravagant/wasteful spending by the government to name a few. How each of these issues forms into an opinion begins with some communication. Once something has been communicated to a social actor, the person forms an impression of how he or she feels toward the idea or issue presented. Most things that occur in our daily lives do not require the formation of an opinion. When the dog runs fast or the water is hot we do not form opinions about running dogs and hot water. Yet we do form opinions about "something." What is it that we form opinions about?

At least three factors are involved in opinion formation. First, we form an opinion about who should make what decisions and, often in the U.S., about how the political system should act. Who has the right to decide whether abortion is legal, whether to bring the troops home from Iraq, or whether gay marriage should be legalized? Do we believe the people should decide these issues, Congress, the Supreme Court, or the President?

Second, opinions provide the core for group identity. People group with other people who share common views. They cluster together because they are born-again Christians, pro-choice, or believe in racial, gender, or sexual equality. Church, pro-choice marches, and membership in the NAACP are contexts which support the opinions a single individual believes in.

Third, people choose those who will lead them in their organizations. There are usually different and often opposing foundations of opinion. U.S. citizens choose a president every four years. It became clear in 2008 that there was considerable discontent with George W. Bush and the Republican party to lead the country. Additionally, there was a large opinion formation that only Democrats could lead the country in the right direction. Individuals sought out those contexts that supported their position.

There is much that needs to be researched in the area of public opinion. We know that some people form opinions before they have any information and then seek out only information that supports their opinion (e.g. Bush building a case for the invasion of Iraq?). We know that some people resist changing their opinions even in the face of overwhelming evidence that they are wrong (e.g. where were the "weapons of mass destruction?"). Sociologists emphasize that people hold different opinions when they are in different contexts. A person in a sociology class may state that same sex marriage should be legalized, but that same person in a Sunday school class may strongly oppose same sex marriage. Opinions are the social glue that holds a person in good light with the social organizations in which he or she is a member.

An individual opinion is not of much interest to sociologists because individual opinions are powerless. But large numbers of people who share the same opinion become a power base. When polls show that the American people are against the war in Iraq, politicians pay attention, since they will not be voted into office if they hold opinions opposed to those who elect them. Public opinion itself is not action. It is a measure of interest that may affect those in power to begin or change a course of action (but not always as George W. Bush continued to send more troops to Iraq in spite of public disapproval of the war).

Since the public reflects a wide range of people, opinions on any one subject will differ depending on the person's age, race, religion, family, community, and networks. The elderly will be interested in social security and retirement benefits while the young will be more focused on keeping the environment clean. Upper class families have strong opinions about what should be done to kidnappers, while the lower class families are unconcerned since all a kidnapper could get for their children is a bubble gum wrapper and one hundred dollars. In contrast, lower class families have opinions about rent subsidies.

Mass Publics

Mass publics are large numbers of people whose opinion is identified by their sharing a common characteristic. Mass publics vary by region (North versus South), occupation (doctors versus lawyers), age (young versus old), race (black, white, Asian, Native American), religion (Episcopalian versus Baptist), political orientation (conservative versus liberal), and sex (men versus women). Sociologists point out the source of information of various mass publics and ask just how well informed they are. One concern is that the mass publics have opinions about issues they know nothing about. For example, they may be for "strong government" but not know how the government makes decisions or even who is running for president.

Rumor

Rumor is an unconfirmed story or piece of information that is widely and rapidly circulated. After Barack Obama (in 2008) won the state of Iowa for the Democratic nomination, all the polls in New Hampshire predicted him (by a wide margin) to be the winner over Hillary Clinton. But Clinton won in New Hampshire. A rumor began that maybe the electronic voting booths had been tampered with. After all, there was no independent check on the validity of the voting machines doing their jobs. It was rumored that a computer geek could easily hack into the system and alter the votes as desired. The rumor was short lived after Hillary began to win more states toward the Democratic nomination.

Rumors are developed and not necessarily false. In the process of developing a rumor social actors may add details, which may also be in error (so a true story may have errors added to it). While psychologists focus on the motivations of those who pass rumors, or upon the process of distortion, sociologists focus upon the interaction between those who pass the rumor. Those in the interaction context may gain by adding or subtracting information from the development of a rumor (e.g. "I know this and you don't"). In effect, they are "in the know." Their ability to add "facts" and to have inside information gives them social status.

Rumor also develops when there is insufficient information, and people fill in what they don't know. One rumor which surrounded 9/11 was that the destruction of the twin towers was an "inside job"—that a plane hitting a building would not cause the building to collapse, so dynamite "had to have been used at the base of the respective buildings to bring them down."

Propaganda

In addition to rumor, another form of communication that affects aggregate phenomena is propaganda. **Propaganda** is any form of communication used to influence public opinion. Public support for the war in Iraq was developed on the basis of a clever media propaganda campaign. Daniel (2008) revealed a study posted on the website of the Center for Public Integrity that President Bush and top administration officials "were part of an orchestrated campaign that effectively galvanized public opinion and, in the process, led the nation to war under decidedly false pretenses." Specifically, the study counted 935 false statements in the two-year period preceding the invasion of Iraq. It found that in speeches, briefings, interviews and other venues, Bush and administration officials stated unequivocally on at least 532 occasions that Iraq had (1) weapons of mass destruction or was trying to produce or obtain them or (2) had links to al-Qaida or both. Subsequent facts have revealed that Iraq did not possess any weapons of mass destruction or have meaningful ties to al-Qaida. "In short, the Bush administration led the nation to war on the basis of erroneous information that it methodically propagated and that culminated in military action against Iraq on March 19, 2003."

Propaganda is pervasive. Television commercials are an example. We are encouraged to buy products because "most doctors recommend." Propaganda thrives because we do not have independent factual information to back up commercial claims. In the case of "most doctors recommend," maybe the only doctors asked were those getting a salary from the corporation making the product.

The propaganda minister of the Nazis was Goebbels. He put together a propaganda machine that brought Adolf Hitler to power and kept him there. Among the principles of propaganda, Goebbels argued that you should tell the truth as often as possible using lies only when they could not be disproved. For example, if someone walks up to you and you begin the interaction by pushing them, and then, they hit you and run, you report the truth. They hit you and ran. This is the most common form of propaganda. Nothing said is untrue. But you lied "by omission." What you said leaves your credibility intact. The worst that could happen is that someday the person would be found and say you pushed them first. You could either deny it or admit it, but either way what you said would be true.

In their classic work *The Fine Art of Propaganda*, Lee and Lee (1971) revealed seven propaganda techniques central to affecting public opinion. In each of these techniques, the goal is to create a symbol and manipulate it toward a desired outcome.

1. Glittering generalities. This propaganda technique involves the use of words which "sound good" but which mean nothing since the words or symbols are not tied to anything. People feel good when they hear the words, but actually, there is no meaning in what they heard. Politicians can use these words since they generate good feelings but obligate the politician to nothing. "Change" was the theme for the Democratic hopefuls in 2008, but the word means nothing (e.g. What is going to change? When? Which changes will benefit whom, how, and for how long?). Other phrases such as "Hope and vision," "American greatness," a return to "basic values," a "drug free society," "democracy," "law and order," and "family values" are glittering generalities which evoke pleasant feelings associated with a candidate for public office (but little else).

2. Plain folks. This technique involves the political candidate using a symbol to convey that he or she is "just plain folk" so that others can have the feeling that the candidate "is just like me." Wearing a hard hat, a baseball hat, a rotary pin, playing horseshoes, or eating a pancake at a diner conveys to the masses that "I am just like you." The idea is to create a symbol, which will help the masses identify with the issue, idea or person. Of course, it is all for show. After the photographs, the politician takes off the hat, leaves the diner, and gets back into the limo.

3. Name-calling. The goal of name calling is to attach a negative symbol to the opposition so as to create avoidance. Hillary Clinton was called a warmonger since she voted to approve the war in Iraq. Mitt Romney was called a "flip flopper" since he changed his position so often. The terms "misguided liberals," "Ivory tower intellectuals," "socialized medicine," and "child murderers" (for pro-choice believers) are all attempts to label someone or some issue negatively.

4. Transfer. This propaganda technique is used when a positive symbol is used as a backdrop for a candidate in hopes that the symbol will transfer to the person. Having a candidate speak with an American flag in the background is a standard transfer technique. Television news journalists routinely deliver their report with a picture of Congress or the White House in the background so as to give their presentation credibility.

5. Testimonial. This propaganda technique involves having a trusted person present a product or idea. The goal of this propaganda technique is to imbue the product with comfort and trust. Academy Award winner Sally Field is featured in a television commercial for the drug Boniva. She is shown holding flowers while she talks about the wonderful effect Boniva has in reducing her

bone loss by taking just one pill a month. (What the television commercial does not say is that Boniva can cause serious problems in the stomach or esophagus.)

6. Card stacking. This propaganda technique presents an argument in such a way that there is only one intended conclusion. A card stacking sequence in reference to the Barack Obama campaign might be that if you want "real change" from "someone who really understands the racial problems of America" and someone who "voted against the war in Iraq," Obama is your man. In effect, the argument builds to only one conclusion.

7. Bandwagon. This technique convinces the masses that so many others are committed to a course of action that they should also join. Politicians use this technique by pointing out the support that they have already received from other groups or associations with the implication that "you" will be left behind if "you" do not also jump on the bandwagon.

Research Methods Used to Study Collective Phenomena

As was pointed out in Chapter One, each social organization is an area of specialization in sociology. Researchers of each social organization develop different explanations (theories) and use different methods to study the organizations. The study of aggregations and collective behavior has its own theories and research methods.

General Theories

1. Functional Theory. Sociologists who study aggregations and collective behavior ask, "What function does propaganda serve for the society?" The answer is that it allows those in power to control an outcome. Propaganda that Iraq was an enemy that must be destroyed resulted in Congress approving an invasion that served to meet the needs of the power elite—the country invaded Iraq and billions of dollars in government contracts were given to persons connected to the power elite.

What is the function of creating and selling the American public new fashions? The answer is that new fashions keep capitalism functioning by creating new needs among the masses. Jobs are created, and the money keeps flowing. If one's existing clothes are "just as good," no new money would be pumped into the economy and no new jobs would be created.

2. Conflict Theory. Conflict theorists believe that the existence of any aggregate phenomenon is the result of conflict. From a conflict perspective, there is a struggle for power, privilege, and prestige within society, and aggregate behavior is the outcome of the struggle. For example, there is a struggle for scarce resources, and the respective social classes develop different mechanisms to assure themselves that they will stay on top. The upper class promotes propaganda that everyone can work hard and make it in America. This belief helps the upper classes feel comfortable giving nothing to the lower classes in terms of support so as to ensure the upper classes stay in power.

Conflict theorists see social change as the outcome of continued struggles between competing groups within society. These groups compete to establish dominance. Conflict never ends. Those who lose will again struggle to succeed.

3. Interactionist Theory. Interactionist theory has its basis in symbolic interaction and focuses on person-to-person interaction. It looks at how symbols are interpreted and acted upon to change the person's opinions and actions in everyday life. Earlier we discussed how propaganda is used to affect public opinion, as well as specific symbols like the American flag or a hard hat.

Specific Theories of Crowd Behavior

To explain crowd behavior and social movements, sociologists have developed a number of theoretical explanations. These go beyond the traditional functional, conflict, and interactionist explanations in that they are focused on the specific content of this subdiscipline. The goal is to explain largely unorganized crowd behavior or organized social movements.

The major explanations of crowd (or collective) behavior are those of contagion, convergence, and emergent norm theory. While there are different types of crowds (casual, conventional, expressive and acting), we must understand why crowds engage in mass behavior.

1. Contagion. **Contagion theory** explains crowd behavior as an infection that spreads through the mass and is so contagious that the crowd develops a sort of "collective mind." Although sociologists have pointed to the fact that Le Bon never explained his "collective mind" and that it does not exist, they cannot discount his approach.

Contagion theory emphasizes that individuals in a crowd become so emotional that they lose their individuality, that a new form of organization develops, and that the crowd acts as one. Contagion spreads until there is a total collectivity that swallows up the individual, dissolves individuality and allows impulsive, irrational, deviant, illegal and highly uncharacteristic responses to emerge.

The individual in a crowd can behave in a manner so uncharacteristic of his or her known "personality," it can be said that he or she is no longer acting on his or her own. Young people who are abducted and put into a cult are understood to no longer be capable of acting rationally—they are assumed to have been "taken over" by the group. Only when they break out of the cult are they free to "return to their real selves."

2. Convergence. **Convergence theory** views the development and action of a crowd as rational—a number of like minded individuals who have the same interests and goals share a common area that leads to crowd action. This theory argues that when you put 50,000 people in a gay pride parade, they form a single action-oriented crowd. They can be one, because all of the members of the group have similar values, attitudes, and interests. It is the commonality that produces the crowd behavior

3. Emergent Norm. **Emergent norm theory** argues that it is neither emotion nor a common focus but normlessness that causes crowd solidarity. Normlessness means that no one knows how to behave or what it is that they should do. Individuals in the crowd look to each other to discover the norms of the aggregation. The terrorist attack of 9/11 created a state of normlessness. People at the base of the twin towers had to choose whether to run for their lives or try to help the people who had been injured? The larger society also wondered how to regard the act and what should be done about it. George W. Bush emerged and led the way to war—"Lets go kick some ass." And in this state of normlessness, the country went along.

Collective Behavior and Social Organization: The Writer's Strike

Collective behavior is expressed in each of the various levels of social organization. For example, the writer's strike of 2007–2008 affected most levels of social organization.

Population

Various segments of the U.S. population watched different television shows and were differentially affected by the writer's strike. Those segments that regularly watched weekly sitcoms were more affected than those who were regular viewers of the evening news broadcast. The former were completely dependent on the writers for new scripts while the latter were not affected at all.

Social Class

When thousands of people from cast members to janitors lost their jobs because of the writer's strike, there was downward social mobility. In contrast, corporate CEOs were still at work and maintained their income since their mobility was not affected.

Groups

A variety of groups were affected by the writer's strike. Close friends who disagreed had strained relationships. Significant others were told that they would not be together because the writer had to walk the picket line. Cast members who usually enjoyed breakfast together had no job to go to and lost their companions. Many different primary groups separated, and secondary groups ended.

Families

An unemployed writer now stayed at home with his or her spouse because he or she no longer had the structure of work and steady income. Being around the house all day and not bringing in an income no doubt affected relationships with one's partner and children. Depending on one's other income sources, the effect on one's family could be devastating. Some families were crippled by the strike.

Communities

Since the entertainment industry IS the whole community of Hollywood, California, the writer's strike was catastrophic. Few sectors of the economy were not affected by the strike. There were no longer hot dogs and sandwiches to sell or cars to rent. Rooms in hotels went vacant, and copy services went out of business.

Associations

The Writer's Guild of America represented two labor unions: the Writers Guild of America, East (WGAE) and the Writers Guild of America, West (WGAW). They received support from a host of other associations including the Horror Writers Association, the Mystery Writers of America, and the Science Fiction and Fantasy Writers of America. The effect was to demonstrate a strong line of support against the opposition.

Networks

Hollywood depends on networks of agents. These agents work across America setting up contracts, contacting writers, meeting with advertising agencies and producers, directors and numerous others, such as lawyers, bankers, and legislators. The network of contacts are all related to the development of television, movies, and electronic media. And these agents depended on the writers to produce scripts to sell. No writers, no scripts, no sales and the networks crumbled.

Societies

As the writer's strike continued (which was eventually settled after almost four months), the effect on the viewing habits of the American public changed. With only reruns to watch, some viewers changed channels and eventually watched less television. As the strike continued, less revenue was produced which in turn affected the tax income for the nation. Additionally, from a society's perspective, there was less water and electricity used when millions of Americans who usually got up at the commercial to use the bathroom developed other activities instead of television watching.

Social Movements

Social movements are another form of aggregation and collective behavior that is typically focused on improving the status and treatment of a specific group of people. The civil rights movement, the feminist movement and the gay rights movement are all social movements specifically intent on reducing prejudice and discrimination against blacks, women, and homosexuals. Tilly and Tarrow (2007) use the term campaign. Their definition of a social movement campaign follows:

> ... *a sustained challenge to power holders in the name of a population living under the jurisdiction of those power holders of concerted public displays of worthiness, unity, numbers, and commitment, using such means as public meetings, demonstrations, petitions and press releases* (p.114).

While we tend to think of a social movement as a regional or national event, Dufour and Giraud (2007) emphasize that some social movements are on an international scale. An example is the European wing of the World March of

Women (WMW), a transnational social movement pulling into its base women from grassroots organizations, labor unions, and leftist political parties in over 150 countries (approximately 6,000 associations).

Stages toward Action

There are five stages in the development of a social movement (Smelser, 1962).

1. Structural Conduciveness. A social movement can only develop in the context of a structure. There can be no women's or gay rights movement as long as women and gays are treated equally. Similarly, there can be no racial mobs in Miami without the presence of different racial groups.

2. Structural Strain. Strain refers to dissatisfaction when a large number of people feel that they are unable to achieve their goals within the existing structure. They may be upset, alienated or generally disagree with the way things are organized. These aggregations include homosexuals, the elderly, and minorities (e.g. Hispanics) who feel constrained by the existing structure of laws, rules, and regulations.

3. Growth and Spread of a Generalized Belief. Once the individuals who feel the strain become known to each other, the aggregation or movement becomes focused on the factor or factors that it believes is causing the strain. The movement targets a specific goal in terms of getting this element changed. For example, members of the writer's strike felt their talent was not being compensated beyond an initial show or program and wanted money for DVD and Internet sales. Illegal immigrants, fearful of being deported, want recognition of the value of their work force to the U.S. economy and an end to their illegal status.

4. Precipitating Factors. After the aggregate forms and becomes focused on a goal, something needs to happen to the crowd or movement to bring the feelings of anger and injustice to a boil. An assassination of a leader will often provide the emotional fuel to move a group closer to action. A verdict a group feels is unjust may increase disenchantment. In Miami, a black man was shot by a Hispanic police officer and that act further escalated tensions.

5. Mobilization of Participants for Action. The final factor which pushes a group from a boil to action is some type of triggering event. It is difficult to separate clearly what precipitates, from what causes the final mobilization. Sometimes they may be one and the same, but more often it is someone in the crowd that takes the leadership role after all of the above factors have resulted in the crowd working itself into a frenzy. Vasi (2006) noted that the success of a social movement (e.g. the anti-war movement) may be in reference to con-

tinued environmental triggers (e.g. more dead bodies in Iraq with no end in sight) and the use of new information technologies such as the Internet (e.g. which makes it possible to send new information quickly). Similarly, Carty and Onyett (2006) noted how contemporary social movements are using advanced forms of technology and mass communication as a mobilizing tool. They also noted how the Internet had enhanced the global and grassroots political mobilization in the anti-war effort in the post 9/11 environment.

Absolute and Relative Deprivation

In addition to responding to prejudice, discrimination, and injustice, social movements come into existence because of the existence of a gap between what people have and what they expect to have. Blacks compare their incomes, jobs, and housing with whites and notice a considerable disparity. There are two types of deprivation. **Absolute deprivation** is based on a factual assessment. If the annual median household income in the U.S. is $46,326 (*Statistical Abstract of the United States 2008*. Table 669), a household income of $5,000 is absolute deprivation. On the other hand, **relative deprivation** is a comparison of one's income to another. Black annual median household income is $30,858 compared to whites' $48,554 (Table 669) so blacks feel deprived by comparison.

Relative deprivation may exist because of an actual discrepancy in numbers or because of what one expects. As one's education increases and one perceives that one's peers are advancing in both promotions and income, these perceptions may encourage feelings of discontent. Perceptions can often create feelings of deprivation, even if the perceptions are incorrect.

Life Cycle of Social Movements

The life cycle of social movements can be seen as progressing through five stages of incipiency, coalescence, institutionalization, fragmentation, and demise (Mauss, 1975).

1. Incipiency. Incipiency is the beginning of a social movement. It begins when a large number of people come together because of frustration and move against the source of their frustration. The mass is not well organized and struggles to identify objectives, tactics, communication, facts, and goals. Various factions of the mass develop spokespersons and leaders emerge. Harris (2006) noted in his article on "It Takes a Tragedy to Arouse Them …" that collective action is sometimes initiated only when tragedy strikes. He noted the impact of the murder of Emmett Till (a 14-year-old teenager brutally killed for smiling at a white woman in Money, Mississippi, in 1955) on activism then and decades later.

2. Coalescence. Leaders emerge who provide a common voice for the masses. The result is greater structure and a stronger organization that coalesces around the key ideas, goals, tactics, and leaders.

3. Institutionalization. At this stage the social movement has become a formal organization. The movement is ordered and has agreed upon, elected or paid leaders. It becomes an entity with power that involves positions and a process to continue to achieve goals and maintain those in power.

4. Fragmentation. The fragmented stage means that the social organization has reached its initial goal and is beginning to break into different fragments, each trying to accomplish something different. The goals and future of the social movement are no longer clear. Indeed, should the social movement continue and if so what should the goals be?

5. Demise. Some social movements may discontinue since their goals have been accomplished. They may leave legacies to the culture in the way of songs or slogans. Woody Guthrie of the thirties went from labor camp to labor camp singing protest songs. But the social movement for the pickers in the labor camps disbanded.

Types of Social Movements

Theorists do not agree how best to delineate the types of social movements that should be studied. One alternative has been to categorize them as revolutionary, resistant, and expressive.

1. Revolutionary. A revolutionary social movement exists when an aggregate seeks to overthrow the existing order and to replace it with something totally new. This type of movement is preceded by enormous discontent, intellectual criticism of the society and an economic justification for change. The revolution occurs and restructures the society's political system. If successful, a new social order replaces the existing one. The tearing down of the Berlin Wall was symbolic of the reordering of the political system in eastern Germany.

2. Resistance. Resistance movements are those that come into being because of a generalized feeling that change is coming too fast or should not have happened at all. Those who resist are those who believe that whatever change has occurred should be stopped, reversed and eliminated. They resist the change as unacceptable to the social organization of life because it will cause irreversible harm. These social movements, such as the Ku Klux Klan, existed to stop those in power who had created a change that destroyed the values (e.g. equality for blacks) they held to be important. Resistance movements occur in all societies that have an "old guard" and "new guard." The new guard protects the changes it has created in the society, while the old guard seeks to join resistance move-

ments which would return the society to the "good old days" when things were "correct." It resists the new ways which are viewed as bad ways.

3. Expressive. Expressive social movements exist for individuals with personal dissatisfactions who join a movement to help them cope with their negative feelings. Walgrave and Verhulst (2006) noted that the Million Mom March in the U.S. was mobilized out of emotions felt by moms over the safety of their children. In response to Columbine and other events where children were gunned down at school, a few mothers set up a website which soon had 500 mothers who moved toward the Million Mom March on May 14, 2000, Mother's Day. Several hundred thousand converged in Washington, D.C. and in 73 other cities and towns around the country in response to the need for school safety.

The purpose of expressive social movements is to change the social actor so that he or she feels better rather than to change the social order. These expressive social movements allow people to escape from the realities of the present into the dreams of the future when the world would be a more perfect place for them. It will be good for them, because they have become the true believers and have accepted the prophecy. Those who do not believe will be gone from this earth.

In the 1830s, William Miller began the Adventist movement, also known as the Millerite movement, which predicted the end of the world (e.g. return of Jesus) on October 22, 1844. Over 100,000 people looked forward to the "blessed hope." Some sold their farms and left their homes to spread the gospel the last days. This movement gave hope to those who joined the movement for a better tomorrow.

Popular Beliefs and Scientific Data: Willpower, Veganism and Social Movement

Elisabeth Cherry (2006) studied vegans and discovered there are two basic groups—those who are vegans who identify with a vegan movement and those who are not part of a movement (primarily those in the punk subculture). Vegans seek to remove animals from every part of their lives, from clothes to food. She interviewed members of the respective groups to find out how they defined and practiced veganism differently. Her focus was the social networks of the punk and non-punk vegans.

While it might be thought that having personal willpower, motivation, and a collective vegan identity would be the necessary element associated with participation in the vegan movement, the researcher found that having supportive social networks was the key. Indeed it was one's social context that created outcomes of behavior, including social movement participation, not motivation or individual willpower.

References

Barr, S. and A. W. Gilg. 2007. "A Conceptual Framework for Understanding and Analyzing Attitudes towards Environmental Behavior." *Geografiska Annaler Series B: Human Geography*, 89: 361–379.

Blumer, H. 1951. "Collective Behavior." In Alfred McLung Lee (ed.) *New Outline of the Principles of Sociology*. New York: Barnes and Noble. pp. 65–122.

Carty, V. and J. Onyett. 2006. "Protest, Cyberactivism and New Social Movements: The Reemergence of the Peace Movement Post 9/11." *Social Movement Studies*, 5: 229–249.

Cherry, E. 2006. "Veganism as a Cultural Movement: A Relational Approach." *Social Movement Studies*, 5: 155–170.

Daniel, D. K. 2008. "False Statements Preceded War." Associated Press, January 23.

Dufour, P. and I. Giraud. 2007. "Globalization and Political Change in the Women's Movement: The Politics of Scale and Political Empowerment in the World March of Women." *Social Science Quarterly*, 88: 1152–1173.

Harris, Fredrick C. 2006. "It Takes a Tragedy to Arouse Them: Collective Memory and Collective Action during the Civil Rights Movement." *Social Movement Studies*, 5: 19–43.

Kornblum, Janet. 2008. "CDC Warns of Deaths, Dangers from Playing 'Choking Game.'" *USA Today*, February 15, 4A.

Le Bon, G. 2002. *The Crowd: A Study of the Popular Mind*, (English translation). Dover Publications.

Lee, A. M. and E. B. Lee. 1971. *The Fine Art of Propaganda*. New York: Octagon.

Mauss, A. L. 1975. *Social Problems of Social Movements*. Philadelphia: Lippincott.

McPhail, C. and R. T. Wohlstein. 1983. "Individual and Collective Behaviors within Gatherings, Demonstrations, and Riot." *Annual Review of Sociology*, 9. Palo Alto: Annual Reviews.

Meyers, C. D. 2007. "Moral Duty, Individual Responsibility, and Sweatshop Exploitation." *Journal of Social Philosophy*, 38: 620–626.

Thomas, W. I. and D. Swaine. 1928. *The Child in America: Behavior Problems and Programs*. New York: Knopf.

Smelser, N. 1962. *Theory of Collective Behavior*. New York: Free Press.

Tilly, C. 2004. *Social Movements 1768–2004*. Boulder, Co.: Paradigm.

Tilly, C. and Sidney Tarrow. 2007. *Contentious Politics*. Boulder, Co.: Paradigm.

Vasi, I. B. 2006. "The New Anti-war Protests and Miscible Mobilizations." *Social Movement Studies,* 5: 137–153.

Walgrave, S. and J. Verhulst. 2006. "Towards 'New Emotional Movements'? A Comparative Exploration into a Specific Movement," *Social Movement Studies,* 5:275–304.

Part IV
More Organized Contexts

Chapter 7

Groups

Committee—a group of people who individually can do nothing but as a group decide that nothing can be done.

Fred Allen, comedian

Groups are the most important contexts in our lives. We are born into a group, marry into a group, go to school in groups, work in groups and die in a group. The last thing that happens before we die is that the call goes out to family members that "the time is near" which results in a gathering for the final hours, death, and funeral. We depend on groups not only for our physical survival, but also for our sense of well-being. The groups of which we are a part also have an enormous influence on our beliefs, values, and worldview. In this chapter, we examine this core topic in sociology.

Foundation of Social Organization

All social organizations begin as unorganized types of individuals who form various groups. These various types follow.

Categories

Categories provide a way for people to identify with each other, which allows for a group to form. Categories are finer distinctions of a population. For example, marrieds can be categorized as husbands and wives, singles can be categorized as never married, separated, divorced, and widowed, and Jews can be categorized as orthodox, conservative, and reform. Categories are important because they provide a connect point of identification with others which then moves the individuals toward the formation of a group. Your sociology class is a group category in part because you share a common characteristic:

undergraduate student at your university. Without first being classified as a student you would not be permitted into the classroom.

Groups

Groups are relatively small social organizations composed of individuals who share norms, values, and goals and who interact with each other. While categories are groups in the sense of being a number of people, in order to become a group individuals must (1) recognize and identify with each other, (2) symbolically and behaviorally interact, (3) share norms, values, and goals and (4) have an emerging structure.

Recognition and Identification. A prerequisite for group formation and interaction is the recognition and identification of the individuals with each other. When you walked into your sociology classroom for the first time, you observed characteristics of the people in the assigned room, which helped you to regard yourself as a potential member of the aggregation. The fact that same aged individuals with notebooks and pens were sitting in desks were signs that they were members of the sociology class you had signed up for. All categories have symbols to assist in their recognition and identification with each other. Within these aggregations and collectivities, groups form. Shriners have tall red hats with tassels, Jews have skullcaps, and sororities/fraternities have pins. Each collectivity creates symbols wherein like-minded individuals may find friends, associates, and colleagues.

Symbolic and Behavioral Interaction. A large number of people in a category do not constitute a group until interaction occurs. The nature of this interaction is symbolic and behavioral. **Symbolic interaction** is the process of interaction between two social actors on the basis of mutually understood symbols. Two individuals wearing a rotary club pin will interact in such a way that acknowledges their belonging to the same group. Symbols may also be words, which are used to permit interaction between group members. Lovers have their pet names (sweetie, sugar pie) and teens have their code words. Some examples of the latter include:

Bounce: To leave.
Chill: Pass time in a relaxed manner, relax.
Down low (D.L.): Secret, covert.
Hook up: To have sex with a person just met.
Phat: Pronounced "fat," means fine, or cool.
Player: Someone who is romantically involved with many people.
Wack: Weird or inappropriate.
Yo: An informal greeting, "What's up?"

Behavioral interaction refers to overt physical behavior that is mutually understood by the two social actors. Two social actors shake hands with each other because each recognizes the meaning of an outstretched hand and responds accordingly. Hence, individuals in a category (20 people in an orientation session for first year college students) recognize each other by symbols (name tag) and behavior (everyone follows the group leader who describes the various buildings on campus), and interacts using commonly understood words to connect ("Yo").

Shared Norms, Values and Goals. In addition to being able to mutually recognize and to use symbols to interact, group members must have shared norms, values, and goals. Without these, the group has no order, no direction, and no future.

The norms of a sociology study group include meeting to exchange pleasantries before and after the study session and sharing notes. The common value of the group is for each member to make a good grade. The goal is to prepare for exams.

A married couple represents a group with its own norms, values, and goals. The norms may include having meals together, watching the evening news on TV together and visiting both sets of parents for the holidays. Shared values may include fidelity, both spouses being employed full time, and attending religious services monthly. Their goals may be to have children, build a home on a lake, and raise organic vegetables.

A focus group consists of individuals brought together for the purpose of focusing the members on a topic and learning what they have to say. Hopkins (2007) emphasized the enormous value of focus groups and discussed their size, location, context, sensitivity of topic, the age of research participants, and the personalities of the researcher as relevant to the information sought.

Structure. All groups have structure made up of positions, roles, and norms. Each member of the sociology study group is a student and the role of each is to share notes and talk about what they believe will be on the test. Each position in the group has an "expectation" of what the other person should do. The positions in the married couple group are husband and wife with the husband's role including the expectation that he change the porch light bulb. If he waits a month before he changes the bulb, his wife may be disappointed, and there will be a clarification of expectations (norms).

Types of Groups

Over the years, sociologists have identified five distinct types of groups: primary and secondary, in groups and out-groups, reference groups, voluntary and involuntary groups, and membership groups. By knowing the groups individuals belong to we can predict the value of the group to the person and its level of influence.

Primary and Secondary Groups

Primary groups are small, relatively enduring groups in which members interact on a personal, intimate, and emotional level. Husband-wife, parent-child, and close friends are examples of primary groups. Primary groups provide a major source of emotional joy and sorrow in life. Just as spouses on their wedding day experience one of the happiest days of their lives, the day of their divorce (if they are among the 42% of couples who divorce) is also a time of great sadness. The death of someone in one's primary group is an occasion of deep loss. Communication is intense in primary group relationships. Two lovers may talk for hours and disclose how they feel about their families, sex, work, school, and important people in their lives.

Personal satisfaction is an important quality in primary relationships. Each person in the primary group relationship seeks to meet his or her own personal needs for intimacy as well as the needs of the other person. A spouse who gasses up the car or leaves a note on the refrigerator that dinner is in the microwave is expressing the desire to please the partner. O. Henry's famous short story "The Gift of the Magi" illustrates the core of altruism in primary relationships. Della, the wife, sells her long hair for $20 so she can buy her husband, Jim, a watch chain for his gold watch. Unbeknownst to her, Jim sold his gold watch to buy a comb for his wife's hair.

Finally, primary groups are havens for front line care. A child with a skinned knee runs "home," a spouse who suddenly becomes sick is taken to the hospital by a caring mate. and a sibling whose house burns down is offered a place to stay with a brother or sister. Primary group members care about you, and take your needs seriously.

The advertising industry uses the emotional comfort people experience in primary groups to market products and services. Companies present themselves as 'family" and imply that their products come from primary group members. Cento Fine Foods has the slogan "From our family to yours." Lowe's presented its Christmas trees as "family trees," Disney Channel Original Programming is "family-friendly", Nationwide Insurance is "on our side" (as any good family member would be), and Allstate has an "accident forgiveness feature" (which is what any good friend would do). Waiters and waitresses in expensive restaurants introduce themselves ("Hi, I'm Pat") to establish the norm that they are on a first name basis with the people they serve. The goal in creating the illusion of a primary group is based on the hope of getting a bigger tip.

In contrast to primary groups are **secondary groups** which consist of individuals who interact in structured formal ways. The individuals may have just met, will interact for only a short time, and may not see each other again. When you buy food at the counter at McDonald's you are in a secondary group relationship with the cashier. Your interaction is short, specific to ordering your meal, and ends when you get your order, and the cashier gets the money. You have no emotional feelings about the cashier and are focused on your burger.

Communication in secondary groups is limited to obtaining the item you are there for. There is no discussion of each other's lives. After the bank teller cashes your check, the interaction is over.

In-Groups and Out-Groups

Primary and secondary groups are differentiated on the basis of the degree of emotional closeness between group members. **In-groups** are groups in which the members view themselves as a unit that is distinct from another group (the **out-group**), which is viewed as having undesirable characteristics. Members of a fraternity or sorority see themselves as being the "in group" in contrast to independents who are literally on the outside or out-group. Politicians (when campaigning) use the term "insider" or "outsider" to their advantage. Promoting one's self as an outsider is designed to convey the impression that one is 'not yet corrupted' (e.g. selling one's votes to lobbyists and special causes).

Physicists emphasize that for every action there is a reaction. In-groups develop an identity for the individuals who belong to the group. The group then acts, which creates a reaction on the part of other groups. The action-reaction of the respective groups results in an in-group and an out-group. Individuals for abortion join together and become a "pro-choice" group. Their visibility results in those who oppose them developing their own group (the pro-lifers).

Some in-groups and out-groups are formed on the basis of population characteristics. The elderly compete with youth for federal monies (Medicare vs. Aid to Dependent Children), blacks compete with whites for jobs, and Republicans compete with Democrats for political control.

Social movements also form in-groups and out-groups. War typically produces collective in-groups and out-groups. For example, the war in Iraq has produced those who want to "bring the troops home" in contrast to those who want to stay in Iraq and "finish the job." One of the functions of in-groups is to label the out-group in negative ways (stereotype them), so as to justify action against them. Pro-lifers call pro-choice advocates child murderers in an attempt to justify their bombing of abortion clinics to save lives.

Both in-groups and out-groups develop group characteristics—they recognize and identify with each other, the members interact, they have similar norms, values and goals, and they develop a structure.

Reference Groups

Reference groups are those groups of individuals whom others use as models for their own values and behavior. Some women use the models of *Vogue* magazine to pattern their hair, make up, and clothes. While they will never be models, they want to look like them. One's peers are often one's reference group. Mack et. al. (2007) found that adolescent females reported higher social physique anxiety than adolescent males suggesting they regarded their female peers as their reference group for their body type, etc. and, if they did not match up, they were anxious about it. Males were less concerned.

Aspiring media journalists may try to model their delivery or presentation on the basis of a celebrity journalist. If they select only one model, such as Brian Williams or Katie Couric, the term **significant other** is used, rather than reference group.

Reference groups help sociologists to explain why some people don't behave the way we might expect them to. For example, we might expect the son or daughter of an upper class family to dress in clothes from the finest fashion stores and to drive BMWs. But some offspring of upper class parents wear cut offs and drive beach jeeps similar to their middle class peers (reference group) at school (rather than their parents). Similarly, punk rockers with tattoos and piercings may make straight A's because their reference group consists of physicians whom they want to be like. Teenage gangs composed of upper class family children may take drugs, steal, and kill. Their reference group is not their parents, but drug dealers.

Voluntary and Involuntary Groups

Voluntary groups, also known as achieved groups, are groups an individual joins by choice. The Masons, Rotary International, and Optimists Club are examples. Voluntary groups also permit easy exit. If you go to a church group, a poker group or a monthly stamp group, you can simply stop going and "unjoin" at any time. Some sociologists believe some newlyweds see marriage as a voluntary group.

Many **involuntary groups**, also known as ascribed groups, are categories an individual is born into and has no input in regard to membership. At birth you become a member of a racial, sex, and age category. You automatically become a member of the white, black, Asian American, Native American, or

Mexican American group category, are automatically assigned to either a male or female category, and are assigned to the category of infant. Sociologists are interested in the involuntary categories that an individual can belong to because they will derive much of their socialization from these groups. Religious cults, drug gangs and prison inmates are involuntary groups to some members. Persons who are drafted to serve in Iraq become a member of an involuntary group. Parents shudder when their children join a tattoo/piercing group, a Nazi sympathizer group, or a gang that deals drugs. Such abhorrence is based on the fact that involuntary group membership becomes important in predicting an individual's values, goals, and life changes.

Membership Groups

Membership groups are groups that require certain credentials before membership is granted. Membership in the Academy of Family Mediators requires an undergraduate degree, 20 hours of training in family mediation, and supervision of 15 cases by an approved supervisor. Membership in the American Association of Marriage and Family Therapy requires a minimum of a master's degree in a mental health field, specific courses in counseling, theory, and therapy, and supervision of 200 hours of the required 1500 hours of therapy by an approved supervisor. Other membership groups require only interest and a check. You can become a member of most fan clubs by stating your interest in joining and by paying annual dues. Most Internet groups require only that you register on the website.

As noted earlier, the reason we classify groups is that they help us to understand human behavior. Knowing the groups to which an individual belongs helps us to make predictions about the way that person will think, feel, and behave. A mother (member of a primary group) who is a female (involuntary group) and a Young Republican (voluntary group) as well as a Mormon (in-group, reference group) is likely to be conservative because membership in these groups tends to produce a conservative individual. An adolescent male who has a father in prison (primary group member) and whose close friends (in-group) are gang members (voluntary group) with known criminals as their reference group is likely to be involved in a life of crime.

Groups: Theory and Research Methods

Sociologists apply certain theories and research methods to the study of groups. In this section, we review theories, research designs, methods of data collection, and patterns of analysis used in studying groups.

Theories

There are both general and specific theories pertaining to the study of groups. Functional, conflict, and interactionist perspectives comprise the general theories while dramaturgical, ethnomethodological, and the social construction of reality are specific theories.

Functional Theory. Also known as structural functional theory, functional theory emphasizes how group structure in terms of positions, roles, and norms of group members function for the benefit of the group. A group of football players is incapable of winning a football game unless structure emerges which is functional for scoring points. Assigning the positions of coach, quarterback, and ends, and identifying the respective roles of calling plays (coach), executing plays (quarterback), and catching the pass (ends) allows the team members to work together to achieve the common goal of getting the ball in the end zone. Status hierarchies are also involved by identifying first, second, and third string players. Functional theory emphasizes how the group structure functions to win games.

Functional theory has been used to study groups in psychotherapy (therapy groups), education (classrooms), and industry (small work groups). In addition, small group research has been applied to small work crews in submarines, spacecrafts, and isolated environments such as Antarctica. These studies have emphasized the relationship between group structure and group effectiveness.

Conflict Theory. Conflict theorists focus on the conflict within or between groups. The first, second, and third string football players compete against each other for the first string position. During practice sessions, each player in each tier tries to outperform his competition so that he will be awarded the first string position. Conflict theorists also focus on competition between groups. In professional football, each team tries to beat the other with the goal of playing in and winning the Super Bowl. These teams are competing against each other for both money and status. The Super Bowl winner not only gets more money than the team they play but also a Super Bowl ring—an artifact accorded great respect in professional football.

Groups may also have conflict over control. Democrats and Republicans fight for control of the House and the Senate, evangelicals and liberals fight for control of the Supreme Court, and the oil industry fights alternative sources of energy (sun, hydrogen, corn, sugar cane) for the dominant fuel source of America. After Katrina devastated New Orleans, the U. S. Department of Housing and Urban Development decided to demolish (rather than rebuild) 4,500 public housing units. In protest were residents, activists, and preservationists. The conflict was intense as the protestors tried to force their way into a council meeting. They were sprayed with chemicals and shocked with stun guns.

Money is sometimes the source of conflict between groups. Bamboo Too is a nightclub overlooking the ocean on Isla Mujures, an island near Cancun, Mexico. Fifty yards away on the same side of the street is the Rocomar, a four story hotel featuring oceanfront rooms. Vacationers fly from all over the world to stay at the Rocomar. What they do not discover until midnight is the sound of blaring lead and base guitars dueling in the night just outside their room. They are shocked, and call the front desk, only to discover nothing can be done. The partying vacationers who want to rock and roll till dawn are in conflict with the hotel guests who want a good night's sleep. The management of both groups derives money from the respective party and hotel groups and is in conflict.

Interactionist Theory. Also referred to as symbolic interaction, the interactionist perspective focuses on the symbols group members adopt and the meaning they attach to those symbols to facilitate their interaction. Group members of a football team must learn the numbers associated with various plays, so that when the coach decides L-3 and the quarterback yells L-3 at the line of scrimmage, the team members know what to do. Without mutually understood symbols, group members are confused about how they are to behave. In the film *The Terminal,* Tom Hanks plays the role of a Russian whose plane has just landed in New York. The immigration officer in charge has no one available to translate the words used by the two men. Without mutually understood symbols available to facilitate communication, the respective parties struggle to transmit their own meaning and to garner what is being conveyed by the other. Their communication breaks down as neither understands the other.

Dramaturgical Theory. Group behavior may also be viewed as an emerging drama in which individual actors play their respective parts. Football team members act out various parts to present the intended show. Six members of the infamous Black Sox team who lost the 1919 World Series on purpose were merely acting as though they were playing baseball. They were so successful in the way they played their roles that the public was largely unaware that the game was rigged.

Teenagers often present an image to parents that they are obedient, trustworthy, and respectful of parental expectations. Research shows that offspring often deceive parents about where they are, who they are with, and what they are doing (Knox et al 2001).

Ethnomethodology Theory. All group members come to develop certain expectations of themselves and others. The ethnomethodologist might focus on the norms that are operative in a group. For example, a dating couple represents the smallest group—the dyad. Date rape (forcing sex on a dating partner) arouses our anger because we expect dating partners to be respectful of each other's personal space. When this is violated, so are our sensibilities. Similarly, the ethnomethodologist may focus on norms in an elevator—people are expected to avoid sustained eye contact, stand apart from each other, and speak superficially ("hello," "this elevator sure is slow").

The ethnomethodologist makes norms visible by violating them. Standing close to a stranger in the elevator makes both individuals aware that the norm of social distance is operative. Other examples of interaction an ethnomethodological researcher might point out are talking loudly on a cell phone in a theater, dominating a class by relentlessly interrupting the teacher, and walking into someone rather than trying to avoid them. A cab driver who refuses to take a tip is breaking a norm.

Social Construction of Reality. Shakespeare's Hamlet said, "Nothing is either good or bad but thinking makes it so." This phrase reminds us that reality is socially created. Five o'clock, New Year's Eve, and sunrise are all socially defined creations. They don't exist independent of others telling us that they exist and label the environment in such a way that the existence becomes real.

Similarly, group members create their own definitions of reality. Two individuals are in love when they define themselves as being in love as a result of their own social construction of reality. Should the lovers find out things about each other they do not like (e.g. the partner drinks too much or is unfaithful), they will begin to define themselves as falling out of love. Once they define themselves as no longer being in love, they will define the love relationship as over. Table 7.1 summarizes the various theories used to study groups.

Table 7.1
Theories Used to Understand Groups

Theory	Theorists	Key Concepts
Functionalist Theory	Emile Durkheim Talcott Parsons Robert Merton	Function, benefit, stability, interrelatedness
Conflict Theory	Karl Marx C. Wright Mills Ralf Dahrendorf Randall Collins	Conflict, struggle competition, tension, change
Interactionist Theory	Max Weber George H. Mead	Interaction, symbols
Dramaturgical Theory	Erving Goffman	Social Scripts
Ethnomethodological Theory	Harold Garfinkel	Common sense explanations
Social Construction of Social Reality	Peter Berger Thomas Luckmann	Creation of reality

Research Design

In order to understand the interaction patterns in small groups, researchers may design studies in a number of ways. Non-participant and participant observation are often used to study groups. In **non-participant observation**, a researcher may observe a group through a one-way mirror as they establish norms, create values, generate a leader and attempt to solve a particular problem. In preparation for the civil trial of O.J. Simpson, Daniel Petrocelli and his legal team conducted a mock trial with a mock jury. After the "jury" heard both sides of the argument to convict or acquit Simpson for the double murder of Nicole Simpson and Ron Goldman, they retired to a room with a one way mirror to deliberate. On the other side of the one way mirror Petrocelli and his team observed the group process—the emergence of a leader, the norms regarding who would speak first, and the focus of the discussion (Los Angeles Police Department or the physical evidence linking Simpson to the murders).

In **participant observation**, researchers become involved in the group they wish to study. For example, studying the Twin Oaks Intentional Living Community (http://www.twinoaks.org/) consisting of 100 members would involve becoming a member and living in the group to study it from "the inside." Swingers, nudists, and gangs have also been studied via participant observation. Regarding the latter, Sudhir Venkatesh (2008), a sociology graduate student, infiltrated one of Chicago's most notorious crack dealing gangs and revealed his insights in *Gang Leader for a Day: A Rogue Sociologist Takes to the Streets*.

Collecting and Analyzing Data

A couple of research methods that are somewhat unique to small group research are those of sociometry and interaction process analysis.

Sociometry. **Sociometry** refers to the measurement of interpersonal attraction between members in a group. A sociometric diagram shows how members in a small group feel about each other and how the members in a group fit together. If you became involved in a study group composed of some members of your sociology class, a sociometric diagram of your group would depict how members of the group feel about working with each other member. If there are five members of your group, some members would like each other more than others. The sociometric diagram reflects the various alignments.

Interaction Process Analysis. In addition to finding out the degree to which individuals in a group like each other, sociologists are also interested in the personality characteristics of group members and how these characteristics influence interaction. **Interaction Process Analysis** focuses on the personality characteristics of the specific persons involved in a group and the pattern of their interaction. One such model of analysis is SYMLOG (System for the Multiple Level Observation of Groups), which examines how group members view and affect each other. More information can be found on their website: http://www.symlog.com/.

Conclusions. The research on small groups has resulted in some knowledge about groups. Some examples of research findings follow.

How leadership develops. Researchers have found that depending upon which member of a group becomes a leader is related to the frequency with which the individual talks, the length of talking once initiated, and the style of communication—democratic rather than autocratic.

How morale develops. Cohesiveness of a group develops as a consequence of group members disclosing, empathizing, accepting, and trusting each other.

How groups help. Groups may enhance a person's ability to cope with stress. For example, Al Anon groups consist of individuals who have spouses or intimates who are alcoholics or drug dependent individuals. Al-Anon groups facilitate coping via sharing one's ordeal, learning that others have similar challenges, and developing new ways of coping.

Relations within Groups: Group Dynamics

All groups develop different patterns of leadership. Groups also have an enormous influence on the behavior of their members.

Leadership Patterns

As members in the group interact, various leadership patterns emerge: instrumental, expressive, authoritarian, democratic, and laissez-faire.

Instrumental. **Instrumental leaders,** also referred to as task leaders, emerge to direct the group's effort to make a decision and to solve a particular problem. In *Treasure of the Sierra Madre* (classic film of the 40s), a group of three men (the "old timer," Curt, and Fred C. Dobbs) set out to find gold in the Sierra Mountains. The "old timer" quickly emerged as the instrumental leader. He had been prospecting before, knew where to look for gold, and how to set up camp. He took charge of the group by deciding what supplies they would take, how far they would travel each day, and how they would deal with bandits. Curt and Dobbs quickly acquiesced to his direction. The "old timer" was aware of his skills and the needs of the group and matched these to emerge as a leader. Van Dijke and Poppe (2007) confirmed that individuals who have power in a group are aware of this power and are motivated to maintain it.

Expressive. **Expressive leaders** are concerned with keeping the morale of the group high and making sure that everyone feels happy and committed to working toward the goals of the group. In regard to the three prospectors referred to above, when tension arose over how much gold they should get before deciding to leave the mountain, how they would divide the gold, and whether or not to shoot an intruder, Curt emerged as the expressive leader. He wanted decisions to result in the emotional comfort of everyone in the group. In the sitcom *Sex and the City*, of the four main female characters (Carrie, Miranda, Charlotte, and Samantha), Charlotte was the expressive leader who always showed compassion for another's feelings.

Authoritarian. **Authoritarian leaders** are instrumental leaders who take control of the group and order people to perform certain roles. The captain of a ship is less concerned about what his crew thinks of him than that they obey him. The pilot of a plane whose landing gear will not go down dictates what the flight attendants are to tell the passengers to prepare for an emergency landing. The instructor of your sociology course is the authority in your class and alerts you to the attendance policy, test dates, and make up policy.

Some authoritarians may be gentle leaders who encourage you to see the "correct path" and follow it. Zen Masters, evangelical ministers, and group facilitators are not heavy handed but ease the group along a predetermined path so that the members feel they are "choosing" the path rather than being commanded to behave in a certain way.

Democratic. **Democratic leaders** are leaders who attempt to insure that group decisions represent input from each member of the group. Democratic leaders are willing to take the time to get agreement about a decision rather than force an authoritarian decision on the group. A group setting out on a mountain hike together may have a leader with a democratic style who ensures that each group member feels that his or her opinion has been heard and integrated into the group decision.

Laissez-Faire. **Laissez-faire leaders** have neither the dictatorial style of the authoritarian leader nor the democratic style, which focuses on a solution that is agreeable to everyone. Laissez-faire leaders prefer to sit by and let the group move at its own pace and make decisions, as it will. The disadvantage of this style is that it may take a long time for the group to reach consensus, resulting in little movement toward an outcome.

Group Conformity

Not only do groups have leaders, they have a number of followers. Conformity is an important aspect of group behavior. When teenagers meet at the mall to see a movie, they may have different preferences about which movie to see. Rarely will any member split off to see a movie alone; rather, pressure for conformity results in all members seeing one film.

One of the greatest predictors of drug use is the fact that one's close friends use drugs. This fact illustrates that reference groups are very powerful in influencing people to engage in behavior they might not otherwise engage in. Falstaff, one of Shakespeare's characters said, "My friends have been the spoil of me."

Groupthink

Groupthink is the tendency of group members to reduce the level of stress they experience by having to personally make difficult decisions by seeking concurrence with each other at the expense of critical thinking. Even though the decisions may not have negative outcomes, it is important to note that many group decisions are the product of members not feeling free to disagree and who drift along with the group will. The decision to invade Iraq involved individuals discounting facts (e.g. weapons of mass destruction?) and "going along" with an agenda identified by President Bush. There was also an element of moral justification—Saddam Hussein was characterized as an evil dictator who must be toppled in the name of democratic freedom. Dissension in the group process was discouraged, and the illusion of unanimity was maintained to support the president.

Functions

All groups have functions. Sjovold (2007) reviewed the four basic functions: control, nurture, opposition, and dependence. Control refers to the structure necessary to accomplish common goals while nurture refers to the predisposition of group members to take care of each other in the sense of listening and working out differences. Opposition refers to being open to questioning the way the group functions and being ready to adapt while dependence recognizes the need for group members to be obedient and focused. For example, Congress has the goal of providing health care for American citizens and sets up committees and subcommittees to examine how this may be done. This is the control function. While debate may be spirited, members of both the Senate and House of Representatives maintain a public politeness to each other

("I respect the honorable Congressman's position, but ..."). This is the nurture function.

The opposition function reflects awareness that politics is influenced by economics, that public opinion is putting pressure on Congress to provide better health care, and that socialized medicine in Canada, France, and other parts of the world is a valid alternative model. Finally, the dependence function recognizes the need for someone to make decisions, drive the bus, and move forward.

Variables Affecting Group Dynamics

The interaction between group members is affected by the size of the group, the physical conditions surrounding the group, and the demographic characteristics of group members.

Size

Size affects group interaction. In general, the smaller the group, the more intense the interaction between group members (and the higher the quality of the communication) (Lowry et al. 2006). The dyad, the smallest and most powerful of all groups, is radically changed by the addition of just one member. A childfree husband and wife having dinner will have a different pattern of interaction than a couple having dinner with a two-year-old child. Not only will the interaction between the spouses be less exclusive and intense because each will be interacting with the baby, but the frequency of exchange will decrease. As the child gets older, the potential for coalitions and alliances to form may weaken the husband-wife bond. One of the spouses may establish a very close relationship with the child and exclude the other parent.

The size of a group also influences the degree of formality, the division of labor, and the clarity of expectations. The interaction in a dyad or a small group is more likely to be informal. Furthermore, in small groups, the division of labor is likely to be rather loose in that expectations may not be specified. In larger groups, interaction is more formal because members have less familiarity with each other. To insure that the tasks of the group are performed, roles within larger groups are usually more clearly defined. There are more roles to perform in larger groups, which are reflected in the increased division of labor. Large groups cannot function with a great deal of ambiguity. Behavioral expectations of what the group members are to do must be spelled out.

In preparing for the civil trial of O.J. Simpson, Fred Goldman asked the law firm of Mitchell, Silberberg and Knupp to take the case (Daniel Petrocelli was the lead attorney). An enormous assault (which included identifying various roles of the members of the legal team and support staff) was mounted to provide a "preponderance of evidence" that Simpson murdered Nicole Brown and Ron Goldman. The carefully orchestrated group effort resulted in a unanimous guilty verdict.

Physical Conditions

Group interaction is also influenced by physical conditions. Where a group meets, at the beach or in the boardroom, is given prime consideration by large corporate firms. Textbook publishers often schedule the annual meeting of their sales representatives at exotic places to create a "fun atmosphere" for the work to be done and decisions to be made.

The size of the room in which the group meets is also important. A relatively small room for a small group is more often selected than a large room for a small group or vise versa. In addition, the size of the table will be commensurate with the size of the group. The shape of the table (round, square, oblong) and the placement of each person at the table may also affect group interaction.

The style and architecture of a room may affect interaction. Professors notice that state of the art air conditioned classrooms with stadium seating, video screens, and DVD equipment enhances the classroom experience and facilitates interaction in a way that meeting in an old basement room with poor lighting and exposed pipes does not.

Demographic Variables

Age, physical size, and sex seem to influence the degree to which an individual speaks in a group. One researcher (Baker, 1988) analyzed the "first to speak" and the "total participation rate" of 218 individuals in 52 groups who were asked to act as a mock jury. After the members of the respective groups were presented the facts of the case, they were asked to state their initial opinions and discuss the case for up to an hour. Being older, larger in size and male were associated with talking during the first minute and having a high "total participation rate."

The Overall Importance of Groups

Being a group member is important because it not only affects one's identity but life experiences. A person who is a black, male, upper class, atheist, stockbroker or a white, female, middle class, evangelical, grade school teacher will belong to different groups, have different group experiences, and be "a different person." Identify the various identities and life experiences which have resulted from your membership in various groups.

Groups provide the anchor throughout life that allows individuals in a complex society to know who they are and who they belong to. People belong to shared occupations, ethnic groups, families, and organizations. They are airline pilots, Hispanics, Mormons, masons, Marines or Americans. They can be identified and gain comfort from knowing where they belong. Groups provide the boundaries and patterns of interaction that tie people together as group members, share values and norms. While social life continues to change, groups continue to act as important guides to everyone in a complex society. In Chapter One we noticed that the Amish allow their youth to leave the fold and to experience the world. Some youth return since they do not know how to function outside the Amish community and they feel comfortable and secure inside the known Amish group world.

Group Composition Affects Survival: A Research Example

In the Antarctic summer of 1911, two teams raced for the South Pole. One team was British and was led by Robert Scott who represented the Royal Navy; the other was Norwegian and was led by Ronald Amundsen. Although both teams made it to the Pole, only one (Amundsen's) survived the return trip. One explanation suggests that it was the attention Amundsen gave to the group's size, composition, morale, and structure, which accounted for the survival of his group; likewise, the lack of attention to group detail evidenced by Scott contributed to the death of all members of his group (Huntford, 1984).

Size Amundsen deliberately limited the size of his team to nine members. Amundsen knew that the larger the group, the greater the chance of cliques forming, and the less control he might have over the group. Scott, on the other hand, "put together a cumbersome group almost three times the size of Amundsen's" (Johnson and Finney, 1986, 330). Cliques did form in the Scott camp.

Composition Groups accomplish their tasks most efficiently when all group members acknowledge the hierarchy of authority and defer to the group leader. Amundsen, who was regarded as a strong leader, selected members of the team who would not question his authority. One of his screening mechanisms was to ask potential participants to complete an obscure work task. If the person questioned Amundsen's directions, the person was considered to be too questioning of authority and regarded as unsuitable for the team. In contrast, Scott was regarded as a weak leader and had little control over the group. Once the group members broke off into cliques, they began to compete for the role of informal leader.

Morale Amundsen made the members of his team aware of the details of the plan to reach the Pole. Scott kept all of this information to himself so that the members of the group were not included. Hence, any consensus of group goals was inhibited by the absence of information about the future.

Amundsen nurtured group morale in yet another way. He understood the importance of lower status positions for inducing an effective and cohesive social unit. "To fill the role of group 'mascot,' Amundsen brought with him a cook named Lindstrom" (Johnson and Finney, 1986, 334). Lindstrom became the group clown and provided humor for the long Antarctic nights. "He functioned to minimize boredom and therefore minimize the potential for group conflict" (Johnson and Finney, 1986, 334).

Social Structure The statuses and roles of the respective members of the group were made clear in Amundsen's group. The members knew their respective positions and what they were to do. Statuses and roles were not made clear in Scott's group. Scott and his crew perished on their return when they were less than 200 miles from the base camp after making it over 1,200 miles to the Pole and back. "The party back at the base camp could have saved Scott's group had there been a clear consensus [over] the various roles" (Johnson and Finney, 1986, 333).

The experience of Amundsen's and Scott's groups emphasizes the importance of size, composition, morale, and social structure in forming a group. Letting a group form at random may not predict well for the ability of the group to accomplish its goals. Attention to group detail becomes particularly important in thinking about future space missions.

Order versus Disorder:
Relations between Groups

All groups have the potential to be both ordered and disordered as can be seen by looking at gender, race/ethnicity, and age.

Gender

Gender groups become ordered in the sense that females stick with females and males with males. Women tend to be more expressive, emotional and open than men, which has the effect of females bonding to other females ("My girl-friends understand me."). Likewise, men target activities around which they bond—watching sports games, duck hunting, and fishing.

Mixed gender groups become disordered in the sense that the sexes have difficulty understanding each other. Deborah Tannen's (2000) *You Just Don't Understand Me* emphasized the different socialization of the respective sexes. She pointed out that boys tend to play outside in large groups with a structured hierarchy like football. The goal of the game is winning. Girls, on the other hand, tend to interact in small groups or in pairs where a girl's social life is her best friend. The goal of the interaction is intimacy. When men and women discuss a problem, the man wants to solve the problem; the woman wants the man to listen and to understand her point of view.

Race/Ethnicity

Racial and ethnic groups are more pronounced than gender groups in their "clannishness." While whites, blacks, Hispanics, Asian Americans, and Native Americans may work in the same factory, after hours, they tend to go their separate ways with members of their own category. While this pattern results in order within the respective white, Black, Hispanic, etc. groups and communities, it creates disorder between the groups. And the racial divide continues—Southworth and Mickelson (2007) noted that segregation of schools continues. They studied the school and classroom organization of schools in the Charlotte-Mecklenburg Schools in North Carolina and concluded, "the operation of this public education system continues to reflect enduring patterns of social inequality in American society."

The Civil Rights Movement testifies to the prejudice and discrimination blacks have continued to endure from whites. Such hatred continues. Jena High School in Jena, Louisiana, was the site of racial discord in late December 2006. Six black teens were charged with beating a white male. But this act was preceded by white students hanging nooses from a tree at Jena High School in response to a black student asking permission to sit under a tree which had become a location where whites would congregate. The Jena 6 incident received national visibility in the form of a march (September 2007) by more than 20,000 protesters in response to the racial incidents in the town.

Age

Age groups are also tightly segregated in our society. Order results because the young and old groups relish their solidarity within their respective groups.

It is a solidarity which differs by the pace of life, music, customs, and culture. Disorder between them results because each views the other with avoidance. The groups are also in conflict for jobs and government subsidies. While youth want financial aid for education, the elderly want increased social security benefits.

Groups and Social Organization

As discussed above, groups are small, but they are integral parts of all other social organizations. They are found within and contribute to the vitality of social life. They have profound effects which we explore below.

Population

As groups change in composition, the nature of populations change. Groups that remain separated from each other and select only members with the same religious, racial or ethnic characteristics maintain similar population separation. In the United States when groups begin to integrate members, the nature of the population changes. When a Greek dates an Italian or a Catholic marries a Protestant, change begins that may ultimately change the entire demographic profile of the population.

Aggregations

The conflict between groups and within groups can cause tension which possibly can erupt. Remembering that groups can change to aggregations, a crowd or a mob, several men, led by their close friend Ted, may suddenly attack a peer group member, John, whom they found kissing Ted's girlfriend. In the heat of the moment, they may seriously hospitalize him with head injuries.

Social Class

Social actors feel more comfortable with friends who share their class rank. Groups form around prestige symbols such as fine wines, yachts, or exclusive clubs at the upper class level. These symbols give rank to members who identify with their social class. This identity can become close, leading to a primary group relationship among some and secondary relationship among others.

Families

Marriage and procreation happen among group members. In some countries the groups that unite are secondary groups. In the United States, most often it is among primary group members who fall in love. These close groups then change over time with each additional child altering the group, sometimes strengthening it and sometimes weakening it. Ultimately, the success of a family depends on the group dynamics within it.

Communities

This is the geographic location for group development. Most social actors meet their friends in the same communities. These groups of friends and colleagues may slowly change locations over time, but friendships last. Within communities there are tens of thousands of groups that, working together, give character and life to all other social organizations, such as associations.

Associations

Groups not only form within schools, hospitals and any workplace but also sometimes become the core of those associations. Colleagues may work together to develop departments at small colleges or become the basis of leadership of churches and organizations. Groups of friends may gather to form new associations dedicated to helping the poor or may influence management in a factory to provide better working conditions. Groups often form the background around which associations grow and develop.

Networks

Over time, groups change in character and form. Close friends move to new communities, meet new friends, and then move on again. Later in life, friends may be able to provide help for each other across the entire country. These friendship networks are becoming more organized by the use of the Internet and may even tie together associates who have never personally met.

Societies

At the macro level of a society, it is important to remember that changing group characteristics ultimately affects the culture and function of society. As the types of groups change, the character of the society also changes. If groups work hard from dawn to dusk across the full spectrum of the society. the nature of that entire society will change. It is often said that everyone is trying to "keep up with the Joneses." In a manner of speaking, groups follow each other and learn from each other. Many groups begin to look like each other in dress and behavior, music, and action. Groups influence society through politics. Groups are the backbone of what a society is all about and what it will become.

Popular Beliefs and Scientific Data: Jury Members Have Already Made Up Their Minds—Juries Don't Deliberate

A jury of one's peers is an American institution. There is the common belief that jury members make up their minds about the guilt or innocence of a case during the presentations of the prosecution and defense in court and that very little deliberation, if any, goes on behind closed doors in the jury room. To provide empirical information, Gastil, Burkhalter, and Black (2007) studied 267 Seattle jurors. Fifty-two percent were female (48% male), 84% were white (16% nonwhite). The median educational level was a college degree, and the median age was 49. These 267 jurors had experienced a total of 60 different criminal trials (assault, drunk-driving, sexual indiscretion, etc.) in Seattle municipal court with only three of the juries failing to reach a verdict. The median juror spent two days in the courtroom, and the median juror was in the jury room for less than an hour—84% deliberating for two hours or less.

Deliberation was defined as jurors rigorously examining a problem and arriving at a well-reasoned solution after a period of inclusive, respectful consideration of diverse points of view.

In deliberation, the group members analyze the case, weigh the evidence carefully, and take into consideration the instructions by the judge. The social context of deliberation is also important including adequate opportunities for each juror to speak with mutual respect given to different points of view by the other jury members. In addition, jurors are admonished by the judge to make up their own mind but to not be afraid to change their opinion if the discussion persuades them to do so. About 10% of trials result in a verdict that is the opposite of the jury's initial preferences.

Findings of the researchers included that most jurors reported that deliberation did occur with similarity of jury members' political knowledge, education, and skill level being associated with greater likelihood of deliberation. Discrepancy of these variables was associated with less deliberation. The perception that the jury had deliberated to reach a verdict was associated with greater juror satisfaction.

References

Baker, P. M. 1988. "Participation in Small Groups: Social, Physical, and Situational Factors." *Small Group Behavior,* 19: 3–18.

Gastil, J., Burkhalter, S., Black, L. W. 2007. "Do Juries Deliberate? A Study of Deliberation, Individual Difference, and Group Member Satisfaction at a Municipal Courthouse." *Small Group Research,* 38: 337–359.

Hopkins, P. E. 2007. "Thinking Critically and Creatively about Focus Groups." *Area,* 39: 528–535.

Huntford, R. 1984. *Scott and Amundsen; The Race to the South Pole.* Stockholm: New York: Anthneum.

Johnson, J. C. and B. R. Finney. 1986. "Structural Approaches to the Study of Groups in Space: A Look at Two Analogs." *Journal of Social Behavior and Personality,* 1: 325–347.

Knox, D., Zusman, M. E., McGinty, K. and Gescheidler, J. 2001. "Deception of Parents During Adolescence." *Adolescence,* 36: 611–614.

Lowry, P. B., Roberts, T. L., Romano, Jr., N. C., Cheney, P. D. and Hightower, R. T. 2006. "The Impact of Group Size and Social Presence on Small-Group Communication: Does Computer-Mediated Communication Make a Difference?" *Small Group Research,* 37: 631–661.

Mack, D. E., Strong, H. A., Kowalski, K. and Crocker, P. R. 2007. "Does Friendship Matter? An Examination of Social Physique Anxiety in Adolescence." *Journal of Applied Social Psychology,* 37: 1248–1264.

Sjøvold, E. 2007. "Systematizing Person-Group Relations (SPGR): A Field Theory of Social Interaction." *Small Group Research,* 38: 615–635.

Southworth, S. and R. A. Michelson. 2007. "The Interactive Effects of Race, Gender and School Composition on College Track Placement." *Social Forces,* 86: 497–523.

Tannen, D. 2000. *You Just Don't Understand Me.* New York: Ballantine.

van Dijke, M. and Poppe, P. 2007. "Motivations Underlying Power Dynamics in Hierarchically Structured Groups." *Small Group Research,* 38: 643–669.

Venkatesh, S. 2008. *Gang Leader for a Day: A Rogue Sociologist Takes to the Streets.* New York: Penguin.

Chapter 8

Social Class, Race, and Ethnicity

… working together we can move beyond some of our old racial wounds, and that in fact we have no choice if we are to continue on the path of a more perfect union.

Barack Obama

Air Force One waits on standby orders for the President of the United States. On his command, the president is whisked by helicopter from the plush lawn of the White House to within a short walk of the jet whose engines have already been started. After he enters, the door is closed, and the jet begins to move toward the runway. By the time it reaches the runway, it has already been cleared for takeoff, and the president is on his way, along with his staff, servants, and selected press corps. In contrast to the president who lives in the White House, a janitor from Washington, D.C., lives in a one-room apartment in a ghetto and must walk everywhere he needs to go. Because of crime, no cabs will come into his area of the city.

The life-styles of these two social actors are different. They occupy radically different positions and have different access to wealth, power, and prestige. Social stratification exists in all societies and influences the other social organizations of which the individual is a part.

Since one's race and ethnic background are major contributors to one's social status and position in the society, we examine the impact of these social factors in detail. First, we will examine the meaning of social stratification.

The Nature of Social Stratification

Individuals in all societies are stratified into various social layers and are treated unequally. Inequality and stratification are interrelated but different concepts.

Social Inequality

Social inequality refers to the unequal distribution of resources. Wealth, power, and prestige are among the resources held differently depending upon one's social position. If everyone had the same amount of money or education, there would be no inequality in those factors. When someone makes more money or has a greater education there is inequality between those individuals. Sociologists measure inequality but are not concerned solely with the differences between individuals. Rather, when these differences become structured into the social organizations of life, they have greater sociological meaning.

Inequality occurs everywhere, but unless it can be perpetuated from generation to generation, it is not of lasting organizational import. Persons in the upper class have considerable wealth, power, and prestige. They ensure that their sons and daughters are taught the right values and sent to the right Ivy League schools so that they continue their wealth, power, prestige and upper class life style. Muhajarine et al (2008) confirmed that married individuals with higher incomes and educations are healthier and report a higher quality of life.

Social Stratification

Social stratification refers not only to the ranking of people from high to low status on the basis of the positions they occupy in society, but more specifically to the continuation of this ranking through time. Persons in high status positions have greater access to wealth, power, and prestige than those in low status positions. The position of President of the United States is associated with higher status than the position of janitor. Social stratification is a measure of the degree to which those in the upper class as well as the lower class pass on their rank to their children and their children's children. If a country is socially stratified, it implies that those who occupy a particular position in society will be able to pass along their wealth, power, and prestige to their offspring. The President of the United States, by virtue of his or her position, will have access to money, power, and prestige and will pass these on to his or her children. A janitor has considerably less money, power, and prestige and will pass, inadvertently, the same class position he or she occupies to his offspring.

Social stratification is often confused with social differentiation. **Social differentiation** refers to the presence of social characteristics which emphasize that one individual is different from another. Age and race are social characteristics which allow for a grouping of individuals into different categories. No social stratification is involved since no ranking is implied. Once a value is placed on these social qualities (i.e. "it is better to be young than old"), then the underlying criteria and justification for social stratification is created. Ageism, racism, sexism, and heterosexism are all evaluations of social qualities which suggest that one category of people is better than another category. Once these social inequalities become visible, social stratification may come into existence.

Examples of Social Stratification

Sociologists have observed the various ways individuals are ranked above or below each other on a scale of inferiority and superiority in a society. These include socioeconomic status, race, ethnicity, religion, reputation, possessions, social knowledge, and social values/attitudes.

Socioeconomic Status (SES)

Socioeconomic status, also known as **social class**, refers to the identification of a person's ranking in a stratification system on the basis of income, education, and occupation. Looking first at income, what do we know about the social stratification of America? The amount of money a person is paid for performing a service is a reflection of the value we place on that service and the person who provides it. We pay thousands of dollars to a physician to perform a two hour surgery and less than minimum wage to a babysitter. Of course, the surgeon spent nine years of medical training in contrast to the babysitter who may not have graduated from high school.

The amount of discretionary income is also an indicator of social class. **Discretionary income** is the amount of income an individual has after paying for rent, utilities, food, car payment, and taxes. One indicator for discretionary income is the amount of household income. Table 8.1 reflects how households vary in the amount of money they have.

The amount of education a person has attained strongly affects the person's income. The median income earned for each level of education is shown in Table 8.2.

In addition to income and education, the level of prestige accorded a particular occupation is used to assess a person's social class. Prestige is a reputa-

Table 8.1
Income Distribution of Households in the United States: 2005

Percent of Households	Amount of Income
14.7%	below $15,000
12.4%	$15,000 to $24,999
11.4%	$25,000 to $34,999
14.9%	$35,000 to $49,999
18.4%	$50,000 to $74,999
11.1%	$75,000 to $99,999
17.2%	$100,000 and over

Source: *Statistical Abstract of the United States: 2008* (127th ed.) Washington, D.C.: U.S. Bureau of the Census, Table No. 668.

Table 8.2
Education and Median Income 2005

| Education | Median Income per Graduate Worker | |
	Male	Female
High school graduate	$30,134	$16,695
Bachelor's degree	$51,700	$32,668
Master's degree	$64,468	$44,385
Doctoral degree	$76,937	$56,820

Source: *Statistical Abstract of the United States: 2008* (127th ed.) Washington, D.C.: U.S. Bureau of the Census, Table No. 680.

tion that a person gets from being a doctor or taxi driver that translates into the ability to impress and influence others. Physicians, judges, and university professors typically enjoy higher prestige than grocery baggers, bail bondsmen, and grave diggers.

Race/Ethnicity

Our society ranks individuals on the basis of racial characteristics and ethnic affiliation. The importance of racial characteristics on identity was emphasized by Decuzzi et al. (2006) who found in their study of racial perceptions among college students, that while both races (black and white) tended to view women and men of their own and the other race positively, there was a pronounced tendency to view women and men of their own race more positively and members of the other race more negatively.

One reason for the low status ranking of blacks is the proportion of that population that has lower incomes. Although the percentage of affluent blacks will increase, less than one percent of the 8.5 million black families in the United States have family incomes of $200,000 or more. In contrast, 5% of the 57.4 million white families have such an annual income (*Statistical Abstract of the United States, 2008*, Table 36). Black families are almost three times as likely as whites to live below the poverty line (22.8% versus 7.5%) (Table 36).

Sometimes a phenomenon is thought to be race based when it may be economically based. Goza et al. (2007) examined U.S. Census 2000 data and found a consistent inverse pattern between income status and infant mortality for white and non-white neonatal and post neonatal death rates. Hence, it is not race but low-income for both whites and non-whites that show infant mortality rates substantially higher than the overall rate for the population.

Social rankings also occur on the basis of ethnicity. An **ethnic group** shares a common cultural tradition and a sense of identity. The Irish, Italians, and Poles are examples of ethnic groups. Poles are sometimes regarded as having less status than Anglos or other ethnic groups as evidenced by the pervasiveness of Polish jokes.

Religion

Churches are also stratified by class. Persons in the upper classes are more likely to attend an Episcopal church. This church is characterized by a great deal of formal ritual and structure with limited emotional expression. In contrast, Americans whose education, income and job designate them as members of the lower class are more likely to belong to the Church of God or a Pentecostal church. These churches rely much less on ritual and encourage open emotional expression including standing and waving one's hands in the air and "speaking in tongues." When people change social classes, they often change churches and even religions.

Possessions

People want to possess certain objects such as a Lexus, Hybrid, Mercedes, or a BMW because these possessions suggest that the owner occupies a high status position in society. Driving the right car, wearing the right clothes, and owning a house in the right neighborhood are all possessions which are seen as boosting one's social image. New York and Paris fashion designers are intent on providing the latest clothes which are sought after as status symbols.

The food and drink one consumes are also social class related. Chivas Regal scotch or a fine wine and filet mignon consumed by the upper class can be contrasted to Mad Dog 20/20 or Boones Farm wine and fatback consumed by members of the lower class. Recently, game food in the form of deer, bear, grouse, and hare has become fashionable and served in upscale restaurants. The important point is that when someone owns material possessions associated with the upper class they feel better and are accorded higher status. Although middle class, some families live in upper class neighborhoods to attain higher status from others than their wealth or income would provide for them. While they may eat tuna fish sandwiches and stay home because they can't afford to go to a movie, they pay for a wealthy home to "look" upper class.

Social Attitudes/Values

The social position that a person occupies influences that person's attitudes. Persons in higher social positions (in contrast to those in lower social positions) are more likely to believe that corporations do not necessarily benefit owners at the expense of workers and that working husbands and wives should share equally in housework and child care. Those individuals in lower social positions are more likely to feel that corporations exploit their workers and that the husband is "the king of the castle."

A person's values vary by social class. Adolescents in the working class value getting married before age 20. They are not going to college, do not think in terms of "establishing a career," and want to escape from their parent's cramped house. Political orientation also varies by social class. The Republican party has traditionally fostered the interests of the wealthy and has become the party of the upper classes. Because the wealthy have their interests to protect, they support conservative economic policies such as limited control of businesses by the government. In regard to social issues, the upper classes are more likely to support legislation for abortion.

Stratification Systems

Differences in inequality are passed on from generation to generation. Stratification systems exist on a continuum from being closed to being opened.

Closed Stratification Systems

Closed stratification systems are those in which there are clear, known, and identifiable divisions between the classes with no movement permitted between classes. When almost no movement is possible between classes it is called a **caste system**. Caste membership results in an ascribed status assigned at birth depending upon one's parents. Once assigned, the person stays in that caste until death. Marriage, and in some cases interaction, with those outside one's own caste is forbidden. The caste system in traditional India provides an example of how individuals were locked into particular social strata. Although the caste system was officially abolished in India in 1949, some people in rural areas are still treated as members of certain castes or varnas. The major castes include the Brahmins (teachers and doctors), Kshatriyas (rulers and politicians), Vaishyas (merchants and artists), Shudras (laborers and service workers), and Hariljans (scavengers). The latter two classes are regarded as "untouchables." Members of a higher caste who touch them are polluted and immediate ritual cleaning must begin to rid one's self of the effects of such contact. An extreme example of the degree to which "untouchables" are social rejects is the belief that if they cross over a bridge, they will pollute the entire stream below. Such beliefs and practices have disappeared in crowded urban areas where the knowledge of one's position in the social hierarchy is unknown.

A similar caste-like system existed in the United States during slavery when southern blacks were denied the right to vote, to be educated, or to use public facilities. Native Americans have also been treated like outcasts by literally being moved "out of town" and put in their own place: a "reservation." Today, some scholars question how much has really changed.

Open Stratification Systems

Open stratification systems or **class systems** are those in which class lines are more vaguely drawn and movement between the respective classes is permitted. Assignment to a particular strata is achieved rather than ascribed and is based on one's economic circumstance. Individuals born into a low social rank can achieve the requisite education to increase their income as well as alter their world view and move upward in class standing. Most societies have some form of a class system.

Karl Marx and Friedrich Engels suggested the existence of a classless society whereby everything was held in common and there was no differentiation of the population into social classes. While Americans think of the former Soviet Union as a "communist" country (which implies a classless society), stratification did exist in the Soviet Union. There was an elite upper class, a small middle class, and a large working class of poor peasants and urban laborers.

Social Mobility

Social mobility is the movement from one social class position to another. The various types of mobility are vertical, horizontal, intragenerational, intergenerational, and structural. Mobility is assessed in numerous ways such as comparing the occupation, income, education and place of residence of one individual at two points in time or comparing children and their parents.

Vertical Mobility

Vertical mobility involves changing positions up or down in a social system. Most people like to view themselves as "upwardly mobile" which suggests that they are climbing the social ladder of success. A few have moved upward. Oprah Winfrey was born in rural Mississippi to a poor unwed teenage mother and grew up in a Milwaukee ghetto. Today, she is known as one of the most influential women in the world, the richest African American in the 21st century, and the only black billionaire. Barack Obama also illustrates vertical mobility. He noted that "I am the son of a black man from Kenya and a white woman from Kansas" Indeed, he was reared in a single parent home (his mother was 18 when he was born).

Other examples of upward mobility include moving from the status of freshman to senior, moving from the status of being a 15-year-old living at home, dependent upon parents without a driver's license to being an 18-year-old with a driver's license, a car, and married. Examples of occupational upward mobility include moving from the position of a head football coach in high school to the position of a head football coach at Notre Dame. Or, from a college football coach to a coach in the NFL (who wins the Super Bowl).

The opposite of upward mobility is downward mobility which is illustrated by moving from a position of high status to one of low status. Flunking out of college and moving from the position of "college student" to "college dropout" is an example of downward mobility. Other examples are moving from the position of being engaged to no longer being involved with anyone, moving from being married to being divorced, and moving from being employed to being unemployed. Tiffin et al. (2007) noted that a drop in income and downward mobility was associated with the perception of greater family dysfunction.

Intragenerational Mobility

Intragenerational mobility focuses on the upward or downward social mobility of a specific individual. Bill Clinton moved up and then down the social class hierarchy as a result of his election to the presidency and his threatened impeachment in reference to the Monica Lewinsky scandal. He regained his status as the scandal blurred over time. Similarly, Barry Bonds might be characterized as being in a relatively low social status position until he became involved in professional baseball and surpassed Babe Ruth's regular season career total of 714 home runs. But he dropped in status when he was indicted on four counts of perjury for steroid use. The important point is that mobility changed for the specific individual within their lifetime. Other baseball players such as Marty McGuire and Roger Clemens experienced a drop in status when their names surfaced for alleged use of illegal substances. Marion Jones started with low status and then won various competitive races which increased her status. She experienced a similar social class roller coaster ride when she "won" five Olympic gold medals, but later admitted to the use of steroids during the period she competed for the medals (and her status plummeted). She was convicted and sent to prison for six months. She had to give up her Olympic medals and all members of her team were forced to return their medals.

Intergenerational Mobility

Intergenerational mobility is the upward or downward mobility of a son or daughter's social class in contrast to that of his or her parents. Kirk Douglas, the well-respected Hollywood actor now in his nineties, observed that his father was an immigrant "ragman" who drove a wooden cart down the street selling rags. This example illustrates intergenerational upward mobility. Michael Douglas, son of Kirk Douglas, has maintained an intergenerational mobility status similar to his father. Oscar winner Angelina Jolie has also maintained an intergenerational mobility status similar to her father, Jon Voight. Skip Holtz, son of famed football coach Lou Holtz, has his work cut out for him to maintain his father's legendary status.

An example of downward intergenerational mobility would be the offspring of a neurosurgeon becoming homeless and living in a shelter. Sociologists are interested in intergenerational mobility because it provides an index of the degree to which the stratification system is open. No intergenerational mobility exists in a caste society.

In general, there is a tendency for intergenerational mobility to be still-born—for people to stay in the same social class in which they were born. Indeed, this caste or caste-like outcome occurs because the institutions of society (i.e. education) perpetuate keeping people in the class of birth. Middle class college educated parents who send their children to state supported colleges ensure the middle class position of their offspring. Launching them into a higher social class is difficult and unusual.

Structural Mobility

Structural mobility exists when changes in the economic or political structure of society affect a person's social status. The invention of harvester machines has replaced farm workers. Similarly, mechanical robots which can weld car doors on assembly lines have displaced automobile workers. No matter how hard the farm worker or machinist worked, they were replaced by structural forces beyond their control and forced downward in social status.

In contrast, new computer technology has resulted in a need for clerical workers to operate computers, thus raising the occupational status of workers who can fulfill this new structural need. The upward mobility of these workers is more a function of changes in technology than of individual achievement.

Social Class and Social Organization

Social class affects each type of social organization. Some examples follow.

Populations

Some populations in our society are more at risk than others. Blacks, who comprise a greater percentage of those in lower class positions than whites, are particularly vulnerable. Specifically, blacks (when compared to whites) are more likely to weigh less at birth, to die during the first year, and to have a lower life expectancy each year. Explanations for these phenomena are not to be found by focusing on the individual, but on the social organizations in which the individual is a part.

Birth weight is the greatest single predictor of a healthy baby, adolescent, and adult. Low birth weight babies are defined as being five pounds and eight ounces or below. Of all babies born, a higher percentage of low birth weight babies are born to black than white mothers. One factor accounting for this discrepancy is the tendency of a greater percentage of black females to have babies as teenagers. In general, as the age of the mother goes down, so does the birth weight of the baby. The percent of low birth weight babies born to black females is 13.4 compared to 7.1 for white females (*Statistical Abstract of the United States, 2008*. Table 85).

Another factor accounting for a higher percentage of low birth weight babies among blacks is less prenatal care. The percent of black mothers compared to white mothers beginning prenatal care in their third trimester or having no care is six percent versus three percent. One of the factors accounting for the fewer number of doctor visits is that, due to increasing mal-practice insurance costs, obstetricians are limiting their services to higher class lower risk mothers. Hence, physicians may not be available to many high risk mothers.

Once babies are born, the inequities continue. The infant mortality rate (number of deaths per 1,000 live births under 1-year-old) for blacks is 13.8 in contrast to 5.7 for whites (Table 108). This means that almost three times as many black babies as white babies die within their first year. Among the primary causes for death in the first year are premature births and low birth weight babies. Just as blacks are more likely to deliver low birth weight babies, their babies are more likely to be born prematurely. While the two factors are associated, the result is the same—more death among black babies.

For those babies who survive the first year, class position influences one's life expectancy throughout life. Black females can expect to live 76.3 years in contrast to white females, 80.8 years. Black males can expect to live 69.5 years in contrast to white males, 75.7 (Table 101).

Death by AIDS is also related to race. Black females are more likely than white females to die of AIDS (13.0 per 100,000 population versus 0.9 per 100,000 population). When black males and white males are compared, the figures are 29.2 per 100,000 population versus 3.8 (Table 119).

Collective Behavior

The magazine industry develops and promotes their products to appeal to a particular social class. Romance magazines and magazines focusing on wrestling are more often consumed by members of the working class. The former appeal to the hope of escape from the lack of romance in the lower class while the latter appeal to the "macho" male image lower class males are socialized to emulate. *Country American*, a magazine for people who appreciate the country lifestyle, was developed specifically for "middle Americans" with "discretionary income."

Magazines such as *Smithsonian*, *New Yorker*, and *Scientific American* are more oriented toward upper middle class readers. The various magazines of the respective social classes are only found within these classes. *True Story* would no more be on a coffee table in the White House than *Smithsonian* would be on top of the television in the ghetto.

Groups

Intimate groups are composed of individuals who belong to the same social class. These groups are usually regarded as being in different places on the stratification hierarchy. High status groups are those in which the individuals play golf, tennis, and polo. Low status groups are those in which the individuals bowl and shoot pool. What is important is that we can explain what individuals do without knowing anything about them. All we need to know is their social class and we can predict with a high degree of accuracy what they will do. If they are in the lower class, they will belong to groups that think a good date is a barbeque, beer and music; in the middle class they will belong to groups that think a good date is dinner and a movie; and in the upper class, a fine meal with opera or orchestra. If you are in the middle class and the group you associate with likes opera, you will feel extremely uncomfortable, as your socialization has not prepared you to understand and enjoy this experience.

Families

Families also vary by social class. Strong kinship ties among families in the lower class are structurally necessitated by the inability of these families to survive in isolated nuclear units. Unemployment, lack of savings, and working in occasional menial jobs requires the pooling of resources among those in the wider kinship system. Sharing meals, housing, and babysitting are necessary and commonplace. Kinship relations are the focus of the lower class.

Middle class families are self supporting and free standing because of their strong link to the occupational sector (associations). One or both spouses have stable professional jobs with secure incomes. Strong kinship ties are unnecessary except for their emotional value. Importantly, middle class family members who lose a job often have no one to fall back upon. Even a sick child may stress the entire family to the breaking point because they don't have extended kinship systems and know few if any people who can watch their sick child while they go to work.

Upper class families literally live apart from both lower and middle class families. They also may own several homes, all of which are isolated (communities). Highfields in Hopewell, New Jersey, was the isolated home of Charles Lindbergh and his wife, Anne. She was definitely of upper class background as her parents enjoyed a home during the Depression complete with 32 full time servants. Today, the president, Warren Buffett and Bill Gates live lives separate and apart of other Americans which means that their families also live distinct and different lives.

Families in the lower, middle, and upper classes teach their children different values. These values may be explained in reference to the work roles of the respective classes. Lower class workers are basically told what to do and learn to conform. These values of conformity and acceptance are passed on to their children. In contrast, middle class professional workers are given more responsibility in their occupational roles and become more "self-directed." They teach their children to be self motivated and make their goals come true. Upper class families own corporations and control markets.

Just as upper class families live apart from lower and middle class individuals, their children are insulated from other classes by attending elite private schools, boarding schools, or private colleges (associations). Mixing with the masses occurs only when politically advantageous (i.e. politicians will go into the ghetto for television coverage that will help them get the poor to vote for them).

Communities

Communities vary by social class distinction. Cities are divided by the cost of housing, crime rates, availability of city services such as schools, police, fire departments, colleges, and trash collection, as well as social class. *Money Magazine* and society as a whole will rank cities by class, and those who live within those cities are labeled with class distinctions by the city in which they reside. Since there are a lot of different communities in cities, living in New York City does not tell you which specific part of the city you come from. In 2000, the data indicate that if you are from the TriBeCa area of Manhattan with an average household income of nearly $120,000, you have all the services, security, and access to safety that you can obtain. If you are from other community areas of Manhattan, your average income is around $47,000, and you have fewer services, less security, etc. Differences by communities change even when considering race. In New York City, black residents of Queens have surpassed whites in household incomes nearing $52,000 and obtain better services, trash collection, and recreation areas for their children than those living in Brooklyn with a median household income of $32,000 per year.

When Hurricane Katrina hit Louisiana, the city of New Orleans and surrounding communities were devastated. On August 29, 2005, Katrina became one of the worst disasters in United States history. As a community, those in the upper classes were more prepared, had better insurance, were better taken care of and more able to evacuate (one couple got into a taxi and said "Drive us to Atlanta") and survive than those in the lower classes. When 80% of the city was flooded, a large proportion of those flooded were in the ninth ward leaving houses uninhabitable. These were later bulldozed to make room for new condominiums for enterprising real estate developers. Other more fashionable communities were rebuilt immediately and residents continued life as usual.

Associations

There are currently about 1.4 million active military personnel (1.3 million in the military reserve, 1.1 million in the ready reserve) and 5 million in the National Guard (*Statistical Abstract of the United States: 2008*. Tables 501, 502, 503, 5046). The military has a basic stratification system of officers and enlisted men. A relatively small percent of the military personnel are officers, and they are given special privileges in terms of salary, housing, and job assignments.

Job assignment becomes particularly critical in that persons with less power are more likely to be given more dangerous assignments. Regarding the war in Iraq, a disproportionate percentage of the combat troops breaking down the doors in Baghdad are members of the lower economic strata as compared to members of the upper classes. One scene of Michael Moore's anti-war documentary, *Fahrenheit 9/11*, showed him asking members of Congress if any of them had sons or daughters fighting in Iraq. Not one had offspring in Iraq. It has been proposed that to develop patriotism in America, all Americans, without exception, should be required to give two years of active service to their country. Conservatives argue that this would create a stronger, safer, more patriotic America. Liberals argue that this would assure equality for men, women, blacks, whites, and the disabled who could use their service to learn skills or clean weapons in a wheelchair. President Bush has two daughters. Would President Bush have ordered the war in Iraq if the association of the military were organized differently, (to include his daughters) prior to the invasion?

Networks

Entry into certain networks requires existence in a certain strata of society. There are economic networks which link business professionals with the same interests. Once a stock is on the rise, the word travels though patterned networks of brokers revealing what stock to buy. The same is true of horse racing. In 2007, the word was passed through a network of betters that the 'groomers' (the men in the stables who groom the horses) believed that Race Car Rhapsody was going to be the winner in an upcoming race. Those placing bets were told "bet all you want" as this was as close to a sure thing as ever happens. Race Car Rhapsody did, indeed, win.

Networks exist at all layers of the business world. Inside trading can only occur among high status individuals who have access to information and who pass this information along closed networks. Similarly, price fixing among major airlines or corporations occurs at the corporate level due to networks about what competitors are doing and agree to do. These networks are class related to activities.

When a heroin addict moves from Fort Wayne, Indiana, to Los Angeles, California, he or she may join treatment centers there to obtain the contacts and information necessary to move and restart life as an addict in the new community.

Societies

All societies are stratified, and the population in each social class is subject to change. In the U.S., the stratification is illustrated in Table 8.3.

In India where most people are poor and some people still occupy caste status, a new middle class has emerged. Over one fourth of the population has become middle class as evidenced by their ability to buy possessions. No longer do these Indians accept a life of drudgery. Enjoying life has become more normative.

Members of this new middle class sometimes use money to bypass (pun intended) the caste system. Marriage advertisements in newspapers often contain the language "caste no bar" which means that a person with money would be willing to marry another with money even though the person was technically a member of a different caste.

Race and Ethnicity

As noted earlier, social class reflects the division of individuals in society on the basis of similar amounts of wealth, power, and prestige. Race and ethnicity are major factors that identify these division lines.

Race

To sociologists, **race** refers to the social significance that is given to biological characteristics. To be black or white only has importance or social meaning because someone else believes that it does and acts on this belief. With the exception of physically challenged or handicapped individuals, the biological makeup of all human beings is very similar—each individual has two eyes to see, a nose with which to breathe, and skin which provides a protective covering. Sociologists point out that, in almost every society, individuals with particular biological characteristics are assigned to a lower social status. For example, Black skin is relegated to a lower status in the United States, which makes it difficult for Blacks to attain high social positions. Indeed, "dark skinned blacks in the United States have lower socioeconomic status, more punitive relationships with the criminal justice system, diminished prestige, and less

Table 8.3
114 Million Family Households by Social Class*

Class Identification	% of Population	Household Income	Education/ Occupation	Lifestyle	Example
Upper Class					
Upper-Upper class (old money capitalists)	1%	$500,000+	Prestigious schools/wealth passed down	Large, spacious homes in lush residential areas	Kennedys
Lower-Upper Class (nouveau riche)	3%	$200,000+	Prestigious schools/investors in or owners of large corporations	(same as above)	Bill Gates, Donald Trump
Middle Class					
Upper-Middle Class	24%	$75,000– $200,000	Post-graduate degrees/ physicians, lawyers, managers of large corporations	Nice homes, nice neighborhoods, send children to state universities	Your physician
Lower-Middle class	33%	$35,000– $75,000	College degrees/ nurses, elementary- or high-school teachers	Modest homes, older cars	High-school English teacher
Working Class	24%	$15,000– $35,000	High school diploma/ Waitresses, mechanics	Home in lower-income suburb; children get job after high school	Employee at fast-food restaurant
Working Poor	15%	Below poverty line of $17,170 for family of 3	Some high school/service jobs	Live in poorest of housing; barely able to pay rent/ buy food	Janitor
Underclass	10%	—	Unemployed/ unemployable; survive via public assistance, begging, hustling/ illegal behavior (e.g., selling drugs)	Homeless; contact with mainstream society is via criminal justice system	Bag lady

*Appreciation is expressed to Arunas Juska, Ph.D. for his assistance in the development of this table. Estimates of percent in each class are in reference to household incomes as published in *Statistical Abstract of the United States: 2008*, Table 670.

likelihood of holding elective office compared to their lighter counterparts" (Hochschild and Weaver, 2007). Barack Obama is the only black person in American history to be given serious national consideration for president. His mixed race parental background is one factor in his being relatively light skinned. One's biological appearance has a social outcome in terms of social status and position in the society.

Ethnic Background

Ethnicity is a larger more generic term that refers to national origin (American, Latin etc.), religion, or distinctive cultural patterns. Examples of cultural patterns are language, dress, food habits and marital customs. A person from Pakistan lives within a stratified society in which the oldest are given the highest respect; they are introduced first, given the best cut of meat, listened to for their opinions and permitted to make the final decision. Additionally, titles have a great deal of meaning, and one is to show respect for titled individuals. Families are private, and questions about a person's wife are inappropriate. Pakistanis eat only with their right hand, and like Muslims, do not drink alcohol or eat pork products of any kind. This ethnic identity of dress, respect, and food is a cultural pattern and sets Pakistanis apart from those cultural patterns which are valued by the majority of members of our society. As an ethnic minority member in America, they are relegated to a lower social status. A person who only speaks Chinese, wears a kilt, or eats dogs can hardly be elected president of the United States because these factors have been labeled as ethnic minority status characteristics by the majority. Like race, ethnic characteristics become important because of the social value (high or low) members of the majority put on these characteristics.

One's ethnic background implies similar norms, folkways, and mores and serves to provide a common emotional bond for minority members. Ethnic minority groups have a distinct way of behaving and relating to the world. Ethnocentric perceptions by the majority result in the minority being labeled as "wrong." This perception also pushes minority group members into a lower social status. For example, Vietnamese and others who eat pickled pig ears (a distinctive cultural pattern) or dog meat are viewed negatively by the majority of Americans and that negative view held widely by the majority makes it difficult for those who eat such foods to move into the upper class.

Other Social Markers of Social Class

Religion. Religion is another aspect of ethnicity. The term "Irish Catholic" illustrates the degree to which a person's ethnic background may be entwined with religion. Religion is important because it also has an effect on one's social class position. Being a "holy roller," typically associated with the Pentecostal Church, is not accepted by members of majority status. Hence, the high status political positions such as President, Speaker of the House, and Governor would probably not be available to a "holy roller." Rather, persons in these upper class positions are more often of the majority Episcopalians or Presbyterians.

Religion may be as decisive an element in social position as race or other ethnic characteristics. In Bulgaria, the Bulgarians are openly hostile against the Turks—an ethnic conflict. However, in Lebanon, the warring groups are religious: the Christians and the Muslims. In America the dominant religions are Protestant, Catholic, and Jewish. A president might be from any one of these three, but would not likely be a Buddhist, Muslim, or Hare Krishna. Among the Republican candidates for the 2008 presidential election was Mitt Romney, a Mormon. His religion was an issue to many majority members and no doubt contributed to his not being an acceptable candidate.

In addition to race, religion, and national origin as factors which separate majority and minority group members, sexual preference and handicapped status are also important factors. These two are becoming more important in America as we begin the twenty-first century.

Sexual Preference. The sexual preference of an individual influences the social positions available to that person. Homosexuals are individuals who are emotionally and sexually attracted to members of their own sex. Although about three percent of the U.S. adult population is predominately gay, they are victims of extreme prejudice and discrimination. While acceptance and tolerance toward homosexuals is increasing, they are called names ("faggot," "pansy," "fruit fly"), regarded as sick or deviant, and denied high status positions. Neither the Republican nor Democratic Party will nominate a candidate for president who goes on record as being a homosexual because of the low social value majority status individuals put on this sexual orientation. When Senator Larry Craig's sexual involvement with other men became public in 2007, his political support waned. Members of the military who clearly announce that they are homosexual are discharged from the service. This "Don't Ask, Don't Tell" philosophy translates into "we don't value homosexuals so if you tell us you are one, you can't work here." Similarly, homosexual elementary school teachers risk losing their jobs because majority status parents may fear their influence in the classroom and force them to be fired.

Physically Challenged. Persons who are blind, in wheelchairs, or are missing limbs are viewed as handicapped in our society and are typically assigned to lower status positions (Franklin D. Roosevelt was able-bodied when he became president; he became wheelchair bound after he became president). The biological difference is given a social significance and persons with these physical differences are lumped into categories that are excluded from certain roles. Waitresses in expensive restaurants must be slim; they cannot weigh 300 pounds. A person whose face has been severely burned from a fire is not hired as a receptionist in an office. There is no reason other than the social label for a person with a burned face to be excluded from being a receptionist.

Majority and Minority Status

Majority status refers to individuals who have full access to the power, privileges, and prestige of the stratification system. This status is based upon their having various identifiable positive characteristics, such as language, dress, or skin color. **Minority status** refers to individuals who have limited access to the power, privileges, and prestige of a stratification system. Their limited access is based upon their having various visible characteristics defined as negative. The significance of majority status is that those in power can identify what are high status characteristics and define characteristics held by minorities as low status. In the United States, being white, having Anglo-Saxon ethnic heritage, being Protestant, heterosexual, and able-bodied are defined as those characteristics which allow them to move to the top of the stratification system. Individuals without these characteristics have limited control over their being relegated to a lower place in the social class hierarchy.

Majority or minority status is defined in societal context. In the United States, being black has a long historical social meaning associated with minority status. In Ghana, being black is associated with majority status and being white with minority status. Hence, skin color has different meanings in different social contexts.

Majority or minority status is not defined on the basis of numbers. The central elements of majority and minority status are power, privilege, and prestige. Irrespective of numbers, those groups with the most valued characteristics have majority status; those with the least have minority status.

In South Africa in the nineties, 12 percent (5 million) of the population was white and 85 percent (24 million) were black—a dramatic example of how a small number of people in the majority controlled a large number of people in the minority. While minorities were gaining more freedom, political control in South Africa was still in the hands of whites. Blacks were restricted in terms of where they lived, worked, and played. Blacks had no voice and **apartheid** (the institutionalization of racism which encourages the development of separate political institutions for each of the racial groups) was still the policy. However, with the speech of President F. W. deKlerk in early 1990, the reform movement toward equality began. Today, while there are still racial issues, apartheid has disappeared.

Race, Ethnicity and Social Organization

The theme of this book is that social context influences and directly affects numerous areas of social life. This section details how each area of social organization influences race and ethnic relations.

Population

Whites, blacks, Hispanics, and Asian Americans may be viewed as different populations. Depending on which racial and ethnic population a person belongs, his or her life experience will be radically different. Blacks, compared to whites, typically have lower incomes and less education. They are also more likely to have more medical problems, shorter life span, and to be unemployed, arrested, and in prison (*Statistical Abstract of the United States 2008*).

The acquittal of O.J. Simpson in the criminal trial for the dual murders of Nicole Simpson and Ron Goldman reflected retribution by the mostly black jury for feelings of racial mistreatment and oppression. That there were no blacks on the jury in the civil trial against Simpson contributed to the unanimous guilty verdict in that civil trial.

Even the sexual behaviors of blacks and whites differ. Blacks are more likely than whites to value delaying sexual intercourse until marriage, to have lower rates of "hooking up" and cohabitation, and to report lower rates of giving oral sex (Knox and Zusman, 2008). To explain behavior, it is not the individual, but the population category that is the best predictor of general differences.

Collective Behavior/Social Movements

Mobs develop and physically attack out-groups. While the HBO drama, *The Sopranos,* was fiction, it reflected mob violence against out-groups. Similarly, the Sunnis, Shiites, and Kurds of Iraq have been out-groups to each other and at war with each other for centuries.

The threat of mob violence provides a mechanism whereby the majority may control the minority. If minorities are made to feel that majority mobs can inflict harm at any time, they are likely to accept inappropriate or outrageous behavior perpetrated against them and hold their behavior in check.

Sociologists who study social movements have focused upon the civil rights movement, the women's movement, and gay liberation as mechanisms for change. Each of these social movements has developed and organized to create change in other social organizations, such as schools, communities, and our society. The civil rights movement led by Martin Luther King, Jr. was responsible for a major structural change in our society. Separate bathrooms for "coloreds" and "whites" reflecting a separate society was forever changed by the movement.

Interracial friends are one index of the level of integration. Briggs (2007) studied interracial friendships for whites, blacks, Asians, and Hispanics and identified the workplace and civic involvement as important contexts for these relationships. Those who reported ties to other races tended to be "joiners." Also, involvement in nonreligious groups, socializing with coworkers, having more friends, and higher socioeconomic status were interracial involvement predictors for all racial groups.

Social Classes

Racial and ethnic backgrounds have a profound impact on the social class of the individual. Barack Obama, Oprah Winfrey, and Denzel Washington are among the 15 percent of blacks viewed as upper class in U.S. society. Other black families in this social class are composed of wage earners who are physicians, lawyers, and successful shop owners.

Marsh et al. (2007) provided data that there is an emerging new black middle class. They created a black middle class index (BMCi) using four criteria of education (e.g. 4 + years of college completed), wealth (e.g. home ownership), per person income ($50,000 or above for single householder), and occupational prestige (using a standard occupational scale). They found that the black middle class is shifting from married couples with children to "SALA Love Jones Cohort." SALA refers to single adult and living alone. Love Jones Cohort comes from the film *Love Jones* about a young black male poet in Chicago who dates a talented female photographer.

The researchers found that in the year 2000, 14.32% of black middle-class households could be classified as SALA in contrast to 48.08% of those consisting of a married couple living with a child. In contrast, the percents in 1990 were 9.05% and 57.78% respectively (p. 749). These data reveal that the SALA

Love Jones Cohort is increasing its percentage share into the black middle class and that no longer should black households be looked at as a dichotomy between single parent and married with children.

Groups

Race and ethnicity are also related to and help sociologists understand group behavior. Groups develop behaviors that can become characteristic of that group and are clearly tied to the social organization of a racial or ethnic background. Rap is characteristic of blacks, observance of Ramadan of Muslims, genuflecting of Catholics. Youth wear baggy pants, get tattoos and sport piercings. The type of pants, nature of the tattoo or the placement of the piercing differs by race, ethnicity, and social class of which it is connected. While the elderly may wear hearing aids, use walkers, and talk about health problems, the type of equipment or problems they discuss significantly differ by their racial or ethnic background. Elderly upper class black surgeons discuss the high cost of malpractice insurance at a Kwaanza celebration. Group membership gives character and predictability to one's behavior. Belonging to a group or being excluded from its membership fundamentally affects what a social actor is and becomes. When the ethnic group you belong to does not drink alcohol (Pakistani), you are unlikely to get cirrhosis of the liver and you don't need organizations to deal with alcoholism.

Families

Family life varies by racial and ethnic background. In the 2002 movie, *My Big Fat Greek Wedding*, Toula, a 30-year-old raised in the ethnic Greek culture meets and secretly dates a WASP (white, Anglo-Saxon Protestant). The importance of families is clear as you watch her grow up in a totally entrenched, exceptionally large Greek family in Chicago. The movie clearly demonstrates the importance of ethnic background to social life. The only thing her father wants her to do as a woman is to marry a nice Greek man. That is the role of a woman (in Greek society), and that is what she is raised to do. However, she falls in love and secretly dates a high school English teacher. When they announce that they plan to marry, Toula's father can't accept such a foreign marriage. He is shocked that her fiancé did not ask his permission. When her boyfriend does ask, he is told "no." Ethnicity affects her choices, clothes, food preferences, family relationships, religious behavior, wedding plans and, as the movie ends, the manner in which she must raise her children.

The movie reveals how racial and ethnic differences affect one's choices and individual experience. Change a family's race or ethnicity and you will change the way that family relates to their children, what they expect of their children, and how they plan for their grandchildren.

Communities

Entire communities are affected by racial and ethnic differences. In the late eighties, blacks and Hispanics in Chicago put together a political coalition to govern the city and elected a black mayor. Chicago is a city that is white by day and black by night. Over a million commuter workers pour into the city during the day and leave in the evening. What remains is essentially a city of minorities which elect their own officials.

While segregation is illegal, it still remains. Notice the residential patterns in the city in which you live. There are both "black" and "white" areas. Race (unofficially) is a primary factor real estate agents use when they show houses to prospective buyers. The important point is that race and ethnic identity characterize areas of cities, and those communities are more or less comfortable to outsiders who do or do not share the characteristics. Additionally, since racial and ethnic characteristics often intersect with social class differences, cities can be divided into communities based upon similarities of racial or ethnic background. Growing up in an ethnic residential area will affect your outcome in life.

Associations

Associations develop to further the goals of both majority and minority groups. Founded in 1865 in Pulaski, Tennessee, by a group of Confederate Army veterans, the Ku Klux Klan opposed the advancement of blacks, Roman Catholics, Jews, and other minorities and resented special programs that were developed for these minorities. There are about 150 Klan chapters today with 5,000 to 8,000 total members. The Klan is a hate group and outside of its members is criticized by mainstream media, political, and religious leaders.

The NAACP (National Association for the Advancement of Colored People) was founded in 1910 in New York by 60 black and white citizens. Today, there are over an estimated 400,000 members who work together to end discrimination against blacks and other minority groups, to sponsor voter education and registration, and to fight against dismissals and demotions of black teachers. The NAACP also urges publishers to produce textbooks that give visibility to the achievements of blacks.

All associations that are purposely created to obtain goals such as schools or hospitals are ultimately affected by racial and ethnic differences. These differences affect the location where members go for services, their feelings of comfort, and the degree to which they can achieve their personal goals in life.

Networks

Minority groups develop networks to circumvent control by the majority group. During slavery, the "underground railroad" was a network though which runaway slaves passed to freedom. Similar networks existed during WWII in France (the "résistance") to help those who wanted to escape the Nazis. Today, networks exist more for economic survival. Elaborate networks exist to get illegal aliens across the Mexican borders into Texas and California. Similarly, networks have been established to connect Polish workers to employers who need laborers for removing asbestos from public buildings.

Societies

The societal policy toward a particular minority influences the amount of freedom and equality accorded that minority. As we discussed above, there is a complex intersection between race, ethnicity, and other markers of social class, such as religion, physical problems, sexual preference, and social organizations. Considering sexual preference, American society is heterosexist, against homosexuals. Only the state of Massachusetts recognizes same-sex marriages. The larger society does not. Without federal recognition of same-sex marriage, long-term homosexual lovers have no benefits accorded spouses. When one heterosexual spouse dies, the other collects his or her social security benefits. When one gay lover dies, the other gets nothing. While "domestic partnerships" (two people who have chosen to share one another's lives in an intimate and committed relationship of mutual caring) are being recognized in some cities, such recognition is not societal. The way we create the social organization has significant consequences for inequality, social class, and sexual preference.

There are exceptions to prejudice against gays. In New York City, the State Supreme Court of Appeals ruled that a long-term, live-in gay couple could be considered a family under the state's rent-control regulations. This meant that when one of the lovers died, the remaining lover (whose name was not on the lease) would be allowed to stay in the apartment. This is a structural change for the city of New York, but such societal changes have not yet occurred.

Popular Beliefs and Scientific Data: Black Men Abandon Their Family Ties

It is a common popular belief that black men abandon their families and have little involvement with them. They are regarded as "absent black fathers" in the context of mother-headed families, and it is believed that street corner networks substitute for family ties. Sarkisian (2007) compared 2,893 white with 590 black men from the larger National Survey of Families and Households.

Contrary to expectations, the researcher found that "black men are more likely than white men to live with and near kin, and they are more likely to frequently see their kin in person" (p. 784). Sarkisian (2007) continues:

> These findings show that despite their lower marriage rates, black men do not necessarily lead lives of social isolation or lack family connections. When talking about families, politicians and social commentators typically focus on the ties between married couples and their children. But this focus on the nuclear family ignores extended family relationships and creates a biased portrait of family life among black men. By taking a broader perspective on family relations and focusing on the often overlooked extended kinship ties, this study refutes the myth that black men lack strong family solidarities (p. 784).

References

Briggs, X. 2007. "Some of My Best Friends Are …": Interracial Friendships, Class, and Segregation in America." *City & Community*, 6: 263–281.

Decuzzi, Angela., David Knox, and Marty Zusman. 2006. "Racial Differences in Perceptions of Women and Men." *College Student Journal*, 40: 343–349.

Goza, F. W., Stockwell, E. G. and Balistreri, K. S. 2007. "Racial Differences in the Relationship Between Infant Mortality and Socioeconomic Status." *Journal of Biosocial Science*, 39: 517–531.

Hochschild, J. L. and Weaver, V. 2007. "The Skin Color Paradox and the American Racial Order." *Social Forces*, 86: 643–670.

Knox, David and Marty Zusman. 2008. "Sexuality in Black and White: Some Data on 783 Undergraduates." Unpublished study. East Carolina University.

Marsh, K., Darity, W. A., Cohen, P. N., Casper, L. M. and Slaters, D. 2007. "The Emerging Black Middle Class: Single and Living Alone." *Social Forces*, 86: 735–762.

Muhajarine, N., Labonte, R., Williams, A., and Randall, J. 2008. "Person, Perception, and Place: What Matters to Health and Quality of Life." *Social Indicators Research*, 85: 53–81.

Sarkisian, N. 2007. "Street Men, Family Men: Race and Men's Extended Family Integration." *Social Forces*, 86: 763–794.

Tiffin, T. A., Pearce, M., Kaplan, C., Fundudis, T. and Parker, L. 2007. "The Impact of Socio-economic Status and Mobility on Perceived Family Functioning." *Journal of Family and Economic Issues*, 28: 653–668.

Statistical Abstract of the United States: 2008 (127th ed.). Washington, D.C.: U.S. Bureau of the Census.

Chapter 9

Gender and Age

The same time that women came up with PMS, men came up with ESPN.
Blake Clark, comedian

The Sopranos and *Desperate Housewives* became a part of American television culture in 2007. While these dramas emphasized the mob in New Jersey and suburban life on Wisteria Lane, what went virtually unnoticed was that traditional and nontraditional gender roles in relationships were a staple of each television episode. Tony and Carmella (*Sopranos*) represented the "man provides/woman stays at home and rears two children" American family. In contrast, *Desperate Housewives* featured Lynette Scavo as the breadwinning wife and Tom Scavo as the husband who stays at home and rears three sons. Both stay-at-home spouses felt a sense of inequality—Carmella felt that Tony kept her in the dark about everything and did not treat her as an equal. Tom felt that Lynette did not understand his exhaustion and contribution to the family in taking care of the three boys.

Age was a focus on earlier episodes of *The Sopranos*. Tony's mother resisted being put into a nursing home and accused him of never caring about her and just wanting to dump and get rid of her. Aging issues also featured Corrado "Junior" Soprano, Tony's uncle, who complained of a failing body and mind. His status in the 'family' was also in jeopardy because of his physical and mental decline. In this chapter we emphasize how both gender and age are meaningful only in social context. We begin by examining the sociological meaning of gender and age.

Gender and Age in America

Lay persons typically think of gender as a woman or a man and age as a number. Various disciplines view these concepts differently. In this section, we review the biological, psychological, and sociological meanings of gender and age in America.

Definitions of Gender

The term **sex** is a biological term and refers to biologically differentiated sex characteristics between women and men. These include different chromosomes (XX for female; XY for male), gonads (ovaries for female; testes for male), different amounts of hormones (progesterone and testosterone), internal sex organs (fallopian tubes, uterus, and vagina for female; epididymis, vas deferens and seminal vesicles for male), and external genitals (vulva for female; penis and scrotum for male).

Psychologists study the psychological differences between women and men. While psychologists have found some differences (violence, emotionality), they are few and the differences are small. Furthermore, the origin of the differences tends to be social rather than innate.

Sociologists study women and men on the basis of **gender roles**—the role expectations for the respective sexes. **Gender** refers to cultural and attitudinal traits associated with being male or female. Those behaviors and characteristics which are typically associated with females are regarded as "feminine," and those behaviors and characteristics typically associated with males are regarded as "masculine." Therefore, masculinity and femininity, or "gender" can only be understood within a specific social context and time period. In the family context, the female is expected to take primary responsibility for the care of infants and children; the male is expected to fix the furnace when it breaks down. Gender is a social creation and what women and men think and do is a result of the social contexts in which they are immersed. For example, women are expected to earn less money which is exactly what happens. The average annual income of a female with some college education who is working full-time is $34,291 compared to $48,369 for a male with the same education, also working full-time, year-round (*Statistical Abstract of the United States 2008*, Table 681).

Sociologists are particularly concerned about gender in reference to the social stratification system. Women and men are valued differently in different social contexts, and their value changes. When 26 million Soviet men were killed in World War II, the value of women for the then Soviet Union increased. Women had suddenly become valuable economic and military assets for the country. In 2008, because men were no longer scarce, women were being displaced (e.g. as physicians), and their status was decreasing. Hence, sociologists emphasize that the value of women and men is structural and social.

Definitions of Androgyny

Androgyny typically refers to being neither male nor female but a blend of both traits. Two forms of androgyny are described here.

1. **Physiological androgyny** refers to **intersexed** individuals, discussed earlier in the chapter. The genitals are neither clearly male nor female, and there is a mixing of "female" and "male" chromosomes and hormones.

2. **Behavioral androgyny** refers to the presence and balance of traditional male and female behavior, so that a biological male may be very passive, gentle, and nurturing, and a biological female may be very assertive, rough, and selfish.

Androgyny may also imply flexibility of traits; for example, an androgynous individual may be emotional in one situation, logical in another, assertive in another, and so forth. Ward (2001) classified 311 (159 male/152 female) undergraduates at the National University of Singapore as androgynous (33.8% men and 16.0% women), feminine (11.0% men and 39.6% women), masculine (35.7% men and 13.9% women), and undifferentiated (19.5% men and 30.6% women).

Androgynous individuals experience less role conflict than their strongly sex-typed counterparts because of their ability to utilize whichever skills are necessary within the given social context. Cheng (2005) found that androgynous individuals have a broad coping repertoire and are much more able to cope with stress. As evidence, Moore et al. (2005) found that androgynous individuals with Parkinson's disease not only were better able to cope with their disease but also reported having a better quality of life than those with the same disease who expressed the characteristics of one gender only. Similarly, androgynous individuals reported much less likelihood of having an eating disorder (Hepp et al., 2005).

Woodhill and Samuels (2003) emphasized the need to differentiate between positive and negative androgyny. **Positive androgyny** is devoid of the negative traits associated with masculinity (aggression, hard-heartedness, indifference, selfishness, showing off, and vindictiveness). Antisocial behavior has also been associated with masculinity (Ma, 2005). Negative aspects of femininity include being passive, submissive, temperamental, and fragile. The researchers have also found that positive androgyny is associated with psychological health and well-being.

Definitions of Age

A person's **age** may be defined chronologically, physiologically, psychologically, sociologically, and culturally. Chronologically, an "old" person is defined as one who has lived a certain number of years. Chronological age has obvious practical significance in everyday life. Bureaucratic organizations and social programs identify chronological age as a criterion of certain social rights and responsibilities. One's age determines the right to drive, vote, buy alcohol or cigarettes, and receive Social Security and Medicare benefits.

Physiologically, a person is old when his or her auditory, visual, respiratory, and cognitive capabilities decline significantly. Becoming "disabled" is associated with being "old." Persons who need full-time nursing care for eating, bathing, and taking medication properly and who are placed in nursing homes are thought of as being old. Failing health is the criterion used by the elderly to define themselves as old (O'Reilly, 1997), and successful aging is typically defined as maintaining one's health, independence, and cognitive ability. Jorm et al. (1998) observed that the prevalence of successful aging declines steeply from about age 70–74 to age 80. Hence, one's health tends to decline most steeply beginning somewhere between age 70 and 74 to age 80.

Research is underway to extend life. Dr. Aubrey de Grey (Department of Genetics, University of Cambridge) predicted that continued research will make possible the ability to add HUNDREDS of years to one's life. Indeed, the paths are known via genetic engineering (we must learn how to switch off the genes responsible for aging), tissue/organ replacement (knees and kidneys are already being replaced), and the merging of computer technology with human biology (hearing and seeing are now being improved). Mercer (2008) noted that the most optimistic predictions are that we are two or three decades away from significant breakthroughs. Some individuals are having their bodies frozen at the time of death in hopes that they will be "thawed out" in the decades ahead when the technology is available to revive the dead and give them a working body.

Psychologically, a person's age is related to his or her cognitive and intellectual capacity. Evidence suggests that there is no automatic diminution of these capacities with advancing age and that the elderly may maintain these capacities until very late in life.

Sociologically, age refers to the social roles a person ages into. In our society, grandparent, retiree, and widow are roles typically associated with the elderly. Like gender, age is a social construct with its meaning embedded in the social context.

Culturally, the society in which an individual lives defines when and if a person becomes old and what being old means. Cultures also differ in terms of how they view and take care of their elderly. Spain is particularly noteworthy in terms of care for the elderly, with eight of 10 elderly persons receiving care from family members and other relatives. The elderly in Spain report very high levels of satisfaction in the relationships with their children, grandchildren, and friends (Fernandez-Ballesteros, 2003).

Differences in Gender and Age

Previously we have noted that education, occupation, income, race, and ethnicity influence a person's social class. Of equal importance in assigning class position are the variables of gender and age.

Roles and Statuses of Women, Men, and the Elderly

Class differences in gender and age have to do with the way in which social structure influences these variables. Recalling that structure consists of roles and statuses, various social contexts assign different roles and statuses to women, men, and the elderly.

The roles most often occupied by women in our society are those such as wife, mother, and waitress, while men are allocated the roles of husband, father, and primary breadwinner. The status, or social ranking of these roles, also varies by gender. Wives typically have less power, and therefore, less social value than husbands.

The role of mother is also accorded less social value, particularly when looking for a mate. Single parent women who place ads looking for a date often downplay or omit their role as mother since doing so may interfere with the fantasy of the available, active, free-for-adventure female stereotype which is more likely to attract a male. In contrast to motherhood, fathers are often stereotyped in positive terms as being the dominant power force in the family (Tony Soprano of *The Sopranos* was portrayed as the more powerful parent).

Similarly, secretaries have less status than the managers (usually men) for whom they work. The elderly are also assigned to lower status roles in our society—grandparent, retiree, and invalid (in contrast to the roles of parent, worker, and able-bodied person).

As a person changes from one role to the next, the status of that person also changes. A man who has a sex change operation and becomes a woman suddenly finds that she is expected to fulfill new roles and that these roles are associated with less status than the roles filled as a man. Similarly, as a person ages, his or her value decreases, more so for women than for men. In general, most people would choose to be a 21-year-old person than an 85-year-old person. Prostitutes note that 18 to 23-year-old blondes are the most desirable sex objects. Female prostitutes age 25 and older become "specialties" in the sense that they are no longer valued for their youth but for their willingness to offer a specific sexual adventure (e.g. bondage and discipline).

The roles and statuses differentially assigned to women, men, and the elderly affect their social class position. In general, single women and the elderly are more likely to be in the lower class than males and individuals in their thirties.

Income Differences

Table 9.1 reflects the differential income earned by women and men in the United States. Women earn about two-thirds of what men earn, even when the level of educational achievement is identical.

Table 9.1
Women's and Men's Median Income with Similar Education

	Bachelor's	Master's	Doctoral Degree
Men	$51,700	$64,468	$76,937
Women	$32,668	$44,385	$56,820

Source: *Statistical Abstract of the United States: 2008.* 127th ed. Washington, D.C.: U.S. Bureau of the Census, Table 680.

The primary reason for lower income among females is that women prioritize family over career or job (they work in occupations with lower expectations and pay, so as to be available to their children). In addition, women tend to be more concerned about the non-monetary aspects of work. In a study of 102 seniors and 504 alumni from a mid-sized Midwestern public university who rated 48 job characteristics, women gave significantly higher ratings to family life accommodations, pleasant working conditions, travel, and interpersonal relationships (Heckert et al., 2002).

Women also earn less money than men because the occupations they work in are regarded as "female" occupations (secretary, elementary school teacher) which have traditionally been low paying jobs. These occupations also have an oversupply of workers for these roles which drives down the salary.

Occupational Differences

As suggested above, the differential incomes earned by women and men are influenced by **occupational sex segregation**—the degree to which women and men are concentrated in occupations in which workers of one sex predominate. Women are concentrated in clerical (secretary, bookkeeper), sales (checker at grocery store, salesperson at mall) and service (waitress) occupations. Men are concentrated in managerial and supervisory positions as well as the skilled crafts of carpenters and laborers.

Occupation is important because it affects income. If only women are concentrated into an occupation, the salary will be lower. Occupation is also associated with status. The role of secretary carries a lower status than manager.

Education Differences by Gender and Age

Table 9.2 reflects that at higher levels, women and the elderly are disadvantaged which results in lower income/status. Being specific about 'advanced degree,' (see table below) women earn 45 percent of doctorates; men, 55 percent (Hoffer et al. 2007).

Table 9.2
Education by Gender and Age

Education Attainment	Women	Men	Over Age 65
High School Graduate	31.6%	31.9%	37.3%
College Graduate	18.1%	18.5%	12.5%
Advanced Degree	8.8%	10.7%	8.8%

Source: *Statistical Abstract of the United States: 2008.* 127th ed. Washington, D.C.: U.S. Bureau of the Census, Table 219.

Education is also structurally induced. Up until 1786, formal education was restricted to men. In that year the first Young Ladies Academy was established in Philadelphia. However, the rationale for women's education during this time was that they played a vital role in the socialization of their sons.

Not until 1832 were women permitted to attend college with men (Oberlin College in Ohio was the first coeducational college). Even though there were some coeducational American colleges by 1872, the more prestigious institutions such as Harvard and Yale denied admission to women. It was believed that women were less intelligent (and would lower educational standards), that higher education might disturb their uterine development which would result in defective babies, and that they would distract men from their studies (Renzetti and Curran, 1988).

While these beliefs are regarded as silly today, they established the perspective that women were second class citizens in regard to education. Even today, subtle forms of discrimination exist in education. Male students are called on more frequently than female students, sex-stereotyped examples tend to be used by teachers (physicians are referred to as "he", nurses as "she"), and references are made to males as "men" but to females as "gals" and "girls."

Just as there is a gender bias in education, there is also an age bias with older people much less likely to be involved in formal education. Only 16.3% of individuals over the age of 35 are enrolled in college (*Statistical Abstract of the United States: 2008*, Table No. 274). Reasons for the relatively low percentage of elderly Americans enrolled in college include their perceived lack of a need for education, their fear of returning to school, and their discomfort in a predominantly "youth context."

Gender, Age and Physical, Psychological and Sociological Health

A person's physical, psychological, and sociological health vary by gender and age. Physically, women have a longer life expectancy than men. A woman born in 2004 could expect to live until she was 79; a man born in that same year could expect to live until he was 73 (*Statistical Abstract of the United States: 2008*, Table 101). This differential may have both biological and social causes. Biologically, females may be wired for greater longevity than males because of the importance of their biological role in conceiving, bearing, and nurturing offspring. Socially, women have received less social approval for behaviors that would jeopardize their health. As a result, lower proportions of women smoke cigarettes, drink alcohol, and work in hazardous occupations. And, there has been no female equivalent of the now deceased risk taker Evel Knievel.

Psychologically, a look at the cover of women's magazines like *Women's Health* or *Cosmopolitan* begs the question, "Are these body images healthy or realistic?" There are more than 3,800 beauty pageants annually. The effect for many women who do not match the cultural ideal is to have a negative body image. Such a negative view of one's body begins early. A team of researchers studied 136 girls aged 11 to 16 years who had exposure to trim and average-size models via magazines and noted that these girls reported negative body images (Clay et al., 2005). The researchers noted the need for early education to help young girls deconstruct advertising and body images

Sociological health refers to the ability of a person to function in his or her assigned roles. A person who does not show up for work has a serious sociological health problem. Similarly, a spouse with Alzheimer's is "no longer there" in the sense of being able to interact meaningfully in a dyad and is, thus, sociologically dead.

Age also influences the degree to which a person is physically, psychologically, and sociologically healthy. Physically, medical problems of the elderly increase—they have a higher frequency of office visits, take more medications and complain more about their health than young people. However, life expectancy seems very much related to social roles. People who live into their eighties usually live in societies that provide meaningful work roles, high status social roles, and regard aging as an accomplishment rather than a misfortune. Earlier we noted that the Spanish hold their elderly in high regard, as do the Danes and Pakistanis.

Theory and Research Methods: Gender and Age Inequality

Sociologists have developed unique theories and research methods to study gender and age inequality.

Theories of Gender Inequality

Three primary theories have been used to explain gender inequality: functionalism, conflict, and interactionism. Functionalism emphasizes that gender roles are based on the biological differences between women and men. Functionalists (Talcott Parsons, Robert Bales) suggest that because women bear and nurse infants they have become primarily identified with domestic roles. Men, on the other hand, because they do not have these biological capabilities (or constraints depending on your point of view) are freer to become engaged in the role of economic provider. The ways in which these "expressive" and "instrumental" roles complement each other is functional for society.

Functionalism has been criticized because it suggests that gender differences are biologically rather than socially determined. Since men can take care of children and women can become breadwinners, functionalism does not give proper credit to the role of social and historical forces in shaping the roles that the respective sexes are expected to fill. Indeed, there are stay-at-home dads who function in the role of the primary parent just as there are wives who work 60 hour weeks and are the sole source of income for the family.

Conflict theorists (Randall Collins, Lewis Coser, Gerhard Lenski) point out that the respective sexes represent power groups who compete for political, economic, and social resources. As already noted, men disproportionately occupy high status, high income jobs while women disproportionately occupy jobs of low status and low income. That men attempt to keep women in subordinate roles is illustrated by the abusive husband who "refuses" to let his wife work outside the home. In effect, he keeps her economically dependent. In addition, as long as childrearing is defined as women's work, men are free to pursue positions of authority and power. Childrearing (as any career woman will testify) is a powerless role and avoiding childrearing allows for the possibility of becoming involved in high status, economically rewarding roles.

The conflict perspective is also relevant when explaining child labor laws. For adults to protect their jobs and incomes, they pass legislation to keep young people out of the job market since they would work for lower wages. Under federal law, 14 and 15-year-olds are prohibited from working more than three hours on a day when school is in session and a maximum of 28 hours during a five-day school week.

Symbolic interactionists (George H. Mead, Herbert Blumer) point out that the ways in which women and men interact with each other in dyads or small groups tend to continue gender inequalities. In a sample of 1,027 undergraduates, 60 percent of the women reported that they had never asked a new partner out, but waited for him to do so (Ross et al., 2007). In addition, while undergraduates tend to "hang out" in groups (rather than traditional dating), eventually there is a pairing process whereby the male-female dominance emerges. The male is expected to ask the female to marry him, and he gives her the promise or engagement ring, not vice versa.

Interactionists also emphasize that the act by a woman or a man is not as important as the interpretation of the act. Thus a woman who perceives a man hugging her as "sexual harassment or a man who perceives a woman smiling at him as a sexual advance will behave differently than if the hug was viewed as affection and the smile was viewed as politeness. Hence, interactionists focus on the fact that inequalities in interaction may occur at the symbolic level.

Theories of Aging Inequality

The same theories of functionalism, conflict, and interactionism are applicable to an understanding of aging inequality. Cumming and Henry (1961) suggested the functionalist perspective which views the gradual disengagement of the elderly from political, social, and economic roles is functional by making way for younger people. Politicians, Boy Scout leaders, and workers retire to provide opportunities for younger people to fill these roles. The latter presumably have more energy to devote to the various demanding roles and they can do so with less stress to themselves. Critics of the functionalist perspective point out that some societies do not "disengage" their elderly but keep them involved in active and meaningful roles.

Conflict theorists view the various age strata as competing for scarce resources. Because the elderly take valuable jobs from those who are middle aged, the elderly are excluded via governmental forced retirement laws. Such social control of who can work and who can't translates into income differentials between those over the age of 65 and those in their middle years. The median income of individuals over the age of 65 is $17,140; for those between the ages of 45 and 54, the median income is \$35,051 (*Statistical Abstract of the United States: 2008* Table 680).

The interactionist view of age inequality focuses on the micro interactions between the young and the old in whom the young telegraph the cultural belief that it is good to be young and bad to be old. The elderly also make negative self referent statements about themselves—that they are an old bag of bones, that they are tired, and that they are physically in pain.

Another theory which helps to explain age inequality is Dowd's (1980) exchange theory. One of the reasons for the retrenchment of the elderly from society is that they are viewed as having nothing of value to exchange. Young people look to peers rather than to the elderly for companionship, and corporations seek ways to dump the elderly so that they can avoid paying their high salaries and pensions.

Data Collection

Sociologists use a range of data collection techniques in assessing gender and age inequality. One source for documenting inequality is the *Statistical Abstract of the United States* published annually by the Bureau of the Census. Table 9.1 (presented earlier) is taken from this source and represents data collected through questionnaires and compilations of existing data.

Each month the government also publishes the *National Vital Statistics Reports* on a variety of topics. Among these are the percentage of males and females dying due to suicide. According to final data for 2004, 25,566 men took their own lives compared to 6,873 women. These deaths for men represent 2.2 percent of all deaths; for women 0.6 percent of all deaths (*National Vital Statistics Reports*, 2007). These data are raw statistics collected by the government.

In addition to data from questionnaires and national data banks on gender and age inequality, sociologists collect data via interviews (e.g. with corporate executive females and househusbands), participant observations (e.g. in the workplace and in nursing homes), and historical documents (e.g. feminist and aging literature).

Analysis

Data are analyzed according to standard statistical procedures to assess any significant differences between respondents. Richey et al. (2008) analyzed 783 questionnaires from female and male respondents who were asked to identify their sexual values. The researchers found that men were significantly ($p<.001$)

more likely than women to select hedonism ("if it feels good, do it") (36.7% vs. 12.5%) as their sexual value. In contrast, women were significantly (p<.001) more likely than men to select relativism as their sexual value (72.4% vs. 51.8%).

Conclusions

Based on the available data, it is accurate to conclude that the economic, occupational, and social status of women and the elderly continue to be un-equal and lower when compared to men and young people. Women earn two thirds of what men earn, work in a narrow range of occupations, and are less advantaged than men.

Similar conclusions can be reached about the elderly who live in a society biased against them. Just as **sexism** refers to discrimination against women based on the assumed superiority of men, **ageism** refers to a deep and pro-found prejudice against the elderly that translates into discrimination against them because of their age. When compared to their younger counterparts, the elderly are more likely to be unemployed, to have lower incomes, and to have lower status.

Gender inequalities also exist in Italy. Mothers are expected to take care of their children even into their forties. Mammoni, meaning "mama's boy," de-notes an unmarried 30- to 40-year-old male who still lives at home. His mother makes his bed, washes and irons his clothes, and prepares his meals. He earns an income and spends it on his own house where he may take girlfriends or have parties, but he lives at home and is cared for by his mother.

Gender/Age Inequality and Social Organization

In this section we emphasize how various social contexts influence gender and age inequality.

Population

It is estimated that by the year 2010, 50.8 percent of the population in the United States will be male and 49.2 percent will be female (*Statistical Abstract of the United States: 2008*. Table 10). Dramatic shifts in these numbers would influence the roles and statuses of the respective sexes. As noted earlier, as a re-sult of 26 million Soviet men being killed in World War II, the need for and value of women in the Soviet society increased. Soviet women were given unique positions in the army with nearly one million in combat. In fact, the 588th Night Bomber Squadron flew over 500 night raids on the Germans to protect Stalingrad. The 588th was entirely female with all mechanics, navigators, fighter pilots and officers being women. Women in World War II were used in all combat that did not involve general hand-to-hand fighting. They were the backbone of the army used particularly as snipers, machine gunners, tank drivers, and communication specialists. While in WWII, women were viewed by the military as better snipers because they were careful, deliberate, patient and could breathe correctly when squeezing a sniper's trigger. Today, when far more men are available, the status of women in the former Soviet Union has decreased again, and they have been mostly removed from the army and air force. The number of young people and old people in a society also has implications for the society.

The view and meaning of age is also affected by population. In 1800, the median age of individuals in the United States was under 16. This means that half the population was under the age of 16 and half were over the age of 16. Hence, the population consisted of mostly young people. By the year 2010, it is expected that the median age will be 37; by 2020, 38 (*Statistical Abstract of the United States: 2008*, Table 10). As the number of young and old in our society change, the equality of the elderly will increase because they will be in a greater position to influence public policy. If there are only a few elderly, the government and everyone else can ignore them. But if 54 million elderly (by 2020) (Table 12) express an opinion about health care or taxes, politicians will listen if they are to be re-elected. Indeed, politicians already have the elderly on radar as evidenced by their talking about "social security benefits."

The elderly as a population also have unique opinions. In a Gallup poll on the death penalty, 72 percent of adults age 55 and older were in favor of the death penalty for a person convicted of murder. In contrast, 67 percent of adults age 18 to 49 were in favor of the death penalty. In effect, the older the person, the more in favor of the death penalty (Newport, 2007).

Social Movements

It is inaccurate to describe "the" women's movement in terms of a group of women at one point in time being politically active to achieve a common goal. Rather, there have been various feminist or women's movements across time with various causes such as the right to vote, pro choice abortion politics, and public education. The result has been to challenge the dominance of the majority (whether male or "white male") and to force recognition of minority rights. While not as visible or powerful, a men's movement has also existed with equally diverse causes—to challenge the traditional prescriptions and restrictions of masculinity, to react to perceived feminist aggression, and to obtain greater equality in the courts for divorced fathers who want access to their children. Both the women's and men's movements have existed alongside the gay rights movement which has sought equality based on personhood not sex or sexual orientation.

Social Class

The genders have differential ranking in regard to wealth, power, and social position. Men as a gender have greater wealth, power, and social position. In contrast, women have less wealth and power. Their numbers are considerably lower than men in Congress. In 2008, 86 women served in the U.S. Congress (16 of 100 in the Senate, and 70 of 435 in the House of Representatives). Hillary Clinton's bid for the presidency in 2008 was certainly a reflection of a political change for women and for America. There are also fewer women on corporate boards. Their social class is still largely regarded in terms of the men to whom they are attached.

On the other hand, age has resulted in some elderly having in their possession a greater amount of the wealth in society. There is a clear intersection between age, sex, and social class. Older Americans worked harder, saved more diligently, purchased less, and now, late in life, find that their social class mobility is higher than they thought. They may have begun in the lower middle class, but now, their children are gone, they have paid off their car, home, and credit cards and have moved suddenly up in social class as they near retirement.

The young, however, have moved downward in social class compared to their parents. They have more education, but less income. They have delayed taking jobs, traveled, purchased new electronics, wasted more money on clothes and gadgets, been indecisive, and switched jobs more often. They now find that they have higher debt in college loans and car payments, in a society where the cost of basic goods like gasoline, insurance, electricity, and food has greatly increased. It will take them years to achieve middle class lifestyle advantages, particularly as they marry, have children, and purchase homes.

This social class's access to wealth is age and gender related. While elderly poverty has declined since the 1960s, it is far more prevalent for women than men. Most youth wait for their intact parents to die to accumulate wealth, but more than that, a significantly greater number of women end up in poverty compared to men, as they lack pensions and receive much less in social security benefits. Women earn less income than men and often work fewer years or work part-time (so they can be home to rear their children). Less time in employment results in fewer contributions to retirement and social security accounts so there will be lower payouts than to men who more often worked more years and did so full-time. This discrepancy, combined with women's longer life expectancy, helps to explain the "feminization of poverty."

Groups

When groups are defined as two or more people engaged in interaction that know each other and develop a pattern based on common expectations, it is clear that women and men develop same sex groups. Women have sororities, La Leche Leagues, and women's basketball. Men have fraternities, poker games, and basketball/football teams.

It is important to note that the gender and age of an individual determines their group membership. Women tend to be much more social than men and, later in life, join far more groups. They also are much more likely to maintain emotionally positive relationships with family and kin networks and, thereby, have greater support systems. Men tend to be less likely to maintain friendship and peer groups or even close relationships with their children. Such group effects help explain disease, hospitalization, alcohol use, and early death. Groups help insulate social actors from harm.

Families

The social organization of the family dictates the roles of wives and mothers and husbands and fathers. In our society, women are expected to give priority to family roles and to take more responsibility for childcare than their husbands. Bragg et al. (2008) analyzed survey data from 293 undergraduates at a large southeastern university and found ten significant differences between women and men in regard to their attitudes toward children. Females were more likely to report that they wanted to have children, to see them as providing a reason to live, to enjoy and to have taken care of infants and toddlers, to not be annoyed by crying infants, to select a marriage partner who wanted children, to divorce a spouse who was against children, to adopt a child if sterile, and to be content with an only child who was of either sex (in contrast to preferring a child of only one sex).

As parents age, it is the father who is likely to die first. It is the mother who is likely to live the longest. This age difference affects families as they must prepare for these differences, or, if not prepared, deal with age-related illnesses. Men are far more likely to have engaged in risky and unhealthy behaviors such as heavy drinking that will affect their family's economic and social relations in later life.

Communities

Some communities are age specific. When communities are defined as contiguous geographic areas wherein people organize to meet their needs and carry out their daily lives, some communities are developed exclusively for the elderly. There are over 40,000 residents in Sun City, a suburb of Phoenix, Arizona, which requires that at least one member of the family unit be over the age of 55. The community features seven recreation centers, eight golf courses, three country clubs, two bowling centers and View Point Lake. The social life and services include more than 400 clubs and social organizations that meet in ten large, community-owned recreational complexes. The residential community also features easy access to shopping, grocery stores, and medical facilities. Sun City (and Sun City West) provides the largest concentration of year round facilities for the elderly in the United States.

Associations

Associations are social organizations that are formed to pursue a specific goal. The university in which you are enrolled is an association whose purpose is to educate students. So is the hospital where you receive medical care and the local police department which provides protection for you. Regardless of the association, salary differentials exist with women being paid less than men. Indeed, for full-time wage and salary workers, the weekly median earnings of men and women in 2006 were $743 versus $600 (*Statistical Abstract of the United States: 2008*. Table 627). As noted earlier, priority to family is a primary reason women earn less money than men. Regardless of the type of association (e.g. academic, medical, and military) women tend to have less training and invest fewer hours due to the concern for their families.

The elderly have their own associations which allow them political visibility and power. The American Association of Retired Persons was founded in 1958 and has about forty million members. The goal of the organization (open to those working or retired) is to emphasize the need for health care, worker equity, and equality for minorities. AARP is the leading nonprofit, nonpartisan membership organization for people age 50 and over.

Networks

Networks tie together a wide range of social services for the elderly. A geriatric caregiver network functions to provide care for an aging parent for an adult offspring who cannot live near his or her parent. There is also a network of Meals on Wheels which delivers food regularly to the elderly who are unable to leave their home. Some social service agencies provide weekly bathing assistance to the elderly who cannot clean themselves.

Women also form networks to help them with business contacts. Advancing women (http://www.advancingwomen.com/) is a site devoted to helping women find jobs. Type in "networks for women" on Google to discover an array of networks.

Societies

Societies represent the largest unit of social structure which affects the role relationships between women and men and how the aged are regarded. In general, societies can be described on the basis of how they get their food which, in turn, influences the role relationships between women, men, and the elderly. In hunting and gathering societies where men hunt large animals and women gather fruits and vegetables, there is little sexual inequality. Since the men may not always be successful killing a large animal, they can return to camp and still have food gathered by the women. Hence, each sex has similar access to the valuable resource of food.

In agricultural societies, where the bulk of hard work is performed by young men, women have less status. Between 1630 and 1820, America was an agrarian patriarchal society. Not only were men the owners of all joint property, women had no legal status in that they could not sign contracts. Men also controlled religious institutions. They alone could speak in church and assume leadership positions.

In our contemporary post-industrialized society, women have increased economic, legal, and religious power. However, our society continues to be largely one which sanctions male dominance. Males continue to earn more money for the same job. Women are relatively absent in terms of total numbers of individuals in Congress and the Supreme Court, and are rare as religious leaders (women are not allowed to serve in positions of power in many denominations and religions, including the Mormon Church). Even so, the position of women in the United States is light years ahead from that of women in Afghanistan. Even though the Taliban was toppled by U.S. led forces in 2001, fewer than 30% of eligible girls are enrolled in schools (Baker, 2008).

Order versus Disorder

As noted earlier, every society must control various aspects of its population. Such order involves caring for the elderly, minimizing hostility on the part of both sexes over gender-based discrimination, and responding to reactions against adversarial movement.

Care and Abuse of the Elderly

As with child and spouse abuse, elder abuse also occurs. It is estimated that about half a million elderly in the United States are abused (Bergeron and Gray, 2003). Cross-culturally, there are 600 million individuals over the age of 60, a figure that will double by 2025, and there is little to no visibility given to the vulnerability of these elderly who are abused (Patterson and Malley-Morrison, 2006). Various examples of abuse include:

1. Neglect: failing to buy or give the elderly needed medicine, failing to take them to receive necessary medical care, or failing to provide adequate food, clean clothes, and a clean bed. Neglect is the most frequent type of domestic elder abuse; more than 70 percent of all adult protective services' reports are for this reason (Fulmer et al., 2005).

2. Physical abuse: inflicting injury or physical pain or sexual assault.

3. Psychological abuse: verbal abuse, deprivation of mental health services, harassment, and deception.

4. Social abuse: unreasonable confinement and isolation, lack of supervision, abandonment.

5. Legal abuse: improper or illegal use of the elder's resources.

Another type of elder abuse that has received recent media attention is "granny dumping." Adult children or grandchildren who feel burdened with the care of their elderly parent or grandparent drive the elder to the entrance of a hospital and leave him or her there with no identification. If the hospital cannot identify responsible relatives, it is required by state law to take care of the abandoned elder or transfer the person to a nursing-home facility, which is paid for by state funds. Relatives of the dumped granny, hiding from financial responsibility, never visit or see granny again.

Adult children who are most likely to dump or abuse their parents tend to be under a great deal of stress and to use alcohol or other drugs. In some cases, parent abusers are getting back at their parents for mistreating them as children. In other cases, the children are frustrated with the burden of having to care for their elderly parents. Such frustration is likely to increase. As baby boomers age, they will drain already limited resources for the lower middle and lower class elderly, and their children will be forced to care for them with little governmental support. Prevention of elder abuse involves reducing the stress for caregivers by linking caregivers to community services (Bergeron and Gray, 2003).

The Possibility of Equality between Men and Women

Equality between men and women will be possible only under the condition that both sexes are aware and conclude that inequality is detrimental to both sexes and that neither profit by denigrating the other. This implies that men, who are the dominant gender in our society, recognize that an identity tied to their work, that the responsibility to be the "breadwinner," and that the lower priority given to their role of fatherhood makes it difficult for them to be anything but a drone or worker. Releasing their grip on political, social, and economic power may free them for a wider range of identities, more flexible schedules, and a stronger emotional bond with their children. Economic sanctions and incentives are also necessary to insure occupational equality. That women earn less than three fourths on the dollar as men for the same education and job is a target for change.

Adversarial Movements and the "Oppressed" Majority

While we have documented the existence of inequality between women and men, reverse discrimination may also sometimes occur. There are rare times when two Ph.D.'s (one female, one male) are looking for a job at the same four year university. Since federal guidelines require that a certain proportion of females be hired, the male may be disadvantaged. In this case, the adversarial movement is the "women's movement" seeking an end to job discrimination and the "oppressed" majority are males competing for the same job as females. There is no perfection in social life and in social organizations, but the majority of adversarial movements work against the oppressed minority.

Popular Beliefs and Scientific Data: Men Drink More Alcohol Than Women

Advertisements for alcohol are most common during the Super Bowl and other televised sports programs. Not only are males targeted as the primary consumer group, there is the belief that men consistently drink considerably more alcohol than women. Researchers Keyes et al. (2008) tested gender differences in a nationally representative sample of 42,693 respondents age 90 and below. The survey was conducted in 2001 and 2002 to assess gender differences in alcohol consumption, abuse, and dependence in four birth cohorts: 1913–1932, 1933–1949, 1950–1967, and 1968–1984. Results revealed that men were significantly more likely to have engaged in binge drinking, to have abused alcohol, and to be dependent on alcohol than women. However, there were decreases in gender differences in more recent cohorts suggesting that the gender gap is narrowing and that women in younger cohorts may be in need of new targeted prevention and intervention efforts.

References

Baker, A. 2008. "The Girl Gap." *Time Magazine*, January 28, pp. 41–43.

Bergeron, L. R. and B. Gray. 2003. "Ethical Dilemmas of Reporting Suspected Elder Abuse." *Social Work,* 48: 96–106.

Bragg, B., D. Knox, and M. Zusman. 2008. "The Little Ones: Gender Differences in Attitudes toward Children among University Students." Southern Sociology Society Annual Meeting, Richmond, Va. April.

Fernandez-Ballesteros, R. 2003. "Social Support and Quality of Life among Older People in Spain." *Journal of Social Issues,* 58: 645–60.

Cheng, C. 2005. "Processes Underlying Gender-Role Flexibility: Do Androgynous Individuals Know More or Know How to Cope?" *Journal of Personality,* 73: 645–74.

Clay, D., V. L. Vignoles, and H. Dittmar. 2005. "Body Image and Self-Esteem among Adolescent Girls: Testing the Influence of Sociocultural Factors." *Journal of Research on Adolescence,* 15: 451–77.

Cumming, E. and W. Henry. 1961. *Growing Old: The Process of Disengagement.* New York: Basic Books.

Dowd, James J. 1980. "Exchange Rates and Old People." *Journal of Gerontology,* 35: 596–602.

Fulmer, T., G. Paveza, C. VandeWeerd, L. Guadagno, S. Fairchild, R. Norman, V. Abraham, and M. Bolton-Blatt. 2005. "Neglect Assessment in Urban Emergency Departments and Confirmation by an Expert Clinical Team." *Journals of Gerontology Series A-Biological Sciences and Medical Sciences,* 60: 1002–06.

Heckert, T. M., H. E. Dorste, G. W. Farmer, P. J. Adams, J. C. Bradley, and B. M. Bonness. 2002. "Effect of Gender and Work Experience on Importance of Job Characteristics When Considering Job Offers." *College Student Journal,* 36: 344–51.

Hepp, U., A. Spindler, and G. Milos. 2005. "Eating Disorder Symptomatology and Gender Role Orientation." *International Journal of Eating Disorders,* 37: 227–33.

Hoffer, T. B., M. Hess, V. Welch, Jr. and K. Williams. 2007. "Doctorate Recipients from United States Universities: Summary Report 2006." Chicago: National Opinion Research Center.

Jorm, A. F., H. Christensen, A. S. Henderson, P. A. Jacomb, A. E. Korten, and A. Mackinnon. 1998. "Factors Associated with Successful Ageing." *Australian Journal of Ageing,* 17: 33–37.

Keyes, K., B. F. Grant, and D. S. Hasin. 2008. "Evidence for a Closing Gender Gap in Alcohol Use, Abuse, and Dependence in the United States Population." *Drug & Alcohol Dependence,* 93: 21–29.

Ma, M.K. 2005. "The Relation of Gender-Role Classifications to the Prosocial and Antisocial Behavior of Chinese Adolescents." *Journal of Genetic Psychology,* 166: 189–201.

Mercer, C. 2008. "Practical Immortality." Unpublished manuscript, submitted for publication. East Carolina University.

Moore, O., S. Kreitler, M. Ehrenfeld, and N. Giladi. 2005. "Quality of Life and Gender Identity in Parkinson's Disease." *Journal of Neural Transmission,* 112: 1511–22.

National Vital Statistics Reports. 2007. "Deaths: Leading Causes for 2004." Vol 56. No. 5. November 20.

Newport, Frank. 2007. "Sixty-nine Percent of Americans Support Death Penalty." Gallup Poll Briefing, October 12, pp. 3–7.

O'Reilly, E. M. 1997. *Decoding the Cultural Stereotypes about Aging: New Perspectives on Aging Talk and Aging Issues.* New York: Garland.

Patterson, M. and K. M. Morrison. 2006. "A Cognitive-Ecological Approach to Elder Abuse in Five Cultures: Human Rights and Education." *Educational Gerontology,* 32: 73–82.

Richey, E., D. Knox, and M. Zusman. 2008. Sexual values of 783 undergraduates. Unpublished paper, East Carolina University.

Ross, C., D. Knox, and M. Zusman. 2007. "Hey Big Boy!: Characteristics of Women who Initiate Relationships with Men." Poster, Southern Sociological Society Annual Meeting, Atlanta, March.

Statistical Abstract of the United States: 2008. 127th ed. Washington, D.C.: U.S. Bureau of the Census.

Ward, C. A. 2001. "Models and Measurement of Psychological Androgyny: A Cross-Cultural Extension of Theory and Research." *Sex Roles,* 43: 529–552.

Woodhill, B. M., and C. A. Samuels. 2003. "Positive and Negative Androgyny and their Relationship with Psychological Health and Well-Being." *Sex Roles,* 48: 555–65.

Chapter 10

Families and Communities

Call it a clan, call it a network, call it a tribe, call it a family. Whatever you call it, whoever you are, you need one.

Jane Howard, anthropologist

An aging marriage and family professor revealed a pattern of always giving the same tests each year. Colleagues thought the teacher both lazy and unfair to students since the tests would get out. But the teacher justified giving the same exams every year on the premise that the answers kept changing. While the family continues to experience massive changes, it remains the most basic of all social contexts in every society. The family is a social organization with which everyone has personal experience. In this chapter, we view the family as an independent variable and examine its effects on family members and the other levels of social organization.

Our families exist in the social context of a community. Communities are the places in which most of our daily needs are met. When we leave the family, we go to school, work, worship, shop, eat out, and interact with neighbors in the community. In this chapter we also examine the various types of communities and how they affect other social organizations. We begin with the family.

Conceptualizing the Family

While all sociologists agree that the family is a social context which affects all other levels of social organization, there are different definitions of the family and disagreements on whether the family exists everywhere.

Definitions and Universality of the Family

It is difficult to identify a definition of the family that characterizes all families in all societies. The **family** as a social context has different forms and functions. A standard definition of the family is that it is a social group whose membership is by marriage, blood, or adoption. When a couple marries, they become a family. Their biological and adopted children also become members of the same family. The husband, wife, and children living as one unit represent the **nuclear family**. In case of divorce, the husband and wife live separately with the children alternating time with mom and dad. This arrangement is called the **binuclear family**. If mom or dad remarries someone who also has children, they begin a **stepfamily**.

While most families in the United States are characterized by their parenting, common residence, and economic cooperation, this definition does not accurately reflect family life in all cultures. Among some groups (Trobriands), the father is of little importance in the lives of his children. Rather, his wife and her parents have the authority and responsibility in rearing their children. In other societies, the father may not even live with his wife and children but only visit them occasionally. This is true of the Kipsigis men of southwestern Kenya who have many wives and rarely stay with any one of them.

As for economic cooperation, in some cultures there is a pattern whereby the wife may grow her own food and be economically self-sufficient. Of course, an absent father and economically self-sufficient mother also characterizes many single parent women in the United States. In addition to single parent families there are childfree couples and homosexual families. Indeed some family scholars acknowledge that family is increasingly being defined in terms of affectional and economic ties. Indeed, there is throughout the world, tremendous variation in the structure and function of various units which may be labeled as family.

However family is defined, all individuals belong to at least one of two family groupings. The **family of orientation**, also known as the family of origin, is the family into which you were born. This group is particularly important as a context for good health. Heaton and Forste (2008) found that positive interaction between spouses has a positive effect on the health of children in the family. In contrast, violence and inequality between the spouses have negative health consequences. Similarly, if one's parents did not smoke, their children are more likely not to smoke and to quit if they (the children) start smoking (Messer et al. 2008). The **family of procreation** is the family you begin yourself. Over 95 percent of U.S. adults marry and begin their own family of procreation. The different types include childfree, one-child, and multi-child families.

Structural Family Patterns

A pervasive theme of this book is that social context affects outcome. The variations in family structure will have differential outcomes for its members. Leininger et al. (2008) examined family structure of 62,193 children ages 0–17 years and found that children in single father homes were disadvantaged in terms of health care when compared to children in two parent homes and single mother homes. Some of the various marital and family structures follow.

Number of Partners

Family structures differ by the number of partners in the marital unit. Marriages of **monogamy** are those in which there is only one husband and one wife. In contrast, **polygamy** refers to having multiple spouses. The primary forms of polygamy are **polygyny** in which a man has several wives and **polyandry** in which a woman has several husbands. Murdock (1949) studied the relative frequency of each of these patterns in 565 societies throughout the world and found that polygyny was approved in 81 percent of the societies. In contrast, less than 1 percent of the societies practiced polyandry. While polygyny was approved in most societies, monogamy was more prevalent in actual practice. Murdock observed that the expense of having several wives and the fact that all societies try to provide regular sexual intercourse for its adults (which would leave out numerous men in a polygynous system or women in a polyandrous system) are the primary reasons for the prevalence of monogamy. The number of partners also affects the interaction patterns of the participants, the issues they must deal with, and the number of potential offspring. Polygynous marriages, for example, not only have significantly more interactions between the members but must deal with a more complex division of labor, sexual sharing, and paternity commitment than monogamous marriages. In addition, the number of children from such marriages is potentially much larger because each wife may have several children. In Bicentennial City, Utah, a man, who is a member of a dissident Mormon sect, may be married to three or more women and have as many as sixty children (there is one legal wife and the others are civil wives). Such a context is quite different from the traditional monogamous relationship between spouses who have two children.

Extended Families

Earlier we noted that nuclear families consist of two married adults and their offspring—either biological or adopted. Nuclear families are most familiar to us in that they are composed of the mother, father, and children. In contrast, **extended families** may involve parents or relatives living with the nuclear family. A typical extended family consists of the husband and wife, the biological children of the husband and wife, and the parents of the husband or the wife or both. Other examples of the extended family may include the nuclear family plus the siblings (and their offspring). All of the people do not need to live together in order to be the extended family.

Nuclear and extended structural patterns are important because they have economic and social consequences for the respective units. Extended families often share their economic resources such that family income can be relatively high where there are several wage earners. This is particularly true of the extended Chinese family which lives and works together. In addition, authority patterns must be worked out as discussed in the next section.

Authority Patterns

Authority patterns may be characterized as patriarchal, matriarchal, or egalitarian. **Patriarchal authority** systems are those in which the power and authority of the family is vested in males with the eldest male usually having the most power. The Hindu, Chinese, and Japanese families are known for their patriarchal structure. In essence, the eldest male controls all family members, and males learn to dominate females. In contrast, females learn to defer to males and accept passivity as their proper role.

Matriarchal authority systems are those in which complete power is vested in females. But their power is weak. Bunger (2008) noted that the closest women ever come to matriarchy is equality. In Tibetan and Burmese societies, for instance, women are the social and economic equals of men, but men still make the political decisions and fill the political roles. There are societies where there are female high priestesses as among the Lovedu of Africa, but the war leaders are still men. However, among the Seneca Indians, the chiefs were men but were chosen by the women, and the women had to approve decisions for war or peace. This is possibly the closest thing to a matriarchy that has been found. Children reared in a matriarchal authority system will experience a double message about female-male authority. While females may exercise formal control, males may be more powerful at the informal level in terms of decisions made which influence the group.

In the **egalitarian authority** system, there is an equal distribution of power and authority between the husband and the wife. Increasingly in the United States, particularly among the middle class, marriages are becoming more egalitarian. Children reared in these marriages are more likely to establish egalitarian relationships themselves than if they had been reared in a patriarchal home.

Descent Systems

Authority patterns are transferred along descent lines from generation to generation. **Descent** refers to the rules which connect a person to his or her relatives. The existence of descent rules emphasize that the family is a social group rather than a biological group. There are three primary systems of descent: patrilineal, matrilineal, and bilateral. **Patrilineal descent** involves the assignment of a person to a social group on the basis of males only. When a wife marries a man, their children become members of the husband's family, and her family is ignored. In contrast, **matrilineal descent** traces kin through females, and the father's family is ignored. **Bilateral descent** involves tracing kin relationships equally—through the mother's biological kin and the father's biological kin. This pattern of descent is used in the United States. Descent patterns are important because they make clear how economic resources are inherited. Males and females born into these respective descent systems will have differential access to resources which will affect their life chances. Males in matrilineal and females in patrilineal systems will be disadvantaged while males in patrilineal and females in matrilineal societies will be advantaged.

Residence Systems

After a couple marries, they may live in one of several places—with or near his parents or her parents or away from both parents. All societies develop rules of residence (patrilocal, matrilocal, bilocal, or neolocal) which determine where the couple will live. The most common residence system, **patrilocal residence**, involves the wife leaving her family of orientation and moving in with or adjacent to her husband's family. It is important to note that the patrilocal rule specifies that the wife will live with the husband's family, not with the husband. While he is often there, the emphasis is on the group (her husband's family) which will have authority over her.

A less common residence pattern is matrilocal whereby the husband leaves his family of orientation and moves in with or near his wife's parents. This **matrilocal residence** system is usually in conjunction with a matrilineal descent system.

Bilocal residence patterns allow the couple to choose whether to live close to his parents or hers. Variables to consider include the wealth of the parents, the needs of the spouses, and the presence of children. Parents and the extended kin often provide support for childcare which influences the decision to live near the set of living grandparents.

Neolocal residence patterns involve the couple deciding to move away from both sets of parents to set up their household. This residence norm is operative in the United States and reflects that the respective spouses have their own economic resources.

Residence patterns are important because they influence the power balance between the spouses. Depending on where they choose to live, one spouse will be in a favored position since the support of kin will be nearby. The other spouse will be disadvantaged by living amid strangers. Residence patterns will also influence the degree to which children will develop strong or weak relationships with their grandparents and the degree to which the parents will develop independence. The neolocal system, for example, will weaken ties with the extended kin and encourage greater interdependence on the part of the couple.

The Process of Change

The marital and family contexts are constantly in the process of change. In this section we review how industrialization changed the family and the nature of some of these changes.

Effects of Industrialization on the Family

Industrialization (the shift from human or animal labor to machines) began shortly after 1800. Towns grew up around factories and created several effects on the family. First, the family shifted from a production to a consumer unit. Prior to the development of factories, everything was produced by the family for its own needs. With industrialization, everything could be produced outside the family. Second, children were transformed from economic assets to economic liabilities. Since the family no longer needed to produce anything, working together as a family was no longer necessary. Since there was less work to do, children were no longer valuable as sources of labor but became liabilities. Today, children (particularly in middle class families), aside from being a tax deduction, provide zero economic benefit for the family.

Industrialization also created a need for mass numbers of workers, including women. Prior to this time, women were restricted to the home and family to prepare meals, spin yarn, and make clothes. A by-product of women working exclusively in the home was that their mate selection was controlled by their parents. Once women began to work outside the home, they could meet men without having to be introduced to them by their parents. More importantly, because they earned an income they could afford to leave their parents' house if they did not like the control their parents tried to exercise over their mate selection choices. Industrialization also created a number of rooming houses so that people could live apart from their families if they wanted to do so.

Industrialization had implications not only for mate selection but for the married couple. As wives began to work outside the home, their power in the marriage increased. Such power resulted in a greater potential for conflict since there was no longer presumed submission on the part of the wife to her husband. It also resulted in an increase in divorce.

From Traditional to Contemporary Marriages

Other changes in the traditional family included that wives were expected to earn an income; that education became important for both spouses to complete; that either spouse's career could dictate the residence of the couple; or that both spouses were expected to participate in childcare and rearing. The family also changed from having a central focus as an institution that was sacred (and therefore no divorce) to a focus on the major functions of providing emotional support, companionship, and intimacy. The marriage relationship became the focal unit with spouses expecting their emotional needs to be fulfilled. One of the reasons spouses began to divorce was the loss of an emotional connection between them. "'til death do us part" became "'til love dies and I get tired of you."

Single Parent Families

Barack Obama has given increased visibility (and hope) to the single parent family. He noted that when he was just two, his father left the family, and he was reared by his mother, a single parent. In recent years, single parent families have become more common. At least half of all children will spend one-fourth of their lives in a female-headed household (Webb, 2005).

It is important to distinguish between a single-parent family and a single-parent household. A **single-parent family** is one in which there is only one parent—the other parent is completely out of the child's life through death, sperm donation, or complete abandonment, and no contact is ever made with the other parent. Obama and his mother represented a single parent family. In contrast, a **single-parent household** is one in which one parent typically has primary custody of the child or children, but the parent living out of the house is still a part of the child's family. In effect the child has two single-parent households.

Single parents enter their role though separation and divorce, widowhood, adoption, or deliberate choice to rear a child or children alone. Jodie Foster, Academy Award-winning actress, elected to have children without a husband. She now has two children and smiles when asked, "Who's the father?" The implication is that she has a right to her private life and that choosing to have a single-parent family is a viable option. An organization for women who want children and who may or may not marry is Single Mothers by Choice.

Bock (2000) noted that single mothers by choice are, for the most part, in the middle to upper class, mature, well-employed, politically aware, and dedicated to motherhood. Interviews with 26 single mothers by choice revealed their struggle to avoid stigmatization and to seek legitimization for their choice. Most felt that their age (older), sense of responsibility, maturity, and fiscal capability justified their choice. Their self-concepts were those of competent, ethical, mainstream mothers.

Lack of money is a frustrating issue for most single parent families, particularly those headed by women. The median income of a single-woman householder is $27,244, much lower than that of a single-man householder ($41,111) or a married couple ($65,906) (*Statistical Abstract of the United States: 2008*, Table 677).

Kwan (2008) examined the effect of family structure on the life satisfaction of 4,502 Chinese adolescents in secondary high school. It was found that in overall life satisfaction, adolescents living with a single mother had similar life satisfaction to adolescents living with two parents, but those living with father only, those with no parents, or a single parent with other adults had a much greater risk of life dissatisfaction.

Families and Social Organization

The theme of this text is how one level of social organization interacts with and affects other levels of social organization and explains why individuals as social actors do what they do. Some of the effects of the family on other social organizations and upon individuals follow.

Population

Families affect the percentage of people in various marital status populations. In general, families in contemporary America encourage their offspring to get married, to be monogamous, and to stay married (not divorce even if there are problems). When families severely disapprove of divorce, there are fewer divorces (Mormon families disapprove of divorce and have a very low divorce rate). If children get divorced, parents encourage them to get remarried. About 80 percent of the divorced remarry. The various populations by marital status in the U.S. are presented in Table 10.1

Table 10.1
Percent of U.S. Adults Age 65 and Over by Marital Status

Married	= 57.8%
Widowed	= 29.9%
Divorced	= 8.7%
Never married	= 3.6%

Source: *Statistical Abstract of the United States: 2008.* 127th ed. Washington, D.C.: U.S. Bureau of the Census, Table 34.

Collective Behavior/Social Movements

The gay rights movement emphasizes the right for homosexuals to have relationships with same-sex partners and to be viewed as members of 'real families.' Due to a strong heterosexual bias, only Massachusetts recognizes same-sex marriages. State legislatures also routinely introduce legislation to restrict or prohibit same sex partners from adopting children or serving as foster parents (Wright, 2007).

Social Classes

Families affect social class position. The greater the number of intact two-earner spouses, the greater the number of middle class families. In contrast, with divorce, the social class of most families drifts downward. The greater the number of divorced families with only one wage earner, the greater the number of lower class families. One way of measuring class is by income. The median income of a single-parent household is $34,177, while that of a married couple is $65,906 (*Statistical Abstract of the United States: 2008*, Table 677).

Groups

The peer group is the most important group of concern to family researchers. The peer group is significant in the life of families in the socialization of sex, clothes, and values that represent generational change (thus the concern of parents in regard to who their children regard as friends). Because the peer group members are of the same age and chosen from neighbors, schoolmates, and playmates, they have the important distinction of being status-equals. They develop egalitarian relationships that are close and help children become self-reliant and independent. These groups are in competition with the family for the child's allegiance and fulfill the role of deepening the child's knowledge of the world.

Communities

There are over a million divorces every year (*Statistical Abstract of the United States: 2008*). These divorces impact the legal, housing, and economic resources of the communities in which they occur. First, domestic courts in these communities become jammed with spouses fighting over custody, division of property, child support and spousal support. Such litigation often pits spouse against spouse and child against parent. The result is a community transformed from domestic tranquility to domestic hostility.

Second, the need for low cost single family housing increases. Divorce usually results in the sale of the family home and/or the respective spouses moving into cheaper living quarters than the couple shared when they were married. As a result, communities become dotted with mobile homes, apartments, and condominiums as single parents scramble for less expensive housing.

Because more than half of the women who are due child support do not receive the court ordered support, communities become burdened with welfare payments in the form of Aid to Families with Dependent Children (AFDC). But lack of money is only the beginning. Single parents need day care, job training, medical and nutritional programs, and safe neighborhoods. When families break apart, community resources are expected to provide the benefits that would have occurred if the families had stayed together. But community resources are limited and cannot meet all of the needs of single-parent families.

Associations

Families look to other socialization agents to help them care for and socialize family members. Boy Scouts and Girl Scouts are examples of associations which have developed to teach specific skills (tying knots) and values (courtesy and parental respect) and provide opportunities for supervised interaction with peers. Families support these socialization associations because they feel they have positive influences on their offspring. Boys and Girls Clubs of America also help families in that they provide recreational opportunities in late afternoon for school children whose parents are still at work.

Other associations develop when the family has been unsuccessful in socializing and controlling its members. For example, successful family socialization can be expected to involve teaching its members not to drink and drive and not to abuse alcohol. These associations include MADD (Mothers Against Drunk Driving) and AA (Alcoholics Anonymous). The former exists to get drinking drivers off the road; the latter to provide assistance toward sobriety for the alcoholic who has the desire to stop drinking.

Networks

Single mothers develop networks to help them with childcare, carpooling to school, and babysitting. The family is also part of larger networks to accomplish more specific goals. Religious, educational, and political socialization is accomplished because of the interplay between various social organizations. While parents may teach their children that there is a God, the church or synagogue may teach them specific passages from the Bible helping to reinforce the parents' beliefs. While parents may teach their children how to spell certain words, the school will teach them how to write a paragraph. While parents may teach their children that America is a great place to live, the school will teach them the Pledge of Allegiance, so that a network reinforces patriotism, and the individual becomes what the network socializes them to be.

Valdez et al. (2008) emphasized that family networks also play a role in non-injection heroin use (e.g. sniffing, smoking). They interviewed 20 Mexican Americans in a poor section of San Antonio and found clear associations between drug use by family members (father, mother, siblings) and use by offspring. Drug use by individuals whose peers were heroin users was less chronic if the family network was not using drugs.

Societies

As families change, so do societies. Aware that unrestricted procreation would overburden the society, China (with its one billion people) looked to the family to decrease its population. The government developed a 'one child' family policy whereby parents who had only one child would get special privileges such as being exempt from paying school tuition, a ten percent bonus on annual income earned by the parents, and priority in nursery school enrollment.

While the policy has not been as successful as planned, it emphasized the need to change family structure to meet societal goals.

Dual earner nuclear families in the United States increase the need for the larger society to provide more services traditionally met inside the family. With 61 percent of wives in the United States working outside the home (*Statistical Abstract of the United States: 2008*, Table 578), the need for fast food restaurants, day care centers, and electronic entertainment for children has increased. Burger King provides food for the family, KinderCare rears the children, and video games entertain them.

Popular Beliefs and Scientific Data: Five Myths about Relationships

There are numerous myths about the effects of various courtship, marital, and family contexts on outcomes. Five of these follow:

Myth One: Marriage is going out of style (fewer couples are getting married).

Fact: Over 96% of U.S. adult women (96.8%) and men (96.7%) aged 75 and older have married at least once (*Statistical Abstract of the United States: 2008*, Table 56). While individuals are delaying marriage into their late 20s and early 30s, there are no data to support that people are opting out of marriage as a lifestyle.

Myth Two: Couples who live together before marriage are more likely to remain married and avoid divorce than couples who do not live together.

Fact: Cohabitants, compared to non-cohabitants, are more likely not only to divorce but to report more disagreements, more violence, lower levels of happiness, and lower levels of ability to negotiate conflict (Cohan and Kleinbaum, 2002). However, if the woman has only one cohabitation experience and that experience is with her husband before marriage, there is no negative effect (Teachman, 2003). It is the serial cohabitant or the person who moves in and out of living together relationships who is at risk.

Myth Three: Couples with children are happier than couples without children.

Fact: Twenge (2003) reviewed 148 samples representing 47,692 individuals in regard to the effect children have on marital satisfaction. They found that (1) parents (both women and men) reported lower marital satisfaction than nonparents; (2) mothers of infants reported the most significant drop in marital satisfaction; (3) the higher the number of children, the lower the marital satisfaction; and (4) the factors that depressed marital satisfaction were conflict and loss of freedom.

Myth Four: Single people have more satisfying sex than married people.

Fact: One-third of a national sample of persons who were not married and not living with anyone reported that they were emotionally satisfied with their sexual relationships. In contrast, 85 percent of the married and pair-bonded respondents reported emotional satisfaction in their sexual relationships. Hence, although the never-married have more sexual partners, they are less emotionally satisfied (Michael et al., 1994).

Myth Five: Conflicts in heterosexual relationships are handled the same way as conflicts in homosexual relationships.

Fact: Kurdek (2004) compared heterosexual married spouses with same-sex partners and found that the latter resolve conflict more positively, argue more effectively, and are more likely to suggest possible solutions and compromises. One explanation for the more positive conflict resolution among same-sex couples is that they value equality more and are more likely to have equal power and status in the relationship than are heterosexual couples (Gottman et al., 2003).

Community Defined

Families typically live in a community more commonly known as a town, city, or suburb. As noted earlier, a **community** is a collection of people who live and interact in a geographic area who have something in common. We now explore the central elements of a community.

Geographic Area

A common question when strangers meet is, "Where are you from?" The answer defines one as living in a specific community—a specific place. New Yorkers define themselves as being from "the East Side," or "Greenwich Village," or "the Bronx." Specific streets may be used to define the geographic boundary of communities. North of 96th Street in New York is a high crime area; south of 86th Street is known as a community for the wealthy elite.

Twin Oaks is a community of 90 adults and 15 children living together on 450 acres of land in Louisa, Virginia. Also known as an **intentional community**, the commune was founded in 1967 and is one of the oldest nonreligious intentional communities in the United States. The community grows its own food, builds its own buildings, and is relatively self-sufficient. Celebration is another planned community designed by the Disney Corporation and is literally adjacent to Disney World in Orlando, Florida. The town of about 2,000 (once it was 5,000) is no longer run by the Disney Corporation.

Social Interaction

Community is also defined in terms of interaction. People who define themselves as belonging to a particular community cooperate with other community members. Such cooperation may involve borrowing a ladder or helping in times of an emergency. In the Amish community, a farmer who loses his barn due to fire will soon find it replaced by a "barn raising." This involves all of the members of the community gathering together to build the new barn. Members of Twin Oaks and Celebration also view themselves as part of a larger community and willing to help fellow community members.

Common Ties

Common ties reflect the social and psychological ties individuals have to a particular community. People from Chicago feel bonded by their commitment to the Cubs baseball team and the Bears football team. New Yorkers have the Yankees or Mets and the Giants. Even though people may move out of an area, they may continue to feel common ties with others who have also moved out of the community. When the New York Giants won Super Bowl 42, Indiana residents who had once lived in New York City savored the victory. Midwesterners, Southerners, and Bostonians may live elsewhere but still feel tied to each other through their common ties with their city of rearing and identity. Wherever they live, they may be New Yorkers or Californians for life. When they meet one of their own "kind" on vacation, they may feel an instant common tie with that person.

Types of Communities

Communities are often categorized as being urban, suburban, or rural. Regardless of the type, the community in which you were reared and the community in which you live as an adult will have a major effect on you. As a college student, your hometown has had an effect on you as does the current "college town" in which you live.

Urban Communities

The United States Bureau of the Census divides communities into those which are urban and rural. **Urban communities** are those with more than

2,500 people. Urban communities may be very large indeed; Tokyo has 12 million, Moscow has 11 million, and New York has 8.2 million people. Peen et al. (2007) examined the prevalence of mental health disorders in an international sample of 7,076 people aged 18–64 and found that increased levels of urbanization were associated with a higher prevalence of psychiatric disorders. The researchers recommended further research to identify the environmental factors important in the etiology of mental disorders. What is important is that the individual is not relevant. Change the size of the community and you change the potential psychiatric profile of those who live there.

Suburban Communities

Surrounding urban communities are **suburban communities**. These are small towns to which urban commuters drive or train to and from work. Suburbs are usually newer and more modern than the cities they surround, are composed of more single family homes than multifamily rented apartments, and are inhabited by a more homogeneous population in terms of class and race than the heterogeneity of the city. Suburbanites also tend to be young, hold white collar jobs, and have higher incomes than city residents.

Living in the suburbs changes the outcome for individuals or social actors. If you move from a large urban area to the suburbs, the risk of being shot, the chance of divorce, and the likelihood of being liberal all decrease. The individual becomes what the context makes him or her. Change the context, and you change the outcome. Move from the suburbs to a rural area and the chance of all of these outcomes decreases yet again.

Rural Communities

Communities of less than 2,500 people are regarded as **rural**. Rural communities may further be broken down into **rural-farm** (those areas in which people live on farms) and **rural-nonfarm** (those areas in which people live in the open country but not on farms). Increasingly people who live in rural areas are not involved in farm-related activities. Nevertheless, persons who want large families move from an urban to a rural area.

Urban, Suburban and Rural Life

Sociologists have examined the development and change of cities as well as the impact of the various contexts of where one lives on individual actions.

The Ecological and Structural Patterns

Ecology is the study of the relationship between individuals and their environment. Ecologists have observed that humans structure their cities in various ways. Three such patterns include concentric zone, multiple-nuclei, and sector (Hoyt, 1943).

Concentric Zone. The **concentric zone** pattern involves a major central business district in the center of the city with banks, hotels, and government offices concentrated in this area. Radiating outward from this central area in a pattern of wider and wider concentric circles is a predictable pattern of other districts. The concentric zone pattern looks like a target. The next circle out from the bull's eye or 'central zone' is known as the "zone of transition" in which those who provide the labor for the low status jobs in the city live. Structurally, the area is comprised of tall but run down apartments, dirty streets, and a high crime rate.

The next rung out is composed of middle class people who live in nicer houses and commute to work. Still further out are the homes of the rich who drive to the city for work and culture. Hence, as the distance from the central city increases, the social status of the people increases. Chicago and St. Louis illustrate the concentric zone pattern of urban development.

Multiple-Nuclei. While in the concentric zone pattern there is only one central district, the **multiple-nuclei pattern** exists where there are several important districts in the city. These multiple nuclei emphasize such different areas as manufacturing, retail stores, and entertainment. Los Angeles is an example of a city where different parts of the city feature different activities.

Sector. The **sector pattern** is one of wedge shaped patterns that grow outward from the center of the city. Hence, a lower class district may extend outward from the city in a wedge rather than a circular pattern. This pattern develops in cities in reference to transportation lanes of water, rail, and interstate highways. Charleston, South Carolina, developed in reference to the water that surrounds the city, and San Francisco developed in relationship to the bay. People moved along known hubs such as subway lines to make it easier to move into and out of the cities.

Structural Patterns of Urban Development

Cities also reflect structural patterns, and these may be viewed as independent variables which impact the life experience of people in the various areas. In regard to the concentric zone pattern, individuals who live in the slum areas next to the central business district will have a shorter life expectancy than those who live among the elite on the outskirts of town. Similarly, those who live next to busy streets and heavy manufacturing will breathe more polluted air and experience greater health risks than those who live in suburban wooded areas.

The Process of Change

If we could position a video camera on a Goodyear blimp and record how a city changes across time, several factors responsible for the change would emerge.

Concentration. Different populations of people are concentrated into different areas of a city. Blacks and whites still live in largely segregated areas. In Greenville, North Carolina, the area "across the tracks on Dickinson Avenue" is largely populated by blacks. Whites live in "Brook Valley" with a few mixed neighborhoods ("Eastwood"). A person of one race moving into an area concentrated with people of another race will experience a very different "neighborhood" than a person who lives in a neighborhood of his or her own race. How people feel, how long they live, what types of problems they encounter has a great deal to do with the community in which they live.

Centralization. While concentration refers to people, centralization refers to activities or businesses. "Downtown" in most urban areas is where large auditoriums featuring cultural events are found. Manhattan is another example of centralization whereby the financial district is located in one area of the city, "jazz" in another, and Broadway theaters in still another.

Specialization. Specialization refers to neither people nor businesses but occupations. Prostitution is often restricted to particular parts of the city. In Baltimore, Maryland, "the block" is known as the area for hookers and bars. In New York, streetwalkers are relegated to Lexington Avenue. In Chicago, "night life" is concentrated in various areas such as the two block area surrounding Rush Street.

Invasion. Invasion refers to a large influx of people moving into a specific area. When a military base is established in a town, it alters the kinds of businesses which develop to serve this new population of people. Since the military is composed largely of single, young, mobile males there will be an increase in the number of bars, prostitutes, furniture stores, and pawn shops in an area. If the military base is moved to another area, most of the bars, prostitutes, and specific stores will also move.

Succession. Invasion and succession are often considered together. Whenever there is an invasion or influx of people, there is a corresponding succession of people who move out. Some residents of a quiet community would move upon learning that a military base was to be established nearby. Similarly, whites in the fifties, moved out of a neighborhood when blacks moved into the area.

Communities and Social Organization

Prior to industrialization, extreme differences existed between rural and urban communities. These differences have decreased because of industrialization, communication, transportation, and the location of businesses in both urban and rural areas. Nevertheless, some important distinctions remain.

Population

The community in which you reside affects various outcomes of your life. The communities may be rural farms, small towns, large towns, or massive urban areas. As an individual moves from a rural farm to a central city, they will have fewer children. As they move from a central city to a farm, they will not only have more children, but change the manner in which they interact and the way in which they feel. Farmers, as a population category, report considerable satisfaction with their lifestyle. Developing one's own abilities and control over one's own life are regarded as the basic rewards of farming. What constitutes a farm today? According to the *Statistical Abstract of the United States* (2008), "a farm is any place from which $1,000 or more of agricultural products are produced or sold, or normally would have been sold, during the census year" (p. 529). The number of family farms has decreased from 1,966,000 in 1978 to 1,910,000 in 2002 (*Statistical Abstract of the United States: 2008*, Table 799).

Social Movements

Rural farming communities have problems that are unique, and social movements develop in response to these needs. When farming was a small family owned business, there was little need for protest movements. Farmers grew their crops and sold them at the local market. As the technology for extensive farming developed and the market for farm products was increasingly controlled by factors beyond the local farmer's control, farmers began to organize. One of the earliest organizations was the Farmers Holiday Association. Over two million farmers in 24 states banded together in 1933 to protest low farm prices in the Depression years of the 1930s. The purpose of the movement was "to call a 'farmers' holiday, a strike in which no food products would be marketed until farm prices were raised" (Rogers et al. 1988).

Although the farmers' holiday strike had little effect on farm prices, farmer's movements today (The American Agricultural Movement and the North American Farm Alliance) borrowed their tactics from the early Farmers Holiday Association. One of the largest contemporary movements is the American Agricultural Movement (AAM), which has had over 1,000 local chapters. Discontent with farm prices led to the movement specifying a strike deadline of December 14, 1977, in which all farm production and marketing would stop. As part of the protest farmers released a herd of goats and a flock of chickens in the nation's capital. Congress reacted quickly, but meaningful legislative changes were minimal.

The movement became visible again in 1978, with its tractorcade in Washington, D.C. Four thousand tractors rolled into the nation's capital and disrupted traffic. Some farmers "scuffled with police and the national networks even broadcast footage of a tractor driving through the reflecting pool on the Capitol grounds" (Rogers et al., 1988, 250). The 1979 tractorcade may have caused more public indignation than support.

The farmer's movement has continued in the form of the North American Farm Alliance and Farm Aid. The latter provided national attention to the problems of farmers by means of televised concerts (organized by Willie Nelson). The 2007 concert took place at Randalls Island in New York City and was recorded in high definition to be broadcasted on HDNet as a two-hour special. The goal of Farm Aid is to help raise money for the family farmers of America. Such crowds, audiences and movements may have little organization, but when they are in existence they have a greater impact than the sum of their parts (individual farm families).

Social Class

When living below the poverty line is regarded as an index of lower social class, people in rural areas are more likely to be in a lower social class than people in urban areas. One explanation for the association between rural area and poverty status is the lack of job opportunities available in rural areas. To increase their standard of living, individuals move to urban areas. A change in community can cause a subsequent change in social class. An individual living in Appalachia who moves to New York City has not only changed the context of his or her community, but also the likelihood that his or her social class will change (upwards). Similarly, poverty is related to the community in which you live. A person in rural Georgia who has $150,000 in a retirement account may be considered much higher in social class than if the person moves to the Hamptons, one of the wealthiest communities in this country. The $150,000 would be nearly worthless in terms of purchasing power for a house in the area.

Groups

Gemeinschaft groups are more prevalent in rural areas and gesellschaft groups are more prevalent in urban areas. People in small rural communities know each other, speak to each other at the grocery store, and have a sense of community. Individuals in large urban areas pass each other routinely without speaking or acknowledging each other. The smaller the community, the more likely that individuals who live there will be emotionally connected and linked to others.

Families

Communities affect families in that small rural communities are more involved in the lives of the individual members than is true in large urban centers. "It takes a village to raise a child" has meaning for rural communities and small towns where everyone knows everyone else. In these areas, when "young people" date, everyone they meet will report to the parents on their activities. If a teenager is seen drinking beer or doing drugs by adults in a small town, the parents are very quickly informed. In a large urban community the behavior would go unnoticed as individuals become anonymous amid the tens of thousands of strangers they would move amongst.

The role of the wife on the farm is not only influenced by the rural community but by the other role commitments of the wife. Farm wives who are employed off the farm (and have an independent income) may view themselves as less subordinate to their husbands than farm wives who work exclusively on the farm. Hence, in assessing the impact of the rural farm family on the role of the wife, it is important to assess her external role involvements.

Size of community also has an effect on the probability of undetected family violence. Jones (2008) studied domestic violence among Native Americans in rural settings. She emphasized that the isolation of rural life provided a context for undetected domestic violence. As with all social organizations, as they change, outcomes change. As the size of the community in which you reside changes, your life also changes.

Associations

A person who lives in an urban or rural context will tend to be a member of different voluntary associations (organizations formed to pursue a specific goal). Clubs for nuclear scientists exist almost exclusively in urban areas. In contrast, rural community members are more likely to be members of the Farm Bureau, 4-H Club, and American Legion associations. Participation in a voluntary association is also influenced by income. Although wealthy farmers tend to belong to the Republican Party, those who are less prosperous may align with the Democratic Party.

The church to which one belongs and the frequency of church attendance also vary by urban or rural residence. Jewish synagogues and Catholic churches are more prevalent in urban areas; Baptist and Methodist churches are more prevalent in rural areas. Regardless of the denomination of the church, attendance is higher in rural than urban areas because there is less competition with other activities in rural areas. Rural churches also draw a higher percentage of women and the elderly than do urban churches. Hence, where one lives has a dramatic impact on the nature and frequency of voluntary association participation.

Networks

Networks tie together one or more social organizations through a common set of activities. The urban area provides a clear illustration of networks. Liebow's (1967) *Tally's Corner* reveals the intricate network of black men who meet regularly in front of the carry-out shop on Tally's Corner in Washington, D.C. and share information about jobs, medical facilities, and rooming houses. Not all of these men may live in the immediate community but congregate at Tally's Corner to share information, resources, and companionship.

Networks may be localized as on a street corner or in a bar. Gay individuals in both large and small communities also establish networks of mutual support and assistance. Most communities will have a particular bar which is known to gays as the place they can meet and connect with others of similar lifestyle throughout the gay network. If someone needs to know of job opportunities where the employers do not discriminate against gay people, they can usually find this information at the network center (the gay bar).

Networks may also involve technology which links rural and urban areas. One of the reasons for the decreasing number of differences between people in rural and urban areas is that communication and transportation networks link the two geographically separated areas.

Societies

Depending on whether the society is capitalist, communist, or socialist, the development of communities will vary. In capitalist societies, wealthy individuals can buy up a large area of a small community, build houses, and sell them to the highest bidder. There may be very little long term planning and those from the small communities who are displaced by the buyout may be accorded little concern.

Communist societies are more organized in the development of their communities. In the past, they would not allow individuals or groups of individuals to buy up land and establish a community. Rather, representatives of the state would decide whether a community would be developed, where it should be built, and determine the size, number, and nature of the buildings to be erected. Nothing would be left to chance; everything would be planned. If people from small communities were to be displaced, some concern would theoretically be given to them.

Socialist societies would allow control at neither extreme. Rather, a blend of top and bottom input would be allowed to produce the desired community. Communities must take into account the needs of all citizens, and society not only limits the rights of those with money, but also the losses that can be experienced by those who are poor. Communities in socialist societies are more controlled so that they serve more of society's general needs.

References

Bock, J. D. 2000. "Doing the Right Thing? Single Mothers by Choice and the Struggle for Legitimacy." *Gender and Society*, 14: 62–86.

Bunger, B. 2008. Personal communication. Department of Anthropology, East Carolina University.

Cohan, C. L., and S. Kleinbaum. 2002. "Toward a Greater Understanding of the Cohabitation Effect: Premarital Cohabitation and Marital Communication." *Journal of Marriage and the Family*, 64: 180–92.

Gottman, J. M., R. W. Levenson, C. Swanson, K. Swanson, R. Tyson, and D. Yoshimoto. 2003. "Observing Gay, Lesbian, and Heterosexual Couples' Relationships: Mathematical Modeling of Conflict Interaction." *Journal of Homosexuality*, 45: 65–91.

Heaton, T. B. and R. Forste. 2008. "Domestic Violence, Couple Interaction and Children's Health in Latin America." *Journal of Family Violence*, 23: 183–194.

Hoyt, H. 1943. "The Structure of American Cities in the Post-War Era." *American Journal of Sociology,* 48: 475–492.

Jones, L. 2008. "The Distinctive Characteristics and Needs of Domestic Violence Victims in a Native American Community." *Journal of Family Violence,* 23: 113–119.

Kurdek, L. A. 1994. "Conflict Resolution Styles in Gay, Lesbian, Heterosexual Nonparent, and Heterosexual Parent Couples." *Journal of Marriage and the Family,* 56: 705–22.

Kwan, Y. K. 2008. "Life Satisfaction and Family Structure among Adolescents in Hong Kong." *Social Indicators Research,* 86: 59–68.

Leininger, L. J. and K. M. Ziol-Guest. 2008. "Re-examining the Effects of Family Structure on Children's Access to Care: The Single-Father Family." *Health Services Research,* 43: 117–125.

Liebow, E.1967. *Tally's Corner.* Boston: Little, Brown and Co.

Messer, K., D. R. Trinidad, W. K. Al-Delaimy and J. P. Pierce. 2008. "Smoking Cessation Rates in the United States: A Comparison of Young Adult and Older Smokers." *American Journal of Public Health,* 98: 317–323.

Michael, R. T., J. H. Gagnon, E. O. Laumann, and G. Kolata. 1994. *Sex in America.* Boston: Little, Brown.

Murdock, George P. 1949. *Social Structure.* New York: MacMillan.

Peen, J., J. Dekker, R. A. Schoevers, M.T. Have, et al. 2007. "Social Psychiatry and Psychiatric Epidemiology." *Dordrecht,* 42: 984–290.

Rogers, E. M., R. B. Burdge, P. F. Korsching, and J.F. Donnermeyer. 1988. *Social Change in Rural Societies* (third edition). Englewood Cliffs, New Jersey: Prentice-Hall.

Statistical Abstract of the United States: 2008. 127th ed. Washington, D.C.: U.S. Bureau of the Census.

Stockwell, R. J. 2003. "Growing a Modern Agrarian Myth: The American Agriculture Movement, Identity, and the Call to Save the Family Farm." Thesis, Miami University.

Teachman, J. 2003. "Premarital Sex, Premarital Cohabitation, and the Risk of Subsequent Marital Disruption among Women." *Journal of Marriage and the Family,* 65: 444–455.

Twenge, J. M., W. K. Campbell, and C. A. Foster. 2003. "Parenthood and Marital Satisfaction: A Meta-analytic Review." *Journal of Marriage and Family,* 65: 574–83.

Valdez, A., A. Neaigus, and C. D. Kaplan. 2008. "The Influence of Family and Peer Risk Networks on Drug Use Practices and Other Risks among Mexican American Noninjecting Heroin Users." *Journal of Contemporary Ethnography,* 37: 79–93.

Webb, F. J. 2005. "The New Demographics of Families." In *Sourcebook of Family Theory & Research*, edited by Vern L. Bengtson, Alan C. Acock, Katherine R. Allen, Peggye Dilworth-Anderson, and David M. Klein. Thousand Oaks, California: Sage Publications, 101–02.

Wright, B. 2007. "Discrimination Is Not in the Best Interest of Children." *Alternatives to Marriage*, Update # 3-2007, p. 1.

Chapter 11

Education and Religion

Education is a progressive discovery of our ignorance.

Will Durant, U.S. author and historian

Religions are many and diverse, but reason and goodness are one.
Elbert Hubbard, American writer

The hope of most parents is that their child will be both educated and moral. The social organizations of education and religion function to meet these goals. In this chapter we examine how each of these associations interacts with other social organizations. We begin with an examination of the educational association.

Education: The Formal Socialization Agency

Education in American society is provided by a formal organization delegated this specific responsibility. Below we define education and how it affects other social organizations.

Definition of Education

Education is the formal mechanism of socialization created to teach people in a society its culture, skills, values, and knowledge of the world. The goal of education is to enable the young to fit into society. The target is almost 50 million children in America attending the almost 100,000 public schools (pre-kindergarten through grade 12) (2010 estimate) (*Statistical Abstract of the United States: 2008*, Table 209).

Formal Organizational Association

As a social organization, the educational association has positions, norms, and roles. Positions include principal, teacher, and student. The norms for teachers include the expectation that they are kind and respectful to students, develop lesson plans, and give tests. Roles involve how the different positions perform their jobs. Students attend class, study for tests, and take tests.

The formal structure of the school system also involves a State Board of Education, a superintendent of education, a local school board, principal, and teachers. All of these elements are coordinated to insure that the basic functions of education are accomplished.

While the formal way of identifying objectives is through the State Board of Education and teachers, the informal patterns of interaction may be more revealing. For example, the superintendent of education may actually meet in private with the presidents of the local PTAs to find out what issues parents feel need to be addressed.

Bureaucratic Structure

The formal bureaucratic structure of education involves various characteristics such as the division of labor, hierarchy of authority, technical competence, written rules, documents, and impersonal relationships (Weber, 1946). Administrators and teachers are delegated specific responsibilities—e.g. administrators are to ensure that funds are available for teacher salaries and supplies while teachers are responsible for assigning the grades students earn.

The hierarchy of authority is also specified. Students are to report to teachers, teachers to principals, and principals to the local school board. Technical competence is also required. Teachers are expected to be certified in the areas in which they teach and secretaries in the administrative office are expected to be able to type so many words per minute.

The educational bureaucracy also involves rules that administrators, teachers, and students are expected to follow. Administrators must hire and fire according to specific guidelines, teachers must give grades according to a specified pattern of performance, and students are expected to attend class so many days per year. The impersonal relationships in the bureaucracy may sometimes supersede formal rules. For example, health teachers may excuse students from class the day after an athletic event although technically it may be against school policy.

Structure of Education in the U.S.

The structure of education in the U.S. involves various age levels of students, ownership of the schools, credentialing, separation of church and state, etc.

Elementary, Secondary, and College

The American educational association is structured into three basic grade groupings: elementary (kindergarten or first through sixth grade), secondary (seventh through twelfth grade), and higher education (post-secondary, including vocational, college/university, and professional training such as law or medicine). Table 11.1 reflects the projected enrollments for 2016 in the public elementary schools (includes kindergarten through grade 8), secondary schools (grades 9 through 12), and colleges.

Table 11.1
Projected Enrollment in Public Educational Associations for 2016

Pre-K through grade 8	9 through 12	College
37,917,000	15,382,000	15,186,000

Source: *Statistical Abstract of the United States: 2008*. 127th ed. Washington, D.C.: U.S. Bureau of the Census. Table 207.

Public, Private, and Alternatives

The educational system is also structured into different arenas such as public, private, and alternative school systems.

Over 46 million children in America attend the 97,000 public schools (prekindergarten through grade 12) (2010 estimate) (*Statistical Abstract of the United States: 2008*, Table 209). Because the schools are public, there is little direct cost to parents as books and transportation are provided by the state (total expenditure on public school education is $495 billion each year) (*Statistical Abstract of the United States: 2008*, Table 208).

The curriculum of public schools reflects the interests of society in general. Because these social, economic, and political interests are constantly changing, the curriculum is always being debated (e.g. should sex education be a part of the public school education, should evolution or "intelligent design" be taught?).

About 15 percent of children in the elementary and secondary schools attend private schools (Table 207). Parents send their children to private school to ensure a particular brand of religious instruction (Parochial—Catholic, Jewish, Fundamentalist, Protestant), to place them in a more regimented academic environment (military school), to avoid racial minorities, and/or to increase their exposure to a particular academic subject (French, mathematics). Today, the primary reason parents send their children to private school is religious, since parents want to increase the control they have over their children's values. Some fundamentalist Protestants abhor what they view as an emphasis in the public school system on **secular humanism** (the belief that gives emphasis to a person's ability to interpret and guide his or her own moral actions) and want their children to value adherence to a higher spiritual authority for their guidance and decisions in their life.

Other parents feel that the public school system is no longer effective in teaching their children how to read and write and enroll their students in private schools to help ensure the academic integrity of their child's high school diploma. Most private schools which advertise for students emphasize that their students make higher grades than those in the public school sector.

Alternative school systems are also private. Also called **free schools**, **alternative schools** developed out of the desire on the part of parents and teachers to organize a curriculum based on student choice and interest. Education is conceptualized as using the interest of the student as a springboard to learning. For example, a student who expressed an interest in the milk he or she had for breakfast would be guided by the teacher to find out about the chemistry of milk and how it is produced and marketed. Groups of students might visit a dairy and talk to farmers.

Summerhill, established in 1923 in England by A. S. Neill, is one of the early free schools. Its premise was that the social context of traditional schools which were characterized by authority and discipline created a destructive and aggressive personality. In contrast, children who were educated in a less restrictive environment and who were allowed to determine what they studied would develop more peaceful personalities.

Alternative schools flourished in the United States during the 1920s and included the Modern School in New Jersey and Manumit School in Pawling, New York. In 2005, there were 4,847 alternative schools teaching 1.1 percent of school age children (*Statistical Abstract of the United States: 2008*, Table 232).

Forced Educational Socialization

In addition to the public, private, and alternative educational structures, our society has a forced educational system. Students are required to attend an approved school from age six through 16. Students who do not attend are considered truant, and the parents and students are held liable for the truancy. Compulsory school attendance is based on the belief that our urbanized, industrialized, technologically advanced society is best served by ensuring that the members of our society have the knowledge and skills which will allow them to function and to contribute to our society. Otherwise, our citizens will not be capable of reading road signs, a menu, or instructions on how to take medicine or operate machines.

Separation of Church and State

Officially, there is a separation between public education and the teaching of religious values. According to the First Amendment of the Constitution: "Congress shall make no law respecting an establishment of religion, or prohibiting the free exercise thereof."

The attempt to separate religion and education is difficult because both are concerned with the moral and social development of the individual. For example, does allowing prayer in the public school system help to ensure a well socialized "moral" citizen or help to indoctrinate individuals with a particular brand of religion? Also, requiring students to say the Pledge of Allegiance (which includes the words "One nation, under God ...") helps to provide a sense of national pride, but also emphasizes a religious and theistic world view. Does allowing members of a particular religion to meet on school property after school imply tolerance for religion or state support for religion? In general, the courts have attempted to keep any semblance of formal religious training out of the curriculum and any expression of religious ceremony off of school property.

Paid Educators and Credentialing

The state maintains control over the educational process through payment and credentialing. Paid teachers must teach according to various professional and ethical guidelines or they can be fired. Individuals who want to teach must be certified and pass the appropriate tests so as to be credentialed. In setting standards and creating guidelines, the state develops penalties which maintain order and control what teachers do on their jobs.

Basics versus Progressive Educational Curriculum

Dead Poets Society, a classic film for which Robin Williams was nominated for best actor, emphasized the confusion over values in the educational system. Is education the imparting of specific skills such as reading, writing, and math or is it the development of minds who critically analyze? Mr. Keating (the role played by Robin Williams) viewed the mission of the school system as the latter. In one scene, he stood on his desk (and asked his students to do likewise) to illustrate that doing something unconventional provides a different perspective. In another scene, Mr. Keating and the headmaster clashed over the school's mission (individuality versus tradition).

There is constant conflict about what schools should teach. The clash centers around the relative need for students to have courses in the basic skills (English and math) versus the need for courses on art, human relationships, and human sexuality. Some argue that the latter courses are "fluff" and only weaken the value of a high school diploma. Others argue that academic programs which do not include socialization in humanity and in relationships are misguided.

Outcomes of Education

There are various consequences for students who progress through the educational system.

Scholastic Achievement

To what degree do schools achieve their basic mission of teaching young people the basic skills of how to read, write, and calculate? When a random sample of Americans was asked, "Overall, how satisfied are you with the quality of education students receive in kindergarten through grade twelve in the U.S. today?" over half responded "somewhat dissatisfied" or "completely dissatisfied" (Gallup 2007). Consistent with the public's concern is the recent emphasis on educational reform in the wake of low academic achievement, high dropout rates, questionable teacher training, and school violence. A recent report by the National Assessment of Adult Literacy (NAAL) described the literacy abilities of a representative sample of U.S. adults 16 years of age or older (NAAL 2007). Three types of literacy were measured— *prose* (e.g. reading a newspaper article), *document* (e.g. reading a transportation schedule), and *quantitative* (e.g. balancing a checkbook)—and evaluated. Data for 2003 revealed that approximately 30 million people in the U.S. are estimated to have below basic literacy skills including seven million non-English speakers. And, 25% of 15-year-old U.S. students failed "to demonstrate the most basic mathematical skills." The result? Fifteen-year-olds in U.S. schools placed 27th out of 30 countries on mathematical achievement (Schleicher, 2006).

Another implication of poor scholastic achievement is the extent to which local schools hide the poor performance of their students. While teachers are not to know the content of the standardized tests, some teachers have been observed "peeking" at the tests to get an unfair early advantage by seeing actual test questions. In rare cases, teachers get a copy of the standardized tests students take and teach them the items on the test and the correct answers. With this specific instruction, the students score high on the national exams, the school looks good, and the school receives an economic bonus for the high student scores.

The characteristics of schools that graduate students "on time" with high academic achievement has been identified. These characteristics include an emphasis on academics rather than sports; parents who volunteer to help in the classroom; a curriculum which reflects the basics rather than fluff courses; and strict attendance requirements. Schools which graduate students who score poorly on standardized tests place greater emphasis on sports, have little parental participation, have a plethora of "fluff" courses, and are lax in their attendance requirements.

Occupational Success, Income, and Mobility

In general, the more a person learns (as defined by an academic degree), the more the person earns. For example, a person studying in the social sciences who earns a bachelor's, master's, and doctorate in 2006 earns $32,134, $42,220, and $48,487 respectively (*Statistical Abstract of the United States: 2008*, Table 291). However, the social conditions of market demand, gender, and race affect the income consequences of earning a particular degree. The greater the number of college degrees, the lower their value. Today, a woman with the same identical education as a man only earns 73 cents for every dollar the man earns. Non-whites are discriminated against in hiring and salary even when their education is identical to whites.

Political Attitudes

One of the goals of education is to socialize individuals in society to be productive citizens. This goal became particularly necessary in the 1890s when large numbers of immigrants began to enter the United States from southern and eastern Europe. **Americanization** involved teaching immigrants the laws, language, and customs of the United States. With the coming of World War I (1917), the Pledge of Allegiance, the singing of patriotic songs, the participation in student government, and other patriotic exercises became a part of the

American school. With the increasing number of immigrants (both legal and illegal) now living in America, the issue of the role of education in Americanization has been revived.

Popular Beliefs and Scientific Data: The Myth of Education and Equality

All associations develop myths to justify their existence. Just as there is the myth in the military association ("The Marine Corps Builds Men") and in the family association ("Two Can Live as Cheaply as One"), there are myths in the educational association as well.

One myth in education is that *education is the great equalizer in our society*.

This myth involves the belief that success can be achieved by making good grades which will allow one entry into the high status, high income professions. Although a person may be born into a poor minority family (so the myth goes), hard work in the educational system will elevate one out of the ghetto. The emphasis of this myth is on the individual. Since the educational association offers the same opportunities for everyone (according to the myth), anyone with intelligence and motivation can overcome his or her impoverished circumstance.

The reality is very different. Olson (1986) observed that students who make good grades are more likely to come from homes in which the parents have high incomes. "The myth of equal opportunity therefore masks an ugly truth: the educational system is really a loaded social lottery, by which each student gets as many chances as his or her parents have dollars" (McLaren, 1989, 224).

> *The real issue is that the education system gives those who begin with certain advantages (the right economic status and thus the right values, the right speech patterns, the right mannerism, the right behavior) a better chance to retain those advantages all through school, and ensures that minority and economically disadvantaged students will remain at the bottom rung of the meritocratic ladder* (p. 224).

In addition, economically disadvantaged and minority students are viewed as not blending into the educational system that is offered. They are labeled as "deviant," "pathological," or "impulse-ridden." If they would only stop being so resistant and accept what they are being taught (so the argument goes), they would get good educations.

McLaren (1989) observed that the problem is more a need to change the educational system than to blame the student. As McLaren stated:

Schools foster programs to correct these problems, to build up the skills and attitudes of ghetto children, to make up for their so-called cultural deficits and motivate their lazy, apathetic souls—rather than considering structural changes in the wider society, changes in school policy, negative teacher feeling, or curriculum implementation that might be exacerbating the problems in the first place. This again amounts to blaming students for their own miseducation (p. 224).

Theoretical Views of Education

Sociologists use various theories to explain the educational system.

Functional Theory

Functionalists emphasize how the educational association benefits society. Some of these benefits include socialization, social control, status maintenance, and occupational placement. In the chapter on socialization, we noted the importance of teaching new members of society the values, norms, and skills that are necessary to function in society. Prior to industrialization, children grew up next to their parents who provided a constant source of learning for their offspring. With the advent of factories and parents spending more time out of the home (90% of fathers and over 60% of mothers now work outside the home), a consistent alternative method of socialization was necessary. This method was the educational system via schools.

Education also exercises social control over all young people by requiring that they attend school six and half hours each day for twelve years. Such a large block of time ensures that they are not roaming the streets during the day, and "homework" helps to ensure that they will have structured time in the evenings.

The status maintenance function implies that high status parents can send their children to private schools to ensure their isolation from other social classes and to prepare them for upper class Ivy League schools. The occupational placement function of education involves the earning of credentials necessary to enter specific occupations.

Conflict Theory

Conflict characterizes the educational association. Among the conflicts include:

1. Language—Should courses be taught in English or some other language? (Hispanics in southern California and other western states argue that their children should be taught in Spanish. Opponents argue that English is the only language that should be used to teach American students.)

2. Religion—Should prayer be required, allowed, or banned in the public school system?

3. Private schools—Should the government subsidize private schools? Should tax credits be allowed for parents who send their children to private schools?

4. Bussing—Should children be allowed to attend the school nearest to them or should they be bussed across town to meet racial quotas?

5. Curriculum—Should schools include art, music appreciation, marriage and the family, or sex education in their curriculums? Should "Little Life's Lessons" be taught (Parish and Rothmeyer, 2007)?

6. Grades—Should grades be the focus of education? Ogden (2007) traces the evolution of education in America and questions our emphasis on test scores as the final indicator of school success. Indeed, he suggests that the love of learning might be a worthy goal.

Another conflict has been in reference to the "No Child Left Behind" initiative begun during the second Bush administration. Henley et al. (2007) noted:

> *The No Child Left Behind Legislation has altered the landscape of elementary schools across the nation. This alteration has left many educators and parents wondering whether children are being robbed of their childhood in order to meet the legislation's many mandates. Across the nation, traditional school days, instructional programs, and programs such as recess, music, and art, along with programs for the gifted and educationally disabled, have been eliminated or altered beyond recognition.* (p. 56)

Henley et al (2007) suggest that there is considerable harm to students in the wake of the "No Child Left Behind" initiative.

Interactionist Theory

Interactionists emphasize that the interaction between teachers and students influences the learning experience of students. Students from lower socioeconomic backgrounds may feel less approval from middle class teachers than students from similar middle class backgrounds. Their incentive to learn may not be nurtured with the effect that they are more likely to drop out.

Other Theories: Exchange and Dramaturgical

Functional, conflict, and interactionist theories are not the only approaches in sociology that attempt to explain education. Exchange theory and dramaturgical theory are additional theoretical perspectives.

Exchange theory focuses on the degree to which time, energy, and cost in gaining educational credentials is viewed as worth the job satisfaction, status, and income which may result from the education experience. As noted earlier, there is a positive relationship between education and income. There is a similar association between education and high status jobs. Entry into the roles of physician, attorney, and university professor require extensive post graduate training. The relationship between education and job satisfaction is less clear than the association between education and income. Some occupational roles require extensive training but may not yield commensurate occupational satisfaction. For example, extensive training is necessary to become a psychiatrist. Yet psychiatrists have a higher suicide rate than most other professionals and there is little evidence that those who enter this profession are satisfied with their decision. In contrast, university professors who spend from five to seven years in graduate school report a very high level of job satisfaction.

Dramaturgical theory looks at the roles individuals play in the educational context. Both teacher and student are expected to act as though they are interested in being in class. While each may prefer to be somewhere else, the image each presents to the other is one of interest. In dramaturgical theory, the explanation for success or failure in the educational system depends on how participants play out their roles. If they play them out well, they are more successful, even if they may not learn much during the experience.

Educational Associations and Social Organization

The theme of this book is that context influences outcome. The educational association represents a social context which results in certain outcomes. The ways in which the educational association influences other social organizations, or is influenced by them, follows.

Population

The educational association is affected by the population of students who make demands on it. The baby boom generation dumped a larger number of individuals on the school system than it was prepared to handle. When the first group of baby boomers graduated in 1964, they had lower SAT (Scholastic Aptitude Test) scores than students had the year before. These scores continued to decline until 1982 when the last of the baby boomers graduated.

In the years to come, racial and ethnic populations will outnumber whites for the first time. The effect on education will be to question the language and courses of the curriculum—should classes be taught in Spanish? At stake at the college level is whether the traditional 'cannon' of Greek, Latin and West European humanities study should be expanded to reflect the cultures of Africa, Asia, and other parts of the world. Many books treasured as classics by prior generations are now seen as not representing the larger world culture.

Collective Behavior

Just as there are fads in music and dress, there are fads in education. Speed reading was a fad of the fifties. Students were expected to take speed reading classes in which they were to learn how to read paragraphs and pages at a glance. Woody Allen made fun of this in his quip, "I read *War and Peace* last night. It was about Russia."

A current fad is the idea that every child in every school needs a computer. This idea is being fostered by computer manufacturers who would like each of the 45 million plus students in the 97,000 public schools to have one of their "computer friendly" machines (at state expense).

Social Class

Schools that serve low socioeconomic districts are largely overcrowded and understaffed, less likely to have teachers with advanced degrees, more likely to have higher rates of teacher turnover, and more likely to lack adequate building space and learning materials (CDF 2004; Viadero 2006; Price 2007).

Tracking and ability-grouping are the primary mechanisms which keep the respective social classes on different educational paths. **Tracking** refers to separating students into college preparatory, vocational, or general curriculums. **Ability-grouping** refers to similar curriculum grouping based on the student's individual ability. Students of higher social class background are tracked into college preparatory courses whereas students of lower social class background are tracked into vocational courses. Students who make good grades are tracked into academic curriculums and keep their advantage until they graduate.

Race is also associated with performance in the educational system. As race and ethnic background in America is an indication of class, Table 11.2 shows the educational attainment by race for persons age 25 years and older for 2006.

Table 11.2
Educational Attainment and Race

Level	Race	Percent
High school graduate	White	86.1%
	Black	80.7%
	Hispanic	59.3%
College graduate or beyond	White	28.4%
	Black	18.5%
	Hispanic	12.4%

Source: *Statistical Abstract of the United States: 2008.* 127th ed. Washington, D.C.: U.S. Bureau of the Census. Table 217.

Groups

Education may provide a social context within which groups form. Small groups of students may form within classrooms which affect educational outcomes. Brighter students seek each other out, study together, and set a high academic bar for the class. Similarly, less advantaged students form their own groups and cope with the escalating academic demands.

Teachers form their own small groups and are drawn to each other on the basis of their age, subject they teach, or number of years taught. Their lives are affected by school structure—what they wear, the absence of tattoos/piercings, and when they can go home.

Families

Families with low incomes have fewer resources to commit to the education of their children. Low-income families have less money to purchase books, computers, and tutors. They also have less money to spend on activities such as dance and music lessons and are less likely to take their children to museums and zoos (Rothstein 2004). Parents in low-income brackets are also less likely to "expect their children to go to college," and this expectation on the part of parents may lead to a self-fulfilling prophecy in their children ("I'm not college material").

Communities

The amount of money spent on a child in the public school system varies by community. Since some of the money for schools comes from the local community, expensive homes in certain communities yield a great deal of tax income while very modest homes in other communities yield meager tax income for the schools in the respective areas. The presence or absence of local industry will also affect local tax money available for schools.

School attendance also varies by community. In rural farming communities, school attendance is lower than in urban areas. Children are needed to "work the fields," and education takes a lower priority. In some states, children are let out of school so that they can work the crops and bring them to the market on time.

Associations

The educational association is in conflict with other associations such as religion. The Amish have objected to the requirement by the public school system that girls wear shorts for physical education. They also have objected to the high school curriculum which includes critical thinking and asking questions. Rather, the Amish emphasize obedience and tradition. The conflict between the Amish and public schools resulted in a case heard by the Supreme Court (State of Wisconsin, *Petitioner v. Jonas Yoder et al.*,) in which the court decided that Amish children would not be required to go to public school beyond the eighth grade. Most Amish have their own private schools and their children, for religious reasons, do not continue after the eighth grade.

Networks

Educational networks are necessary for the system to function. Students who move from one community to the next may request that their transcripts be sent to the new school. Without a network linking the respective educational associations, it would be impossible to move between these associations. Students may begin their educations in a private school in California, move and continue in a religious school in Idaho, and then move to New York City to complete their education in a public school. If the network functions, they may lose a few credits, but should not be at a major disadvantage in timely completion of high school.

Societies

Many societies have no formal mechanism for educating the masses. There are 781 million illiterate adults around the world, and 100 million children who have little or no access to formal education (UNESCO 2005, 2006). Where formal education exists, there is a wide range of effects worldwide with some countries educating their population longer and some not very long at all. For example, the average years of schooling for those over the age of 15 in China is 6.4 years, in India, 5.1 years, in Iraq, 4 years, and in the Sudan, 2.1 years (Nationmaster 2006).

Societies vary in regard to how they provide education for their citizens. Japan hires professionals to develop and implement a national curriculum and to administer nationwide financing for its schools. In the United States schools are often run at the local level by school boards, and parent teacher organizations and associations are composed of laypeople. In effect, local communities raise their own funds and develop their own policies for operating the school system in their area. There can be no doubt, change the society and you change the outcomes for education and vice versa.

In addition to education which emphasizes the socialization of societal members, we examine the association of religion which exists for the purpose of providing information about how to relate to the supernatural. In the following pages, we look at how religion varies by culture and how religion impacts other social organizations.

Religion Defined

We have noted that associations are social organizations that are created for the attainment of specific common goals, that associations are a context, and that contexts create outcomes. As a person's religion changes, so will the thoughts, attitudes, and behaviors of that person. Aside from these general statements, what is religion?

What Is Religion?

As a social organization, **religion** is an association created for the purpose of relating to the supernatural and for providing meaning for society's members. Religion may be best understood by looking at its various elements which include sacredness, beliefs, and rituals.

1. Sacredness. Durkheim (1858–1917) emphasized the dichotomy of the sacred and the profane. That which is **sacred** refers to the spiritual, supernatural, and transcendental. The transcendental refers to an ultimate power to which the person gives deference. This ultimate power is assumed to know everything and can be responsible for the creation and order of the universe. Harrison (2008) studied Southern gospel music and noted that it "seems to

trample the intellect and stampede straight to the heart, the soul, the spirit...." (p. 36). In contrast, the **profane** refers to the everyday world—the empirical and the scientific. The Bible is sacred; an iPod is profane.

2. Beliefs. Religion also involves an acceptance of certain beliefs on the part of a social actor as he or she relates to the sacred. Catholics believe in the immaculate conception of Mary, Jews believe that they are the chosen people of God, and Hindus believe in reincarnation.

3. Rituals. All religions have various rituals or ceremonies which are designed to communicate with the supernatural (e.g. prayer and meditation) and to provide a social bond for their members. In regard to the latter, communion in the Protestant church is designed to bond believers together who share the sacrament.

Formal Religious Organizations

As long as religion is conceptualized as an individual and personal experience, sociologists have no interest. However, when religion is conceptualized as a set of beliefs or rituals about the sacred that are shared with other members, a social organization has evolved, and the sociologist becomes interested. The sociologist examines the ways in which a group of people formalize and systematize their behaviors in reference to the sacred and set up mechanisms to recruit and maintain others in the religious organization.

Hence, formal religious organizations consist of individuals who are bound together into an association for the purpose of achieving specific goals such as getting into heaven. The organization then develops rituals which allow members to communicate with the supernatural (prayer) and allow members to progress toward heaven. For Baptists, such progression involves "giving their heart to Jesus by professing Him before the congregation as Lord and Savior."

In addition to getting people into heaven, religious organizations must make money to survive. Watch one of the religious services on television and notice the pleas for money—"love offerings," "help us reach others for Jesus," and "send in your money for a prayer towel" are all designed to garner economic support. (A country western song mocks the commercial aspect of religion by asking "If this money is for Jesus, why am I making the check out to you?").

Although religion is most often thought of as providing a context for understanding "God and the supernatural", from a sociological perspective, a God-centered belief is not a central element of religion. Rather, a sense of the sacred, beliefs, and rituals make up a "religion." Robert Bellah (1967) describes civil religion in America as a system of symbols, values, beliefs, and practices which give sacred meaning to a nation and its people. Nationalism or patriotism are not "religions" in the traditional sense but provide a framework of meaning for members of a society, that serves the purpose of a foundation of morality and social cohesion. Therefore, even in secular nations, where there is (at least in theory) a separation of church and state, a form of religion (civil) surfaces which meets a basic need of the larger community.

Major Western Religions

Less than 15 percent of adult Americans identify themselves as having "no religion." Of those identifying with the Christian religion (160 million), 68% identify as Protestant and 32% as Catholic. Of the almost 8 million "other" religious members, 36% identify as Jewish, 14% as Muslim/Islamic and 13% as Buddhist (*Statistical Abstract of the United States: 2008*, Table 74).

Our focus will be on the degree to which behaviors and perceptions are influenced by the social context of the respective western religions.

Protestantism

Different churches within the protestant faith teach a different doctrine. As an example, if we focus on the approximately 35 million members of the Baptist church we find a complete set of beliefs that will differ from others within Protestantism. Strict Baptists give a tenth of their income ("the tithe is the Lord's") to the church, do not drink alcohol, and believe that baptism is the necessary ritual to profess one's conversion experience. Baptists also believe that they will go to heaven if they "accept Jesus Christ as their personal Savior" and will go to hell if they reject Jesus Christ.

Catholicism

There are about 60 million Catholics. Members are socialized to go to "mass" on Sunday morning, to go to confession, and to use no artificial means of birth control. Catholics are also taught to give special reverence to Mary, the mother of Jesus. They believe that their souls go to purgatory at death and may be prayed to heaven by those who remain. The important aspect of beliefs is that they influence outcomes.

Judaism

Jews are socialized to believe that God exists for all people, not just Jews. They also believe that they have been chosen to bring the message of love, a need for social justice and the ethical code of the Ten Commandments. Traditional Jews put on a sacred robe, pray daily and read the *Talmud* (sixty-three volumes of tradition that explains every act that an orthodox Jew should perform). Jews wish to keep kosher, where meat is carefully prepared and blessed in the traditional way, separating milk products from meat products, with no pork permitted. They believe that following traditions that go back thousands of years have created a culture prepared for survival and based on knowledge.

Cultural Differences in Religion

The various religions differ by content and religious leaders. These differences are important in considering why individual social actors raised in different religious backgrounds become very different after their socialization.

Symbols, Values, Norms, Rituals, and Sanctions

Symbols are concrete artifacts which are given meaning by a particular group. Symbols are useful in creating a social bond among group members who share them. For example, symbols among the Sikhs who practice Sikhism in Punjab, India, include long hair, turbans, a wooden comb in the hair, a bracelet on the right wrist, and special underwear called Kachhehra. Similarly, Catholics identify with a statue of the Virgin Mary, and Jews identify with a small hat called a yarmulke. A wooden gate called a torii is the symbol of those who practice Shintoism; the wheel is an important symbol in Buddhism.

Values, standards of behavior which guide how a person is to behave, also vary by religious association. Traditional Southern Baptists believe in virginity before marriage, no alcohol, and no dancing. Muslims embrace and enjoy their sexuality, but only within the context of marriage. And, for Muslims, only vaginal intercourse is acceptable (oral and anal sex are not).

There are other ways in which religious values impact societies. In Egypt, where 84% of the population is Muslim, and the other 16% are Coptic Christians (the largest Christian church in Egypt and a part of Orthodox Christianity, but with its own particular notions about the nature of Christ), the crime rate is extremely low. This can be traced to the fact that both Islam and Copticism prohibit alcohol consumption (some Muslims refuse to even handle alcohol unless their employment in the tourism industry requires it). This means alcohol and drug abuse are almost non-existent social problems in Egypt, and subsequently, crime that is often associated with those behaviors in the U.S. (theft, drinking and driving, physical assault) doesn't exist in Egypt. These different values create differences in how religious people live out their lives and make demands upon other social organizations, from society to communities.

Norms are also different in various religious associations. Muslims pray five times a day. Amish don't own cars. Evangelicals wave their hands in the air and speak in tongues during a church service.

Rituals in the Catholic Church (communion, lighting candles) are different from those in the Jewish synagogue (carrying a Torah scroll, reading in Hebrew, and chanting).

Sanctions also vary from eternal damnation to feeling guilty when you don't follow the values of the religion. Catholics take the position that abortion is a mortal sin which jeopardizes one's soul. Unitarians are less likely to view abortion as a spiritual transgression and, therefore, do not assign a spiritual consequence. The Amish "shun" a member who disobeys one of their norms (going into business with someone outside the Amish community). Such shunning involves the entire community not speaking to the person who has violated the norms of the group.

Religious Leaders

Cultural differences in religion are not limited to symbols, values, rituals, norms, and sanctions. Each religion has its own leader or leaders as prophets, messiahs, founders, and has developed a set of functionaries who carry out the work of the association. **Prophets** are charismatic leaders who construct a new vision for people to follow and from whom a sacred text evolved. Moses' teachings resulted in the Old Testament, Jesus' in the New Testament, and the *Qu'ran* was revealed to Muhammad. Muslims regard Moses and Jesus as Prophets, as well as Muhammad. However, they believe the Holy *Qu'ran* (the final word of God) was revealed to Muhammad, who is regarded to have been the *last* Prophet.

Prophets claim to have had a special revelation or visit from God which is designed to give the prophet credibility. The prophet Moses, an Old Testament prophet, claimed to have heard the voice of God and to have been given the Ten Commandments by God. Joseph Smith, prophet of the Mormons, claimed that he was visited by both God the Father and His son Jesus, the Christ.

Messiahs do not represent God but claim to be God. Jesus said, "If you have seen me, you have seen the Father." George Baker, known as Father Devine and who established the Father Devine Movement in the early 1900s, claimed to be God. Local pastors in Valdosta, Georgia, were not impressed and had him declared insane. Messiahs take the position of having ultimate power. Jesus made it clear that people who did not accept Him would end up in hell. Messiahs are important in that they define the norms and sanctions to which followers are to subscribe.

Founders are responsible for beginning a religious group and may be either a prophet or a messiah. Founders sometimes name the religious group or it becomes named after them—Confucius was the founder of Confucianism, Buddha was the founder of Buddhism, and Bhagwan Shree Rajneesh was the founder of Rajneeshpuram, a spiritual commune in central Oregon which was developing into a religion. The survival of the movement is sometimes dependent on the founder. Rajneeshpuram, which began in May of 1981, flourished (several thousand members) in the eighties until their leader left the country in 1984 on charges of arranging fraudulent marriages to enable foreign disciples to stay in the United States. With no leader, Rajneeshpuram soon ceased to exist.

Once a leader of a religious organization surfaces, a group of **functionaries** must emerge to carry out the work of the organization. A church cannot survive with a pastor alone. There must be deacons, music directors, and secretaries. These functionaries ensure that others are recruited to the organization, music is prepared for services, and letters are typed to communicate with the external world. Functionaries not only adopt the values, norms, and sanctions of the religious organization, they script it for other people in the organization. A deacon in the Southern Baptist church is expected to avoid the consumption of alcohol and to "witness" to others (set a good example and encourage others not to drink).

Religion and Social Organization

As an association, religion interacts with other social organizations.

Population

Religion influences the birth rate of its members. Commitment to Catholicism is associated with the use of the "natural family planning" method of birth control with the result that Catholics have higher birth rates and larger families than Protestants.

Different populations are more likely to be involved in the religious association. Those who are elderly, female, and black are more likely to attend church than those who are young, male, and white.

Collective Behavior

Religion may provide the social context within which collective behavior emerges. In April 1984, a night worker was returning home and observed "a large, two dimensional image that he identified as the Virgin Mary" (Duggan, 1990, 84) on a cement wall that forms most of the Starr Presbyterian Church in Royal Oak, Michigan. The next day he told his family and friends, and soon after 25 to 50 people were gathering nightly to observe the scene.

At its peak, about 500 persons gathered nightly to see the apparition of "Our Lady of Royal Oak." Sociologist Thomas J. Duggan visited the scene every second or third night over a period of two months and made some observations on this religious collective behavior. First, he noted that the gatherings on the lawn consisted of small clusters of people who would talk about what they had or had not seen. He characterized the entire group as altruistic—although the members were strangers to each other, they interacted with openness, warmth, and cooperation. Duggan also observed that group roles emerged. "Facilitators" would walk from cluster to cluster to help newcomers identify the place to look on the wall where the images had been seen. As the crowds diminished across time, "cheerleaders" emerged, urging those present to "see" and to believe.

Duggan observed that collective behavior in reference to religious sightings are not unusual. During the year after his participant observation study, he became aware of six such events that had occurred in the northeastern quarter of the United States.

Social Class

Various religious groups attract members of different social classes. Upper class individuals are more likely to attend the Episcopal or Presbyterian churches; members of the lower social classes are more likely to attend the Pentecostal or Church of God. As a person changes his or her social class, he or she is likely to change religious affiliation. The electronic church also draws its audience differentially from the various social class levels. Those who comprise the electronic church tend to be blue-collar, poor, old, less educated, black, and from the South. They are also most likely to be evangelical Protestants by faith which suggests that they are conservative in religious beliefs and values.

Groups

Religion provides a social context within which groups form. Prayer groups meet to pray for a particular individual to get well. Similarly, groups form to visit "shut-ins," to organize the church's Homecoming, and to raise money for the building fund. When a church member dies, a group may form to prepare a meal after the memorial service.

Families

Religions attempt to control family behavior. Religion emphasizes marrying someone of similar faith (religious endogamy), having a large family (Mormons), and attending religious services regularly ("the family that prays together stays together").

The mechanisms of control are parent to child and spouse to spouse socialization. Parents take their children to church, and spouses socialize each other that "we are a family now and want to bring up our children in the church." Children reared in homes where their parents attend church are very likely to attend church themselves.

Religion also affects the probability that a couple will stay married versus get divorced. Mormons are very family oriented and keeping the family together (avoiding divorce) is a strong value. It comes as no surprise that Mormons have lower divorce rates than non-Mormons.

Religion may also affect the health of family members. Some Pentecostal churches encourage their members to handle snakes to prove their faith. Other churches (Christian Scientists) do not believe in medical attention for a physical problem but "pray" for better health (sometimes resulting in death). Religion also serves as a coping mechanism. Lumpkin (2008) studied grandparents who had assumed the role of parents in taking care of their grandchildren and observed that the grandparents used their "faith" to help them cope with the stress of rearing children.

Communities

Churches in rural communities are different from churches in urban communities. Church membership is higher in rural communities than in urban communities (fewer distractions), the physical size of the church in rural communities is smaller than in urban communities (less money), and women are more active in rural churches than in urban churches (fewer career wives and more time). Also, in regard to participation of women, rural churches tend to be more fundamentalist in doctrine which suggests a traditional division of labor between the sexes. Women's place, according to fundamentalist doctrine, is in the home, family, and church.

Small rural communities are also much more likely to have Protestant and Catholic churches; Jewish synagogues are much more likely to be in large urban communities.

Associations

Religion has an effect on all other associations. For example, Alcoholics Anonymous was created to help alcoholics remain sober. While formally denying that it is a religion, AA has elements of religion: ceremonies (meetings) and symbols (chips). AA members accept the existence of a "higher power" which they appeal to for help in overcoming their desire to drink.

Other associations such as drug abuse recovery programs offer "faith-based" programs to help people chart and stabilize a new path in life. Rays of Sonshine in Monroe, Louisiana, helps formerly drug addicted persons by providing them with a place to stay, food, and a faith-based perspective. Faith-based programs have also been used in prisons both in the United States and in Britain (Burnside et al., 2005).

Networks

Religious denominations are connected to each other through networks. When a member of a Baptist church moves to another state, he or she can join a new Baptist church in the new community "by letter." The procedure involves the new church writing to the church in the prospective member's former community and asking for his or her "letter" to verify that the person was a member of that church. Honoring the "letter" for membership in the new church reflects the network between the specific Baptist churches in the larger society.

Societies

Some societies are dominated by religion. Catholicism in Spain, Islam in Iran, and Buddhism in Thailand are examples of how religion dominates a society. The domination is revealed in the religious values that permeate the society. For example, until recently, divorce was not permitted in Spain. In other societies, religion may informally dominate a society. For example, both the U.S. and Egypt are secular (non-religious) nations, at least in theory. However, in both countries, the calendar of holidays revolves around the religious holidays of the dominant religious group. For example, in the U.S., government offices and schools are closed for Christmas Eve and Christmas Day, and many are closed for Good Friday. In Egypt, the holidays (and daily work hours) are centered around Muhammad's birthday, Ramadan, and the celebrations surrounding the Hajj, or holy pilgrimage to Mecca, which all Muslims are required to do. In the U.S., the "weekend" is Saturday and Sunday to allow for Sunday as a day of worship for Christians, whereas in the Middle East, the "weekend" is Friday and Saturday, so Muslims may attend mosque on Friday, and Jews may celebrate the Sabbath from sundown Friday until sundown on Saturday.

Religion may also move a society toward adopting new values. Douglass (2008) noted the degree to which environmental concerns have become evident in Catholic pronouncements. "Papal statements about the environment, stewardship, and moral duties to future generations provide background for interpreting the initiatives in the U.S. Catholic church" (p 117).

References

Burnside, J., N. Loucks, J. R. Adler, and G. Rose. 2005. *My Brother's Keeper: Faith-based Units in Prisons.* United Kingdom: Willan Publishing.

Bellah, Robert Neely. 1967. "Civil Religion in America." *Journal of the American Academy of Arts and Sciences,* 96 (1): 1–21.

CDF. 2004. Educational Resource Disparities for Minority and Low Income Children. Available at http://www.childrensdefense.org/education/resources-disparities.

Douglass, Keith. 2008. "The Greening of American Catholicism: Identity, Conversion, and Continuity." *Religion and American Culture,* 18: 113–143.

Duggan, T. J. 1990. "Our Lady of Royal Oak: The Natural History of an Expressive Crowd." *Sociological Analysis,* 51: 83–89.

Harrison, Douglas. 2008. "Why Southern Gospel Music Matters." *Religion and American Culture,* 18: 27–59.

Henley, J., J. McBride, J. Milligan, and J. Nichols. 2007. "Robbing Elementary Students of Their Childhood: The Perils of No Child Left Behind." *Education,* 128: 56–63.

Lumpkin, J. R. 2008. "Grandparents in a Parental or Near-Parental Role." *Journal of Family Issues,* 29: 357–368.

McLaren, P. 1989. *Life in Schools.* New York: Longman.

Nationmaster. 2006. "Average Years of Schooling of Adults by Country." Educational Statistics. Available at http://www.nationmaster.com/graph/edu.

Ogden, W. R. 2007. "Mountain Climbing, Bridge Building and the Future of American Education." *Education,* 127: 361–368.

Olson, P. 1986. "Methods, Interpretations, and Different Views of Aspirations." *Interchange,* 17: 78.

Parish, T. S. and R. Rothmeyer. 2007. "ABC's of Life's Little Lessons." *Education,* 127: 610–610.

Price, Hugh B. 2007. "Diversity Goals Help Kids in School—and Later in Life." *The Press-Enterprise,* February 16. The Brookings Institution. Available at http://www.brookings.edu.

Rothstein, Richard. 2004. *Class and Schools.* Washington D.C.: Economic Policy Institute.

Schleicher, Andreas. 2006. "Elevating Performance in a Flat World." *Education Week,* 26: 79–82.

Statistical Abstract of the United States: 2008. 127th ed. Washington, D.C.: U.S. Bureau of the Census.

UNESCO (United Nations Educational, Scientific, and Cultural Organization). 2006. "Literacy Statistics." Available at http://www.uis.unesco.org.

UNESCO. 2005. "United Nations Literacy Decade: 2003–2012." Available at http://portal.unesco.org/education/en.

Viadero, Debra. 2006. "Rags to Riches in U.S. Largely a Myth, Scholars Write." *Education Week,* October 25. Available at http://www.edweek.org.

Weber, Max. 1946. *From Max Weber: Essays in Sociology.* Translated and edited by H. Gerth and C. Wright Mills. New York: Oxford University Press.

Chapter 12

Politics and Economics

Government's view of the economy could be summed up in a few short phrases: If it moves, tax it. If it keeps moving, regulate it. And if it stops moving, subsidize it.

Ronald Reagan

Supreme Court rules on abortion
President calls halt to strike
Dow hits all time record
General motors opens plant in Mexico
China buys property in Manhattan

These headlines illustrate that the issues of political and economic associations are the most visible topics in the United States. The latest Supreme Court decisions, presidential acts, Dow Jones average, labor competition in foreign markets, and the purchase of American property by foreign nations are among the foci of the news media. Our political freedoms and economic well-being depend on what happens in the political and economic associations.

Political and economic associations exist for the attainment of certain goals. Political associations are of many kinds—political action groups, democratic and republican parties, and the House of Representatives. Economic associations also come in different varieties—corporations, national accounting firms (H&R Block), and capitalism. Both political and economic associations are part of even larger political and economic institutions and tied into networks that have major effects on our lives. In this chapter we show how political and economic associations and institutions interact. We begin by emphasizing that political associations have their basis in power.

Power, Legitimacy and Authority

Political associations are associations of power. Max Weber defined **power** as the ability of one group to accomplish its goals even against the resistance and resources of competing groups. Power is the raw exercise of the will of one group being imposed on another. Power may involve either legitimate or illegitimate expressions of authority. For example, power is viewed as legitimate authority if it is generally approved of by the members of society. We view the stopping of our cars for sobriety checks and paying taxes as legitimate government mechanisms for helping to keep our highways safe and paved.

Sometimes the exercise of power is viewed as an illegitimate use of authority. When Joseph Stalin controlled the Soviet Union, Beria (the chief of KGB security) is said to have motored through the streets of Moscow pointing out women he wanted picked up and taken to his room for sex. While he had the power to abduct women, the use of such power was regarded as an expression of illegitimate authority.

To sociologists, the sources of power or authority have three bases: traditional, charismatic, and rational-legal.

Traditional

Traditional authority is based on custom. The Pope has power because the role has been associated with power for centuries. Any person occupying the role of Pope is in a position to influence Catholics throughout the world. Similarly, British royalty are given their authority through tradition.

Charismatic

Charismatic authority is based on what are perceived to be stunning qualities of a particular personality. Gandhi, Dr. Martin Luther King, Jr., and John F. Kennedy were regarded as charismatic individuals and were able to influence people to behave in certain ways primarily through the strength of their personalities. Some regard Barack Obama as charismatic (Obamania).

General Charles de Galle, the French leader, was also able to use his charisma to convince his country to form the French Resistance. On June 18, 1940, de Galle made a stirring radio broadcast from London urging French people to contribute to the struggle against the Nazi forces. The people were so moved by his charisma that they acted with strong patriotism.

Rational-Legal

Rational-legal power is embedded in formal law. The Supreme Court has ruled that officers of the law may stop cars on the highway to ascertain if the driver is under the influence of alcohol or drugs. The right of the police officer to stop individuals is embedded in law. It does not come from tradition or the charisma of the officer. Similarly, Congress has given the government the power to tax citizens of the U.S. and to seize their bank accounts if they do not pay the taxes they owe. This power is given to the state by formal means.

Political Systems of Power

Political sociologists study power and view it as the central issue in sociology. Again, power is sociological. It does not reside in an individual but between individuals. It is located in positions, roles, and norms. If you are a policeman, you have in that position certain authority and power, which you will not have if you leave that occupation and become a salesman. Power also forms into more macro systems of governance at a higher level of society. Some of the different political systems include those of monarchy, democracy, authoritarianism, and totalitarianism.

Monarchy

A **monarchy** is a political system of power in which a person inherits a throne and is head of state for life. Monarchies exist in Jordan, Morocco, Nepal, and Saudi Arabia. Monarchs have different titles including king, emperor, or sultan. Traditionally, the power of the monarch was absolute; the monarch was responsible only to God and this power became known as the divine right of kings.

Monarchs viewed themselves as literally owning the people and their property. Under monarchy, individuals in the society are referred to as "subjects"; under democracy, they are referred to as citizens.

Revolutions, particularly those in England and France, destroyed much of the power of monarchs. For example, in the 1630s, the English Parliament raised an army, defeated King Charles I, and condemned him to death. In France, the French Revolution of 1789 limited the power of Louis XVI, and in 1793, the revolutionists put him to death. As a result, the concept of **constitutional monarchy** developed in which the power of a monarch was relegated to ceremonies and symbols. In modern constitutional monarchies, the executive power is usually exercised by a prime minister and Cabinet. Great Britain, Norway, Denmark, Sweden, and Japan are modern constitutional monarchies.

Democracy

A **democracy** emphasizes that the purpose of government is to benefit the masses in society and maintains that the people being governed have the right to participate in their government. Such participation may involve selecting and voting for leaders, approving or disapproving certain laws, and deciding what penalties will be associated with what violations of law.

Democracies also permit the right of controlled dissent. Individuals may challenge anything but are controlled by the system itself. For example, individuals may challenge the right of the government to force them to pay income tax. But the courts may rule that the person must pay or be put in jail. Similarly, while having divergent ideas is tolerated in the United States, the idea of overthrowing the U.S. government and replacing it is not tolerated.

The right of legitimate opposition has been tested in the courts over the issue of the right to burn the American flag. Those in favor of this right contend that the fundamental issue is that of freedom of opposition. Those who oppose this right say that there should be limits to the rights of U.S. citizens which do not include flag burning. The Supreme Court has ruled that citizens do have a right to burn the flag. What is important is that the citizens of the U.S. still have input into the laws which govern them. A constitutional amendment would involve elected officials discussing and voting on the issue of flag burning.

While we tend to assume that the United States has always been a democracy, this is not the case. Our government was originally an **oligarchy** in which a few privileged individuals controlled the republic. Furthermore, there were numerous restrictions on who could vote. In the presidential election of 1824, only 350,000 votes (about ten percent of the population) were cast. Blacks, women, and persons under 21 years of age were not allowed to vote.

Totalitarianism

A **totalitarian** political system is one in which those who govern or rule, control everything—the military, media, education, religion, and economic system. Right of dissent is not tolerated as illustrated in the brutal attack by the 27th Army on 5,000 students who refused to leave Tiananmen Square in China in the summer of 1989. The Nazis of Nazi Germany also represented a totalitarian state and were responsible for the death of over six million Jews and other minorities. More recent totalitarian states include North Korea, Burma, and Iraq (under Saddam Hussein).

Totalitarian political systems control their citizens by force and terror. Following the Tiananmen Square incident, the Chinese government issued a most wanted list suggesting that those who participate in dissent will be punished. These tactics are identical to those operative at the time of Joseph Stalin in the Communist U.S.S.R. Stalin tolerated no dissent, and millions who were critical of Stalin in the media, education, and politics disappeared and were executed.

Our concern in this book is to emphasize the importance of social context on outcome. People born and reared in the respective systems will experience different lives. For example, students reared in the political system of totalitarian China may lose their life for dissent, whereas those who dissent in the United States may be featured on the evening news to discuss their cause.

Economic Systems of Property Control

The power reflected in a political system is often expressed in the economic system of property contol in a society. The three major systems are those of capitalism, socialism, and communism.

Capitalism

Karl Marx viewed **capitalism** as a system in which the ruling classes (capitalist or bourgeoisie) owned the means of production. Such means included land, raw materials such as gold mines, and machinery used to get and refine the gold. Those who worked in the mines and factories were the **proletariat**, or workers. Marx felt that capitalism exploited the workers because their labor produced much more profit for the owners than the amount they were paid for their labor. Hence, the owners profited at the expense of the workers.

A key element of capitalism is that anyone could own anything. Theoretically, the workers could save enough money, buy some land, and open their own store. They could then employ their own workers, make money from their labor, and increase their own profits. As profits increased, the person would have greater access to the political system which created the laws of the society. Hence, capitalists may not only own their own car, house, and store, they may have a larger power in the political system. Those who make the most money may be able to translate that money into political power. Those who make the greatest amount of money may, indeed, hold the most political power in the society.

In this book we have emphasized the importance of context as it creates outcomes. In a capitalistic system, the owners of capital, of business, define the value of the worker's labor and dictate the worker's behavior. An old man with a bad back is of no value to a construction firm which needs strong young workers. No matter how motivated that individual may be to work, the context may find him useless. The system, not the individual, is in control of the outcome.

Similarly, capitalism permits owners the power to dictate the educational criteria for employment. A person without a college degree is not considered for the job. The homeless in America can be viewed as victims of the capitalist system which has defined them as without value because they do not meet the criteria set by the owners of business and industry. Were these same individuals living in another economic system (socialism), they would be valued and would have a job available to them.

Communism

To rectify the problems of capitalism, Marx suggested **communism**. A true communist state, as envisioned by Marx, is one in which everything in the society is held in common. It is a classless society in that everyone is a joint owner of everything so that the opportunity for exploitation of the workers by the owners is nonexistent. In addition, in the communist state, there would be no distinction between manual and mental labor. The bricklayer for a building would be just as valued as the architect.

Marx never specified how his ideal communist society would be developed. The details of how everyone would own everything was never spelled out. The closest approximation to communism is socialism.

Wright (2008) noted that citizens under communist rule come to accept the system as best. She found that the emergence of capitalism in China has brought into existence both greater economic inequality and new forms of dependence on the state. In effect China's economic reform has created disincentives to oppose the authoritarian political status quo. Many come to believe that communism is a system that works.

Socialism

Socialism is an economic system in which the state or government, rather than the individual, owns the means of production (land, raw materials, factories). Theoretically, decisions about when goods are produced are made by political leaders who have the interests of everyone in the society in mind. The goal of these leaders is to ensure that everyone is taken care of by the government.

Another key element of socialism is the belief that a collective egalitarian society can exist in which all people are treated equally, and their needs are met. In theory, people are more important than property or profit. Denmark, Sweden, and Austria are examples of socialist states in that the major industries (medicine, railroads, airlines, and education) which are essential to the welfare of the people are controlled by the state. Making a profit in these respective industries is not as important as ensuring that the medical, transportation, and educational needs of the citizens are met. Not so in the capitalist societies where profit in, say, the heath care industry, takes precedence over people. For example, Michael Moore interviewed a male for his 2007 award winning documentary *Sicko* (on the U.S. healthcare system). The male had been sawing wood and cut off the last unit of his middle and third finger. The male took these units to the local hospital and was told it would cost $60,000 to attach the unit on the middle finger and $40,000 on the smaller finger. He had the unit on the smaller finger attached since he could not afford to have the unit on his middle finger attached. Such a situation occurs in a capitalist country which is focused on profits, not on caring for individuals. If the man lived in Canada whose government provides the medical care for its citizens, the man would have had the units of both fingers attached at no cost. Again, context creates outcomes. The healthcare a person receives depends on where they live, not who they are as individuals.

Socialist societies are also adamant in their attempt to avoid the exploitation of workers. Factory workers in Sweden and other socialist countries must be paid an acceptable wage to allow them to maintain a reasonable standard of living. Not so in a capitalist society where workers are paid as little as possible while corporations may become wealthier and wealthier (e.g., Exxon).

Socialism is a philosophy between capitalism and communism. Socialism has elements of capitalism in that some production may be in the hands of individual owners, but distribution may occur according to the dictates of the state. Also referred to as the **welfare state**, socialism ensures that regardless of who produces it, the citizens of the state may benefit from it; under capitalism, if citizens can't pay for something they can't have it. The mechanism which provides the basis for the redistribution of the goods and services in socialist societies is taxes. Citizens are heavily taxed on their incomes but these taxes are used to take care of their medical, educational, and employment needs.

One of the problems of socialism is massive inefficiency. It is a problem also in communism. Once a decision is made, as was done in the Soviet Union, that there would be no unemployment, a large bureaucracy must be created to ensure a job for everyone. Numerous people are unnecessarily involved in getting anything done, which results in an inefficient state.

Table 12.1 is an attempt to identify the political and economic systems of various countries. Another way to look at political systems is to consider the degree of political rights and civil liberties. Countries with very limited political rights and civil liberties include North Korea, Saudi Arabia, Rwanda, Pakistan, and Syria (Puddington, 2007).

Table 12.1
Societies by Political and Economic Systems

Society	Political System	Economic System
United States	Democratic*	Capitalism
Sweden	Democratic	Socialism
China	Communism	Centrally-directed Capitalism
South Africa	Democratic	Capitalism
Mexico	Democratic	Free market
Australia	Democratic	Capitalism
France	Democratic	State Directed Capitalism
United Kingdom	Democratic	Socialism/Capitalism

*Democratic is defined as one person, one vote, competitive elections and party system, rule of law, civil liberties and human rights.

Popular Beliefs and Scientific Data:
Politics and Homophobia

It is commonly believed that individuals who are against homosexuality and same-sex marriage remain that way. But researchers Lewis and Gossett (2008) found that persons who self identified as liberals, Democrats and the "less religious" became more accepting of homosexual relations since they turned age 18. In effect these social contexts may have had a liberalizing effect. In contrast, individuals who self identified as Republicans, Protestants, and African-Americans did not change their disapproval of homosexuality over a 20 year period.

Political and Economic Relationships

The political and economic systems of a society are intertwined. We illustrate how in the following sections.

Political-Economic Culture

The degree to which the political and economic relationships in a society become intertwined is illustrated in the development of a political-economic culture. This culture reflects various norms, values, and symbols. In the democratic capitalistic political economic culture of the United States the norms include minimum wage, a specific number of breaks per number of hours worked, and payment made directly to the person who performs the work. Values include protection of workers from injury, an eight-hour day/forty-hour week, and payment for overtime. Symbols include the American flag and the letters GM which are displayed on all automobiles produced by General Motors.

Cultural entrenchment of the political economic system is pervasive and subtle. For example, elementary math books ask students to work problems which suggest a capitalist context. "Jane buys sugar and lemons for one dollar to make a gallon of lemonade and sells it for two dollars. How much profit has she made for herself?" This example could not be included in a math textbook in communist China.

Large Corporations

The political economic system in the United States is dominated by large corporations. There are over seven million manufacturing corporations alone in the United States (*Statistical Abstract of the United States: 2008*, Table 970). The largest corporations are Wal-Mart, Exxon, and General Motors.

In order to survive, corporations must stay free of political control. American Telephone and Telegraph (AT&T) had a virtual monopoly of the telephone business until it was taken to court by MCI. The courts forced AT&T to give up its monopoly which resulted in AT&T diverting more of its resources to advertising to keep its customers.

Corporations also develop links to other countries so that they can escape the various restrictive laws that develop in a particular country. If taxes get too high or a product is banned, corporate executives simply find another market for their product. The tobacco industry has been under assault in the United States. In response, the tobacco industry escalated the sale of their products overseas. China now has 350 million smokers—more than the total population of the United States.

PACS and Interest Groups

In order for corporations to remain in power, their interests must be protected by the decisions of those in political power. To ensure that politicians vote for issues which benefit a particular corporation and against issues which would hurt those corporations, **Political Action Committees** (PACS) are formed. PACS (there are over 4,000 PACS) (*Statistical Abstract of the United States: 2008*, Table 408) donate money to politicians who support a particular position or cause. Unlike individual contributions which have a $25,000 limit, there is no limit to the amount of money a PAC can give to a candidate. Hence, candidates vote in a social context which includes the existence of PACs. If they do not vote consistent with the will of the PAC, they will not receive the donations necessary to help them win an election. One explanation for the high cost of medical care and medications in the United States is that PACs contribute enormous sums of money to legislators who support legislation consistent with the medical corporations.

Governmental Regulations of Industry and Trade

Prior to the Great Depression, the U.S. government took a **laissez-faire** (hands off) attitude toward the economy. It was believed that the country would best be served by letting the market dictate how much of what items were produced at what price. When businesses failed and people were out of work (e.g. The Great Depression), the government reevaluated its involvement and responded with President Franklin D. Roosevelt's New Deal. This program was designed to boost the national economy through putting people to work which would provide more money for them to spend which would create the need for more goods and services.

The government also recognized the need to control certain industries for the welfare of its citizens. Today, virtually all industries (food, medical, airline, railroad, financial, postal) regarded as essential to the well-being of U.S. citizens are regulated in some way. Food must be inspected before it can be sold, hospitals must maintain a specific doctor/nurse/patient ratio in order to open and must provide emergency service to patients even though they have no money or insurance, airline companies must inspect their planes at regular intervals, railroad passenger trains must not exceed a certain speed, banks must insure their deposits, and letters must be delivered within so many days of being mailed.

The agricultural industry is also heavily regulated to insure that we have the right amounts and variety of agricultural products. Otherwise we may have an overabundance of wheat and no soybeans. Farmers are paid not to produce certain crops and paid subsidies to produce other crops. This program ensures that the agricultural market is profitable to farmers so that they will continue to produce the items necessary for the good of society. In addition, McHughen and Smyth (2008) emphasized the regulatory powers of the federal government over plant agricultural biotechnology in the USA.

Government Control of the Money Supply

It is important that the government control the supply of money in a society. If there is an over supply of money, money has no value. Only by limiting its supply are people motivated to work for money.

Similarly, if there is too little money in circulation, goods are not manufactured since there is no profit for doing so. In effect, too little money means that there are few items to spend it on. One of the economic consequences of the Great Depression was that people had no money and the economy was still. Roosevelt's New Deal pumped money into the economy by creating jobs (Works Project Administration) for which people earned money they could spend. A specific example is the Blue Ridge Parkway in North Carolina and Virginia. This highway on the crest of the mountain provided the unemployed with jobs and pumped money into the economy.

The government defines what constitutes money and controls its supply in two ways. The government defines American currency as the only currency that may be exchanged for goods and services in the U.S. French, Swedish, and Mexican currency are not accepted.

The U.S. controls the supply of money through its fiscal and monetary policies. Fiscal policy defines how much money is to be spent on what. Table 12.2 illustrates how the federal government has decided to budget its money. By deciding that such a large proportion is to be spent on national defense, by implication, less money will be spent on housing. In essence, the homeless may be thought of as individuals who live in a society where relatively little priority is placed on housing. There are very few homeless in Sweden because those societies give higher priority to the housing needs of their citizens.

The federal government also controls the supply of money in the society by controlling the interest rate. The Federal Reserve Board decides the interest rate the federal government charges banks who want to borrow money. By increasing the interest rate, the Federal Reserve Board can decrease the amount of money banks borrow and therefore decrease the amount of money citizens will borrow (since there will be less money available to borrow). By decreasing the interest rate the federal government charges banks, banks will borrow more money and allow their customers to do likewise.

Government, Military, and Industrial Triad

Governments are concerned not only with the day to day welfare of its citizens through controlling various industries (food, medical, transportation) and

Table 12.2
The Federal Outlays for 2007 (est.)

Category	Amount
Defense	$2,784,300,000,000.
Housing	39,000,000,000.
Natural Resources	35,200,000,000.
Air Transportation	18,000,000,000.
Social Services	17,300,000,000.

Source: *Statistical Abstract of the United States, 2008.* 127th edition. U.S. Bureau of the Census, Washington, D.C., Table 459.

through the control of the supply of money, they must also be concerned about resisting other countries who might want to take them by force. Such resistance is possible by creating an effective military machine in the form of weapons and troops.

There is a clear interrelationship between the government, military, and industrial segments of the economy. The government defines the level of military machines and weapons that are necessary for a society's protection and gives defense contracts to various industries to produce the needed hardware. The government also funds troops and operations. The cost of the war in Iraq is estimated to be $275 million per day (in 2008). For an up-to-date cost of the war in Iraq, go to http://www.nationalpriorities.org/costofwar_home.

Politics and Work

There is an interrelationship between the political and economic sectors. All societies share certain aspects of each type of economic system. There is some socialism in capitalism and some capitalism in socialism.

Unionization

A **union** is a social organization of workers in an industry whose purpose is to improve the wages, benefits, and working conditions of its members. Unions exist in certain political-economic systems (capitalism) and not in others (socialism). Under capitalism, unions emerge because the workers have little control over wages, benefits, and working conditions unless they band together. One individual who asks an employer for a salary increase will be less effective than everyone in the industry or plant asking for the same increase. The Writer's Strike of 2007–2008 resulted in writers being given a share of the revenue generated from their work that is broadcast on the Internet and downloaded. An individual writer would have been laughed at (and fired) if he or she made such a demand.

Prior to the early 1800s, unions were illegal in the United States. Two or more individuals who conspired to deprive a third person of his or her property (factory owner) were said to be involved in a criminal conspiracy. In 1806 the Massachusetts Supreme Court (*Commonwealth v. Hunt*) ruled that the act of forming a union was, by itself, not illegal. After the death of the criminal conspiracy theory, the purpose of unions was debated in the courts over the next 100 years. In 1900, only three percent of the labor force of the United States belonged to labor unions, but by the end of World War II in 1945, almost a fourth of the labor force was unionized. Union strength peaked in 1954 with 35 percent of the work force. Today, only about 13 percent of wage and salary workers are members of a union (*Statistical Abstract of the United States: 2008*, Table 642).

Reasons for the decline in membership include fewer gains to be made, the success of firms not honoring union contracts, foreign competition, and reluctance of white collar workers to join unions. Initially, unions were successful in getting increased wages, benefits, and improved working conditions (e.g. safer, cleaner). New workers took these gains as givens and became complacent about joining unions. In addition, even though unions were successful in getting a good contract with management, they were not assured that the gains they fought for would actually occur. The company might be sold, and the new owner would not honor the agreements made by the previous owner.

Foreign competition has also made unions reluctant to ask for huge salary increments and wide ranging benefits. If unions were unreasonable in negotiating with management, the latter would move their operation to foreign soil where labor demands are almost nonexistent. For example, union leaders at General Motors might win the right for their members to be paid $40 an hour only to have the whole plant closed and moved to Mexico. In addition, Skerry (2008) noted the legitimate concern that day laborers today have over the presence of immigrants, who are a serious threat to the development of a union. Immigrants can replace workers. They will work for lower wages and do not require benefits. It is important to point out that employers are rarely held accountable. They are willing to hire undocumented workers because they can exploit them by paying lower wages and are not forced to provide benefits. When it comes to debates about immigration, the behavior of employers is often overlooked, and blame is placed on the immigrants, rather than the Americans who willfully employ them illegally because of the benefits for doing so.

Unions collectively bargain for greater shares of the economic system. Unions recognize that profits are based on the labor of their membership, and they want what they view as their fair share. They use both mediation and arbitration to achieve their goals.

Mediation and Arbitration

Mediation and arbitration are the primary mechanisms for negotiating more power. In **mediation**, the two sides, labor and management negotiate with the help of an impartial third party called a mediator. They try to reach a contract spelling out the terms and conditions of employment. Labor attempts to protect its workers, increase their wages, and their benefits of employment. If mediation succeeds, an agreement results which works for management and labor.

Sometimes agreements between labor and management are not clear, or individuals are fired by management for what the union considers unfair reasons. **Arbitration** is a means of settling a grievance between the parties. Both labor and management present their respective positions to a third party (arbitrator) who makes a decision that is binding for both parties. For example, some unions have negotiated contracts which permit an employee who is fired after drinking alcohol on the job an automatic second chance to return to work (if the employee admits guilt and goes through mandatory drug treatment). If an employee, after two drinks, comes to the factory to obtain his or her paycheck on his or her day off and is fired by the company, the person may refuse mandatory drug treatment and argue that drinking off hours to pick up a paycheck is not what was meant in the original contract about employee drinking. The union and company may then attempt to resolve this dispute through arbitration. An arbitrator would hold a hearing, allow both sides to present evidence and make a decision.

Political/Economic Associations and Social Organization

In this section we emphasize how the political and economic associations interact with other social organizations in society.

Population

Within a society are various population groups which influence the political and economic decisions of a society. The elderly (65 years and older), for example, represent about 13 percent of our population. By the year 2050, they will comprise about 20 percent of our population (*Statistical Abstract of the United States: 2008*, Table 10). Sometimes their voting is not protected. Karlawish et al. (2008) surveyed nursing and assisted living facilities about their procedures for facilitating voting by the elderly and found substantial variability existed in procedures used for registration and voting. In effect, about a third of the elderly in the nursing homes and assisted living facilities surveyed wanted to vote and were unable to do so, largely due to procedural problems. Current procedures in many facilities fail to protect voting rights.

The needs and interests of the elderly impact political and economic issues such as social security, Medicare, and pension benefits. Social Security is expected to run out of money in 2041 meaning that the system will only be able to pay a percentage of the benefits currently promised. Politicians will be scrambling to "fix" the system so as to get the vote of the elderly to keep them (the politician) in office.

Population and economics also have reciprocal effects. As large numbers of people begin to live in an area, the demand for food and services in that area increases. During the summer months, resort areas become packed with affluent vacationers who want food, lodging, and beach towels. The impact of these vacationers is to strengthen the local economy. However, when the summer is over and fall begins, vacationers leave the area and the local economy constricts.

Social Movements and Crowd Behavior

Most social movements (women's movement, gay rights movement, pro-choice/pro-life movements) are in reference to political issues (sexism, homophobia, and abortion). When the Supreme Court is scheduled to make a decision on a controversial political issue, crowds form on the steps of the court to voice their positions (collective behavior).

Similarly, when labor and management cannot settle their contract disputes through negotiation, mediation, or arbitration, picket lines may form in front of a workplace. These publics carry signs exposing their political opposition to the economic policies of their employer. The power labor has over management (in the form of boycott, walkout, and strike) is aggregate power. As indicated earlier, individuals have no power. Power exists only in social organizations.

Social Class

Political behavior is class behavior. Men who are white, professional, affluent individuals are likely to be Republican, while women, blacks and the working class poor are more likely to be Democrats. The lower class is often politically powerless. They are uninformed, do not have the socialization necessary to vote, do not have the economic resources to manage an effective resistance to their employer, and are victims of the political system. One of the reasons for homelessness is that these individuals have no political power to alter their situation.

Lack of political power is particularly true for the black "underclass." Due to social factors, these individuals are chronically unemployed, welfare dependent, and socially immobile. Even in the wake of the civil rights movement, positive political outcomes have not occurred.

Groups

A central theme throughout this book (and of sociology as a discipline) is that behavior is a function of social context. One of the most influential contexts a person experiences is his or her reference group. Such a group consists of significant others to whom the individual looks for approval, attitudes, and behaviors. The political affiliations of individuals usually mirror those of their reference groups. For example, workers in a particular industry (e.g. textile) may belong to a union (the American Textile Union) which protects the rights of those workers. The voting behavior of the union members will reflect the ideas of this reference group (union).

Families

The socialization of children involves teaching them various attitudes about political issues (abortion, the importance of voting, nuclear power). While parents may not formally indoctrinate their children with specific political positions, their political behavior (voting or not voting), and their informal discussion about political candidates or political issues in the presence of their children will bias their children toward various candidates and positions consistent with their parents.

As children become adults and establish their own families, they may diverge from the political leanings of their parents. Their new peer groups, work groups, and voluntary associations will all impact their new political commitments.

Kwon (2008) observed the widening gap between the need for long-term care and the capacity of welfare programs to fulfill that need in Korea. In essence, the political association feels responsible to take care of the elderly, but the economic resources to do so appear to be lacking. Korea is likely to introduce social insurance for long-term care rather than tax-based financing. Whatever the decision, the impact of the political and economic associations on the family is evident.

Communities

Communities represent a microcosm of politics and economics. The smaller the community, the lower the tax base and the fewer the number of services (garbage pickup, water, sewer, paving of streets) that the community provides. Rural communities have limited amounts of money to spend for parks and recreation, fire protection, and schools, and their members may suffer from these deficiencies.

Communities also represent how power and politics are used to govern an area. From November 1955 until he disappeared on December 20, 1976, in his sixth term, Mayor Richard J. Daley ruled the city of Chicago. Known as the Chicago machine, Daley held political control of the city for over twenty years. During his reign, nothing happened in Chicago without Daley's approval. It has been reputed that Daley was instrumental in the election of John F. Kennedy. After his death, the machine (political social organization) that Daley built continued to place individuals (including his son) who supported his politics in various political offices. Richard M. Daley (the son) was re-elected for his sixth term in 2007 and is expected to remain in office beyond 2010.

Associations

The interaction of the political association with other associations is illustrated in the example of religion. Fundamentalists believe that it is important to live by a strict set of religious guidelines. There are various fundamentalist groups (Mormons, Jehovah's Witnesses, and the Pentecostal churches) who view themselves as being on the sole path to a moral life. The political expression of their religious views is in the form of the New Christian Right. They are against abortion on demand, homosexuality, and sex education in public schools. They are also influential in supporting for political office politicians who are favorably disposed to conservative issues such as George W. Bush. In 2004 he received almost 80% of the white evangelical vote. Presidential Republican candidate Mike Huckabee in 2007 was also supported by the New Christian Right who felt that John McCain was not conservative enough to warrant their vote.

Networks

A **political party** may be defined as a social organization whose purpose is to get and maintain legitimate political power. Such a party consists of an extensive network of small groups operating at the county, state, regional, and national levels. A candidate for the Democratic or Republican party's nomination for president is dependent on building support through the network at the various levels.

The business community also has a network which binds them together for a common cause. There are over 4,000 political action committees. In an election year, they will contribute over $300 million to the candidates they feel will support their causes (*Statistical Abstract of the United States: 2008*, Table 408 and 409).

Economic networks are also essential for the manufacture and distribution of goods throughout the society. In regard to food production, farmers depend on a network of laborers to harvest the crops that are taken to market. There, the goods are sold and shipped to wholesalers who, in turn, sell and distribute to retailers. The buying public then consumes the food which began at the other end of a network chain. A breakdown at any point in the network or a delay can be a disaster. For example, if migrant farm workers or truck drivers are on strike, food can lay in the field or in warehouses until it rots. Pati et al. (2008) noted a network system involved in waste management and pointed out that what might be economically profitable might not be environmentally good for the society.

Individuals who participate in a political protest are also recruited and maintained by social networks. Within these networks, people share grievances such as their fear of a nuclear power plant being built in their neighborhood. In effect, people socialize their peers to be attentive to causes they regard as important.

Societies

The political and economic policies of different societies create contexts which influence how people think and live. In Sweden, a country that is politically socialistic and economically a blend of capitalism and socialism, individuals have little fear of unemployment, lack of medical care, or starvation. However, they do feel burdened by high taxes which are necessary to pay for these benefits.

Citizens in the United States live in a democratic capitalistic society but are not immune to being unemployed (4.9% in January 2008) are often without medical insurance (16%), and do not have a home for shelter (750,000 are homeless). However, the tax rate in the United States is relatively low when compared to other countries.

References

Karlawish, J. H., Bonnie, R. J., P. S. Appelbaum, R. A. Kane, C. Lyketsos, P. S. Karlan, B. D. James, et al. 2008. "Identifying the Barriers and Challenges to Voting by Residents in Nursing Homes and Assisted Living Settings." *Journal of Aging & Social Policy*, 20: 65–79.

Kwon, S. 2008. "Future of Long-Term Care Financing for the Elderly in Korea." *Journal of Aging & Social Policy*, 20: 119–130.

Lewis, G. B. and C. W. Gossett. 2008. "Changing Public Opinion on Same-Sex Marriage: The Case of California." *Politics & Policy*, 36: 4–30.

McHughen, A. and S. Smyth. 2008. "U.S. Regulatory System for Genetically Modified Organism, DNA Crop Cultivars." *Plant Biotechnology Journal*, 6: 2–12.

Pati, R. K., P. Vrat, and P. Kuman. 2008. "A Goal Programming Model for Paper Recycling System." *Omega*, 36: 405–417.

Puddington, Arch. 2007. "A 2006 Freedom House Survey. The Pushback Against Democracy." *Journal of Democracy*, 18: 125–137.

Skerry, P. 2008. "Day Laborers and Dock Workers: Casual Labor Markets and Immigration Policy." *Society*, 45: 46–52.

Statistical Abstract of the United States: 2008. 127th ed. Washington, D.C.: U.S. Bureau of the Census.

Wright, T. 2008. "State-Society Relations in Reform-Era China: A Unique Case of Post Socialist State-Led Development?" *Comparative Politics*, 40: 6–23.

Chapter 13

Networks and Societies

The value of a social network is defined not only by who's on it, but by who's excluded.

Paul Saffo, a Silicon Valley forecaster

It's not just enough to change the players. We've gotta change the game.
Barack Obama

People who move from one state to another are likely to change schools, banks, and churches. In moving, they will experience the importance of networks. As a student who wants to transfer academic credit, the respective associations will transfer the credit through their network linkage. In addition, funds from one bank can be transferred to a sister bank within the bank's network. Similarly, as noted in Chapter 11, individuals may transfer membership from the church they are leaving to a new church "by letter." Networks not only tie schools, banks, churches, and voluntary organizations together, but they also tie together communities, states, and nations. Networks are central to the functioning of associations within and between societies.

Networks also exist in the context of a larger society—the largest form of social organization. We define society by identifying its various elements and types. We end the chapter with how society interfaces with the other levels of social organization. First, we examine networks.

Networks: The Lost Area of Study

Look at the table of contents of any sociology textbook. The various chapters reflect the basic areas of sociology. Sociology professors teach and specialize in such areas as family, education, politics, economics, population, social class, communities, minorities, religion, deviance, gender roles, and the aged. Rarely does a professor emphasize networks. While social networks are central to what sociology is all about, networks are rarely discussed and not an area that is heavily funded for research. Funding agencies looking at two proposals, one on "Drug Usage among High School Students" and one on "Social Networks among High School Students" are likely to fund only the former, and those teaching sociology will find fewer research studies on networks.

Networks: Definition and Types

In general, **networks** are a set of interdependent links that tie numerous social organizations together. They are the social glue that ties together a wide range of social organizations and allow individuals to navigate all aspects of their lives. The type of a network depends on whether the network is of a macro or micro variety.

Macro networks are a pattern of interconnected and interdependent lines which tie together large scale organizations concerned with similar activities in pursuit of common goals. The schools, banks, and churches mentioned in the first paragraph have macro social networks which help individuals move between institutions in pursuit of degrees, banking services, and church membership. A key element in the definition of a macro social network is "goal." Prison networks exist with the goal of keeping prisoners confined, legal networks exist for the purpose of moving individuals through the legal system with speed and ease, and economic networks have the goal of moving food from the farm to the table. Table 13.1 summarizes some of the macro networks in our society.

Table 13.1
Macro Networks: The Linkage of Associations

Macro Network	Associations Linked Together
Political	Local and national governments, political parties
Educational	Public and private schools, universities, community colleges
Economic	Factories, transportation systems, businesses
Religious	Churches and synagogues, seminaries, religious orders
Military	Army, Navy, Marines, Air Force, Department of Defense
Communication	Local and national radio and television stations, magazine and book publishers, newspapers
Socialization	Family, day care centers, Boy Scouts, Girl Scouts, Sunday school
Medical	Schools, hospitals, public health clinics

Micro networks, also called **social networks,** link individuals together most often for companionship, emotional aid, or small-scale services. Hinduja and Patchin (2008) emphasized that today's youth have embraced online social networking sites such as MySpace or Facebook as a way of meeting their social and relational needs. Heartchoice.com is a relationship website which includes message boards which link individuals who are single, married, and divorced.

Figure 13.1 illustrates the micro friendship network of person A. Person A is connected to each of four other people, and they are connected to each other through person A. Hence, Ric can call Joseph, Jacqueline or Maria to ask for a favor because each is connected to the same person. Notice that Joseph, Jacqueline and Maria are connected to each other even though they may not interact with each other on a regular basis. Each person in the diagram is also connected to others who provide a linkage of each person to those additional people. For example, Jacqueline is a medical student and has close contacts with a heart specialist. Joseph has high blood pressure and wants to talk with a cardiologist about his condition. He asks Jacqueline to call her friend and set up an appointment. One of the reasons the cardiologist agrees to meet with Joseph is Jacqueline's connection with Joseph.

Figure 13.1
Micro Friendship Network

```
                        Joseph
                          *

                          *.

                          *
    James * * * * * * * * * Person A  * * * * * * Jacqueline
                          *

                          *

                          *
                        Maria
```

Examples of micro networks are those which exist on the basis of family, proximity, demography, and interest. **Family networks** can be seen at a family reunion in which all individuals at the reunion are linked to all other individuals through family ties. However, each of the members at the family reunion may not know or interact with everyone else.

Proximity micro networks exist as a result of individuals living in the same neighborhood with others or seeing others on a routine basis at a particular place. People who wash their clothes, drink coffee, jog, or play tennis at a particular location on a routine basis establish a network with others in that specific context. Students who study at the same table in the library, eat at the same restaurant on campus, or hang out at the recreation center form a network. People who live in condominium complexes may meet and interact at the mailbox center.

Demographic network ties develop between individuals who share particular characteristics such as race, sex, or age. As the nomination for the 2008 presidential candidates approached, blacks identified with Barack Obama, women with Hillary Clinton, and the elderly with John McCain.

Interest networks develop because people share a particular focus. Computer gamers, skateboard riders, and owners of Airstream silver trailers develop a network so as to be in touch with others who share their interest. Regarding the Airstream trailers, 5,000 owners of these vehicles travel to the campus of Notre Dame in Indiana every year for a convention to interact with fellow travelers. These networks form across America to find parts and learn about the different model Airstreams for future purchase. They continue their networks online where they have created several Airstream clubs.

Individuals in a micro network may or may not know each other. Some medical schools have such large numbers of medical students entering at one time, that although they represent the same class, the students may be tied to those they do not know personally through a network.

Individuals are in both micro and macro social networks at the same time. Individuals as new army recruits in basic training will be in a micro network on a particular army base. If they meet at a bar they will identify with each other as members of the same boot camp network. At the macro level, these boot camp recruits are part of a network linked to all other individuals in all other boot camps. Similarly, graduating seniors in a particular high school are tied into a network of "seniors" in their particular high school. They are also tied into a network of all other seniors in all other high schools in that their college entrance exams are looked at as an aggregate, and their chance of being accepted is dependent in part on how many other seniors are applying to college at the same time.

Micro network interactions affect macro networks. Networks can be normative or deviant, as networks tie together all levels. At the micro level, a person in a large city who is looking for illegal drugs will contact a friend who knows a friend who has a "drug" contact. At the macro level, the source of the drug comes from a foreign country that is delivered through an elaborate network of traffickers involving organized farmers, communities, boats, planes, businesses, and sellers. In contrast, macro networks affect micro networks. Price fixing by large corporations affects the discretionary income available to individuals. This, in turn, affects the money friends have available to see a movie, rent a jet ski, or go to a concert.

Networks versus Groups

Networks are sometimes confused with groups. While the characteristics sometimes overlap, Table 13.2 lists some of the differences.

Table 13.2
Differences between Networks and Groups

Networks	Groups
1. Network members are more dispersed.	Group members are more contained.
2. Network members have less interaction.	Group members have more interaction.
3. Network members have a loose identity.	Group members have a strong identity.
4. Network members are usually in secondary group relationships with each other.	Group members are usually in primary group relationships with each other.

Dispersed, infrequent interaction, loose identity, and secondary relationships tend to set networks apart from groups. Taking computer gamers that are connected by computers to all other gamers as an example of a network, and a baseball team as an example of a group, it is clear that the gamers are more spread out, probably do not interact with everyone in the network with any frequency, don't strongly identify with each other, and regard the relationships as emotionally distant. In contrast, the members of a baseball team practice, work/play together, travel together, stay in shared rooms, interact frequently, identify with each other, know the families of many players, and have closer emotional ties.

Developing and Sustaining Networks

As one of the most crucial aspects of social life, where do networks come from, what maintains them, and how do they operate?

1. Formation. Some networks are already in existence. Individuals connect to these existing networks by being born into them. Newborn infants take their place on the family tree and are immediately connected to an extended kinship network.

Individuals may also join existing networks by becoming involved with a bank, church, or school. Most banks feature the service of being able to withdraw money anywhere in the country as long as one belongs to a particular bank or has a particular card. Similarly, American Express emphasizes that it has a worldwide network and can replace your lost traveler's checks the day they are lost. This network was in place before the individual entered the American Express system.

Other networks develop to meet the needs of various social organizations. Political parties are dependent on local community networks to provide labor to campaign for the candidate. Hillary Clinton, Barack Obama, and John Mc-Cain could not have run their campaigns for the 2008 presidential nomination without the support of local community networks. Finally, some networks develop out of the need to form ties with others for mutual sharing and survival. College students often meet individuals with whom they form a network of friendships throughout their adult years. Fraternities and sororities are particularly known for forging friendship networks at both a micro (within the fraternity or sorority) and a macro level (between other chapters of the same fraternity or sorority) throughout society. These associations may have a secret handshake and greeting which allows members to confirm for each other that they are a part of the network.

2. Maintenance. Networks are maintained on the basis of the need to continue to connect a number of social organizations together so that organizational goals may be met. One of the functions of the organization of the family is to produce and socialize new members for society. However, the family in industrialized society is incapable of accomplishing its goal without the help of other organizations—hospitals to help with the birth of babies, schools to help educate them, and churches to help socialize them. Hence, maintaining networks connecting the family to the various other social organizations is essential.

The networks within each organization are also essential to maintain the networks of the respective organizations. For example, in order for the hospital to function, it must have links with drug suppliers, surgical equipment, and nurses' associations.

Personal social networks must also be maintained. Markert (2008) noted that an important source of one's positive self-image is one's social networks. Retirees often do not acknowledge the importance of their social network for their self image until they have detached from it. The researcher noted that social networks are crucial to how an individual feels about him or herself. A retiree removed from the occupational network of contacts may suddenly feel depressed and, in fact, have a shortened life.

3. Operation. Networks operate or function in a number of ways. Micro social networks function to help a person find a job, someone to marry, or solve a problem. Individuals often report that they become aware of a job "through a friend." Similarly, individuals often meet a mate through a friend or through a dating network such as Match.com or E-Harmony. Finally, computer owners quickly discover that their machines break down so they ask others who own computers (a network of users) to suggest someone who might be able to fix it.

Macro networks function to tie social organizations together. Families link themselves together by requiring that individuals marry someone outside the family of origin (the **exogamy rule**). Hence, brothers and sisters are not allowed to marry because no new economic resources would be available to the parents. When the children marry someone from another family, several families (and their resources) are linked together.

Insurance companies are also tied together by networks. Insurance companies cooperate with each other by sharing information on "high risk" clients. Persons with extremely high blood pressure who have been denied life insurance are placed on a list which enters the insurance network. All insurance companies have access to this information so that they can deny insurance to the person with high blood pressure who applies to their company. The criminal justice system has similar networks so that a detective in one city can call another for information about a suspect who has moved.

Networks and Social Organizations

Networks are connected to other social organizations.

Population

Population characteristics have meaning only to the degree that these characteristics affect a person's access to networks. A person of a particular sex, race, age, and sexual orientation has access to networks specific to these particular characteristics. First year college students who are gay benefit from finding other gay individuals on campus (the network) so that they can learn gay friendly stores, restaurants, and bars. The elderly develop a network with others their age to find out about pharmacies with the best drug prices, recreational facilities, senior discounts, and retirement villages.

Collective Behavior

Before a social movement comes into existence, there must be a number of like-minded individuals. One of the functions of networks is to both collect and socialize individuals into feelings and thoughts about a particular cause. Unless individuals are aware of a cause and motivated to join, there is no collective action. Gay networks alert members of an upcoming gay pride march and encourage them to go and join the march (collective behavior). Not only does the network provide the individual with a group of others to go with, but the network provides the transportation to assure the person is at the march.

Collective action is also dependent on communication. The telecommunications industry results in a network of emails, text messages, and cell phone calls which connect individuals instantly. When Congress begins to consider a bill on abortion, social security, or global warming, networks are mobilized, and a collective reaction begins.

Social Class

Each social class tends to have its own social network. Low status individuals have networks primarily composed of family and friends. These become particularly valuable for survival in the lower classes. A person who needs a babysitter, a ride to the grocery store or doctor, or to borrow someone's lawnmower can usually find someone in the network to provide this service.

Upper class networks include more formal organizations which serve as a source for advantage to affect career chances. Upper status individuals attend prestigious universities and are members of clubs and corporate boards which connect them to other high status individuals who have the resources of wealth, power, and prestige. The adage, "It is not what you know but who you know that is important" means that high status networks provide an advantage across the entire country to meet and connect with others of similar social class.

Some people engage in "networking" whereby they go to parties, join clubs, and seek entry into networks as a means of collecting important "connections." Marla Maples, former wife of Donald Trump, reported that she "networked" her way to her intended husband and identified the people she went through to get to him. Most people who would like to meet and have dinner with a celebrity will never have the opportunity since they have no entry into the network that will eventually lead to that person.

Finally, the "good ole boy" network is often a white upper middle class network which gives information, jobs, and preferences to those in the network. Minorities who do not have access to this network do not obtain jobs. Some are aware that there is an intricate network designed to deny anyone access to a job who does not have membership in the "good ole boy" network.

Groups

A person's network is not necessarily a group because not all members of the network interact. However, a network may contain groups since some members in a network do interact with each other. For example, a person may be a member of a computer gamer network across the United States. This network is not a group since the members do not interact and know each other.

However, some of the members (e.g. a small group in Ames, Iowa) are group members because they do interact by playing video games together.

Networks are valuable because they link people to certain groups. People who have friends have access to the groups and organizations of those friends. For example, a person whose network of friends includes one who plays in Toby Keith's (country western singer) band has a connection to the band members (including Toby Keith).

Families

Families are connected by elaborate kinship networks. **Kinship** is a social network of people related by common ancestry, adoption or marriage. Fielden and Gallagher (2008) noted the importance of parents who are connected into strong family kinship and community networks (thus high social capital) which provide a positive context where their children's social, emotional, and educational needs are met.

One goal of society is to replace its dying members with new socialized members. While families play a major role in this socialization process, families are part of a larger network of agencies such as nursery schools, secondary and elementary schools, youth groups, and churches. When one segment of the network fails to socialize a child properly, other segments in the network are expected to provide support. For example, when a family does not teach a child to say "thank you" it will be taught in schools, youth groups, and churches until the network produces the culturally acceptable outcome of saying "thank you" at the appropriate time.

Communities

Large urban communities frequently become the hub of network centers. Historically, this was true of places such as Egypt and Rome, but it is also true today in cities such as Paris, where all surrounding cities have rail links to the city. Similarly, New York City, Los Angeles, Washington D.C., Ottawa, and Zurich, Switzerland, have become central network centers that have ties to the rest of the world. Awareness that cities represent networks to the rest of the society is illustrated in the phrase, "If you want to be successful in the arts, theater, or finance, you have to live in New York and establish your connections." Communities are also linked with the needs of individuals. If you need a transplant in Dallas, Texas, your blood may come from Loredo, Texas, your heart for the transplant from Los Angeles, and the surgical team from Minneapolis, Minnesota.

Associations

Table 13.1 presented earlier in this chapter identified some of the various associations connected by networks. To repeat, examples of these networks include economic, political, educational, and legal networks. A desalination plant is also an association and must be connected by a series of networks both to the saltwater and to the network system providing fresh water for a community (Helal et al., 2008).

Economic associations are sometimes linked by having members who sit on the board of directors of one corporation also become members and sit on the boards of other corporations. Such a network connects board members to inside information about what is going on in other corporations. In contrast, the heads of other corporations may also sit on one's own corporate board.

Regarding the political network, the associations linked to this network include local, state, regional, and national political associations. Local governments are often linked to state governments and state governments are linked to regional associations, which are dependent on the national government. When a disaster (e.g. flood or forest fire) strikes a community, the mayor may contact the governor who may then ask for the help of the federal government to declare the area a disaster and to obtain federal funds.

Educational associations are similarly linked. The fact that elementary, secondary, high school, and colleges are linked in a systematic network makes it possible for a person to enter school in the first grade and have his or her records passed on to the next educational association. If the network functions properly, they can move from private to parochial to public schools in several states without losing any academic credits.

Legal associations are very visible networks. When a person is stopped for "driving under the influence," he or she enters the criminal justice network. After being taken to jail, he or she is arraigned and required to enter another part of the network: driving school. For repeat offenders, longer jail terms or prison sentences are used. The point for us here is that once a person enters the network, he or she is passed along from association to association dealing with police, attorneys, bail bondsmen, courts, judges, jails, prisons, parole boards, and others who will assure that the network functions properly.

Societies

Societies consist of large numbers of social organizations (family, health, political, economic, education, etc.) that are tied together by networks. Suppose a mother and her 15-year-old daughter live together. Suppose also that the mother becomes suddenly ill and faints at the kitchen table. In response, the 15-year-old uses the family network and calls her aunt to come immediately. Together, the aunt and the 15-year-old decide to use the health network by calling 911 and asking that an ambulance be sent. This ambulance exists because the city government (political network) decided to appropriate special funds for rescue service for the city. Such an appropriation was made by interaction with the economic network to determine the available funds for such a rescue service. In order to encourage citizens to use the 911 number to avail themselves of the rescue service, the educational network began a program of socializing the community's awareness of the service through the news media network.

Another way of viewing **society** is that it represents the sum of the interrelated networks of the social relationships existing within the boundaries of the largest social system. Historically, the largest social system was a clan, tribe, or family. Today, the largest social system is the nation-state.

Society: The Largest Element of Social Organization

Societies are the largest and most important of all social organizations. Their importance results from their power over all other social organizations. For example, Bridget M. Mathew was a student at Omaha Westside High School in Omaha, Nebraska. She wanted to form a club of Christian students which would meet after school in one of the classrooms to pray. School authorities denied her the right to form a religious club on school property. She took the matter to a lawyer, and five years later the Supreme Court ruled that religious clubs did have the right to meet on school property. By an 8 to 1 decision, the court upheld the constitutionality of Congress' 1984 Equal Access Act. The act says that no public secondary school receiving federal funds may bar any student clubs on the basis of their "religious, political, or philosophical views" if the school permits any group to meet after school hours.

This case illustrates the power of the larger society over the educational association. In the rest of this chapter we review the elements which help to define societies, how they are classified, and how they interact with other social organizations. Our basic theme remains the same—the social context largely produces the outcome. The society in which a person lives literally affects their ability to survive. In Tanzania, almost half a million children die every year due to diarrhea and dehydration—very preventable causes. Their society of

34 million people does not allocate its resources to saving the young but lets them die, which arguably becomes a method of population control.

The Elements of Society

In defining a society, it is helpful to look at its various elements. These are territorial boundary maintenance, independence, power and decision authority, allegiance and common culture.

Territorial Boundary Maintenance

All societies have a territory in which the members of the population live. Maps help to define the territory of various societies and define for their members the land they must fight to maintain. Disputes such as those between the Israelis, Jordanians and Syrians have, in part, been disputes over territorial boundaries. Similarly, the war between Mexico and the United States (1846–1848) was a war between societies over boundaries. If Mexico were to decide to annex Texas, the two societies would be at war again.

Independence

Independence refers to freedom of control. All societies are given the responsibility of taking care of the needs of their members. Societies are less dependent than any other type of social organization on another entity for their well-being. While the United States may trade with other nations for oil and foreign goods, it is largely capable of standing alone. No other society dictates to the United States how it will be operated. The Declaration of Independence was basically a document specifying how the United States was independent of British rule.

Power and Decision Authority

Societies are also the major foci of power and decision authority. The society of the United States through the Supreme Court has decided that burning the flag is a legal right of all Americans. What local groups feel about flag burning will not prevail in light of the will of the larger society. Similarly, in the early sixties when George Wallace, governor of Alabama, called out the National Guard and stood in the admission's door of the University of Alabama to prevent blacks from registering to attend school, he was exercising his local authority. But President Kennedy, exercising his authority of the larger society of the United States, nationalized the guard which brought its power and might under the will of the federal government. Civil rights legislation reflects the will of the society at large rather than specific pockets of influence within the society in communities, families, schools, or other social organizations.

Allegiance

Allegiance is loyalty. Societies consist of people who are loyal to its causes and, in some cases, are willing to die for it. Wars depend on the allegiance of people in the society to fight for them. Japanese kamikaze pilots in World War II were willing to crash their airplanes into United States destroyers as an act of loyalty to their country and to God. Suicide bombers for Al-Qaeda routinely kill themselves in Iraq out of loyalty. While this suicidal level of allegiance is not necessary, a modicum level is necessary in order to protect the interests of the society.

Individuals are socialized by their family and by other institutions (education, religion) to be loyal to their country. Parents pay taxes, and let their children know that they do so. Schools require their students to learn the Pledge of Allegiance, and churches support allegiance to one's country. For example, the Bible reads, "Render unto Caesar the things that are Caesar's and render unto God the things that are God's." This translates into being loyal to one's country and to one's God.

Common Culture

Societies are also characterized by a **common culture**. Defined as ways of thinking and doing, culture is a way of binding people together. Americans celebrate the Fourth of July, and the French celebrate the 14th of July. Iranians celebrate the death of Ayatollah Rudolph Khomeini, and the Saudi's celebrate the birth of Mohammed.

Food is also a cultural trait. Americans love hot dogs, and Vietnamese and Koreans love dogs. The French have wine with their meals while Americans drink a variety of beverages. While milk is a predictable liquid in the American diet, the Chinese rarely drink milk. They do not have an enzyme which helps to break milk down into a digestible substance when consumed.

A common culture binds people together by making them similar to others in the society. When people observe others eating, dressing, talking, and behaving as they do, they feel a sense of commonality with them. Societies are composed of people who feel connected to each other via a common culture. Whether culture is unique to humans is the subject of scientific debate.

Popular Beliefs and Scientific Data: Culture Is Unique to Humans

It is commonly assumed that only humans have culture. However, researcher Jeff Galef, a McMaster University psychologist, noted that female quails look to other females to point out the best mates. He also noted that groups of Japanese macaque monkeys have been observed washing sweet potatoes and wheat before eating their food (Christie, 2005). Seemingly, these practices are learned by observing others in the group, not by directly being taught. And, baboons have used stones as weapons.

While these examples suggest a rudimentary level of cultural development by nonhuman birds and primates, there is no evidence of more sophisticated levels of culture. While John Tyler Bonner's (1980) *The Evolution of Culture in Animals* is an interesting read, only humans seem to have developed elaborate sporting events, religious rituals, and marriage systems. However, Wey (2008) noted that animals live and interact together, forming complex relationships and social structure and emphasized the need to study these patterns using social network analysis.

Classification of Societies

Like types of institutions, societies may be classified in a number of different ways. We begin by looking at classification by size.

Size

The larger the size of a society, the more difficult it is to defend and control. Russia today is the largest country in the world, almost twice the size of the United States. Defending such a large land mass is very difficult. In the wake of 9/11, the United States has recognized that it is impossible to prevent terrorists from entering via the Canadian or Mexican borders. As the geographic size of a society increases, it becomes more difficult to exercise control.

Size also affects the degree to which people interact with each other. The smaller the society, the greater the interaction between the members for purposes of cultural bonding. Size also affects the level of control a society has over its members. In a small society of a few thousand people, almost absolute control can be assured. In contrast, China has over a billion people. The problem of issuing an order in Beijing and having it carried out thousands of miles away in Shenzhen requires a very sophisticated level of control. In addition to size, societies may be characterized by subsistence strategies.

Subsistence Strategies

Societies may be identified on the basis of how they provide food and shelter for their members. Each of these strategies has implications for the individuals in the society; context creates outcomes. Lenski et al. (1991) identified various subsistence strategies as follows:

1. Hunting and Gathering Societies. The Negritos of the Philippines and the Mubh pygmies of Central America are examples of **hunting and gathering societies**. These societies consist of a relatively small number of members who spend their time in specified functions of hunting wild game and gathering berries and fruits for immediate consumption by members of the society. The society must remain small because large numbers will consume food faster than the members can find it. The life expectancy in a hunting and gathering society is short. Those members who get sick or break a limb cannot go on the hunt and contribute to the survival of the society. They must be left behind.

2. Horticultural and Pastoral Societies. Between 7000 B.C and 3000 B.C., individuals learned how to plant crops (**horticultural societies**) and domesticate animals (**pastoral societies**) for food. Being able to develop one's own food source allowed individuals to settle in one area rather than to be constantly on the move in search of new food sources. Such societies could also sustain a larger number of people than hunting and gathering societies. Staying in one area meant that a division of labor was necessary—houses needed to be built, and the community (its people, land, and houses) needed to be protected. Hence, the roles of carpenter, weapon maker, and warrior emerged. These changes illustrate again that the context creates the outcome. Only in societies which need houses, weapons and warriors will positions emerge to fill such roles.

3. Agricultural Societies. **Agricultural societies** developed with the invention of the plow which allowed large land masses to be tilled for crop development. These land masses produced more food than individuals in a given community could consume so that a surplus occurred. This surplus represented value which the community could use to amass power against other societies in trade or in warfare. Rome, Greece, and Egypt were agricultural societies which had huge surpluses of grain.

4. Industrial Societies. **Industrial societies** developed in the 1700s in England with the advent of the Industrial Revolution. The shift from human and animal power to machine power characterized the Industrial Revolution. While

some machines such as combines were used on the farm, most were housed in factories where mass production of other machines (e.g. automobiles) and goods (e.g. clothing, dishes, shoes) occurred.

The effect on society was enormous. Individuals no longer worked in rural areas at home but moved to large urban centers to work in factories. Once under strong social control of their parents and kinship system, they were anonymous in cities and could largely do as they pleased. The result was more crime and individual freedom. Regarding the family, wives began to work away from home in factories where they earned their own income. Such independence provided them greater power in the marital relationship and the financial independence to leave their marriages if they were unhappy. With the advent of the Industrial Revolution, the divorce rate increased.

5. Post-Industrial Societies. **Post-industrial societies** are those in which machines have become increasingly important in the economic sector. Rather than 500 people and 10 machines needed to produce a product, 15 people and 20 machines can turn out the same product. Entire factories may consist of robots that do not need food, healthcare, or coffee breaks. They also do not need lights or heat so they can work full time in the dark without heat in the dead of winter and without complaint. The post-industrial society has spawned a new brand of employee: the service workers who repair the machines. They sell their knowledge rather than their labor as they keep the machines operative. Computer geeks are examples of a labor force that services machines that need to keep operating.

Developmental Changes

In addition to classifying societies by size and survival strategies, societies differ on the basis of their development.

Gemeinschaft and Gesellschaft. Ferdinand Tonnies (1887) conceptualized societies as moving from Gemeinschaft to Gesellschaft. **Gemeinschaft**, a German term, means "a community" which is characterized by personal, informal, and caring interaction patterns between people in primary groups who have a common bond. Gemeinschaft societies are small and are found in preindustrial societies including hunting and gathering societies, horticultural/pastoral societies, and some agricultural societies. Individuals in these societies know each other on a first name basis, interact with each other frequently, and care about each other. Some small communities in America still reflect Gemeinschaft qualities.

As societies become industrialized, they become Gesellschaft in nature. **Gesellschaft** societies are very large, impersonal, formal, bureaucratic societies in which secondary relationships predominate. Individuals in Gesellschaft societies do not know each other on a first name basis, may see each other never or only once in their lives, and are unconcerned about each other's personal well-being. Tonnies originally viewed Gemeinschaft and Gesellschaft communities as dichotomies. An alternate view suggests conceptualizing these communities on a continuum showing elements of both types. The ideas put forth by Tonnies have been extended to societies, but are equally relevant at the community level.

Mechanical and Organic Solidarity. Emile Durkheim (1893) suggested another way of conceptualizing societies. He focused on the nature of those mechanisms that bond people together and identified two types of social glue which results in radically different societies. **Mechanical solidarity** operates in pre-industrial societies such as hunting and gathering societies in which people are bound together by similarity and common culture. Every individual in society has a role which is directed toward a common goal. Among hunters and gatherers, someone stalks wild game, someone gathers berries, someone collects wood, and someone builds the fire with the common goal of survival. Everyone works together and feels that his or her participation is important. Everyone also uses a common language, dresses in a predictable way, and knows the accepted norms.

In contrast, **organic solidarity** operates in industrial societies. People behave in civil ways toward each other not because they are similar or share a common culture but because they need each other. The grocer is kind to his or her customers because they will shop elsewhere if they are dissatisfied. In return, customers are kind to the grocer because they need the grocer to cash checks.

People on assembly lines in factories cooperate with each other out of interdependence. When automobiles are assembled, each worker must finish a particular part (and on time) so that the next person can begin to do his or her part. If there is no cooperation, the products are not produced, and the factory will close causing all those involved to collectively lose their jobs.

As in both Gemeinschaft and Gesellschaft societies, mechanical and organic solidarity may be viewed on a continuum. As societies move from pre-industrial to industrial or from simple to complex, the type of solidarity shifts from mechanical to organic. Whereas people in preindustrial societies get along with each other because they want to, people in industrial societies get along because they have to.

Traditional and Modern Societies. Max Weber (1921) viewed societies as those in which individuals behave on the basis of traditional or rational values. In agricultural societies, people cared about what each other thought and believed that custom and tradition were adequate guidelines for behavior. When two farmers disagreed over what should be planted in their jointly-held land, they discussed it between themselves and arrived at a settlement acceptable to both. Custom and tradition dictated that their relationship was more important than who planted what crop. In modern societies, when two farmers disagree over what should be done with their jointly-held land, they each retain their own lawyers who become legalistic about who has the right to do what. This "what is legal and right" is the rationalism which Weber observed became characteristic of modern societies.

Societies and Social Organization

As noted earlier, society is the ultimate social organization because decisions at the societal level affect all other areas of social organization. Society is an independent variable as it acts on other social organizations as dependent variables. In this section we review the ways in which these effects occur.

Population

The laws developed by the society regarding immigration affect the composition of society. **Immigration** refers to the admission of individuals from foreign countries into a new society to be granted legal permanent residence. Every year about 1.2 million immigrants are given citizenship in the United States (*Statistical Abstract of the United States: 2008*, Table 45). They are admitted on the basis of certain quotas—so many professional individuals, skilled individuals, refugees, ministers of religion, foreign medical students, orphans, and Cubans/Haitians. By changing the immigration laws, the society will change. An example of this effect can be seen in Miami in which large numbers of Cubans have immigrated. Similarly, the border towns of Texas (e.g. San Antonio, El Paso) are heavily concentrated with Mexican Americans. Cetron and Davies (2008) note that one effect of increased migration is growing acceptance of diversity.

Birth rates can also be affected by social policies dictated at the societal level. Faced with the burden of overpopulation, China instituted a one-child family policy whereby the government provides inducements to parents to restrict family size to one child. Such inducements include health care benefits amounting to a ten percent increase in annual family income. After January 2008, cities in China prohibit couples from having more than one child, and strong penalties are being enforced. Parents who elect to have three or more children must pay a special tax equal to ten percent of their income for the first 14 months of that child's life. Other privileges such as free school tuition and priority employment for the "only child" are not available for the third and fourth child. As a result of the one child policy, China's birth rates have dropped significantly. Since 1979, China has had over one half billion less children. This has improved the economy of China and made it a world power.

Death rates can also be affected by societal decisions. A society that does not permit a person to terminate his or her life or others to assist in doing so will have a lower death rate than a society which permits these acts of death. Hence, societies have the power to constrict or expand their population on the basis of the decisions they make.

Collective Behavior

Individuals band together for collective action and initiate social movements when societies become unacceptably oppressive. Blacks in South Africa, representing 70 percent of the population, initiated riots (throughout the eighties and early nineties) in protest of their treatment at the hands of the minority whites (representing 20 percent of the population). Similarly, pro-democracy Chinese students crowded into Tiananmen Square in the summer of 1989 to protest the totalitarian Chinese government. In October 2007, Burmese people were angry about the sudden fuel price increase. Pro-democracy activists (about 400) led the initial demonstrations in Burma's main city, Rangoon. It was the largest demonstration that had been seen in the military-ruled nation for several years.

In all three cases, the repressive context created the collective action. However, the larger society limited the degree of resistance it would tolerate. Black South Africans are still required to live in certain areas and are not accorded full citizenship. The pro-democracy students were annihilated by the 27th Chinese Army—5,000 citizens died in one brutal attack in Tiananmen Square on June 4, 1989. In Burma, the authorities moved swiftly to quell the protests, rapidly arresting dozens of activists.

Social Class

The number of members in each social class depends on the economic policies of a society. Societies develop different economic structures, including different inheritance policies, tax codes, and welfare laws which determine how many and which of its citizens will have money, education, and higher occupations. The George W. Bush administration passed legislation favorable to big business and to the rich, which resulted in an increase from 11.7% to 12.3% of the population living below the poverty line since Bush became president.

Groups

The society defines what groups are legally permitted to form and for what purpose. The Supreme Court has ruled that prayer groups may meet on school property, that anti-abortion protest groups may not meet within so many yards of an abortion clinic, and that individuals may meet in a group to burn the American flag.

In the summer of 1990, Canadian police officials in Oka, Quebec, (18 miles west of Montreal) were carrying out the will of the society by shooting bullets, tear gas, and stone grenades at a group of 200 Mohawk Indians (three deaths resulted). The latter were protesting the expansion of a private golf course on tribal land. The Indian protests were overruled by the larger society. Again, the larger society dictates what behaviors are acceptable for collectives.

Family

Gillies (2008) noted how society targets the family as the way social ills such as crime and poverty are to be remedied. Indeed, the family is seen as transmitting social values crucial to society's well being. Societies also determine what type of marriage they permit. In the United States, **monogamy** (the marriage of one husband to one wife) is the only legally approved form of marriage. Polygamous marriages whereby spouses have more than one partner are not officially allowed. Other societies permit different marriage forms. Among the Yoruba of Nigeria and the Pokomo of Kenya, **polygyny** (one husband, several wives) is permitted. **Polyandry**, in which one wife has more than one husband, is practiced among the Buddhist Tibetans.

Societies also determine who may marry whom. Prior to the mid sixties, it was against the law for blacks and whites to marry in the United States. Age restrictions make it illegal in most states for men and women to marry below the age of 18 without the consent of their parents. In the United States, a 40-year-old man may not marry a 14-year-old girl. In France, the legal age for marriage is 15.

Not only do societies control who may marry whom and at what age, they dictate whether or not the spouses may divorce and under what conditions. While most societies recognize some form of divorce, some societies have more permissive laws than others. Divorce in India is very rare (three to five percent of marriages end in divorce) whereas the divorce rate in the United States is one of the highest in the world. The conditions of divorce are also specified by the society. Among the ancient Hebrews, a husband need only hand his wife a bill of divorcement stating, "Be thou divorced from me," and the couple would be divorced (Deuteronomy 24:1–2). In the United States, a couple must sign legal documents specifying how their children will be cared for (visitation and child support), as well as how property will be settled.

Community

Societies affect whether the community people live in will be gemeinschaft or gesellschaft. Small, rural, folk, hunting and gathering societies will produce gemeinschaft communities characterized by intimate primary group relationships. Large, urban, industrialized societies will produce gesellschaft communities characterized by formal secondary group relationships. Indeed, the lifestyle, health, and happiness individuals experience are in reference to the community in the society in which they live. If society changes the laws with regard to pollution standards, water use, the use of plastic grocery bags or required recycling, the entire community will be affected.

Associations

Societies decide what associations can form and for what purpose. Until recently, former Soviet citizens were not allowed to become members of associations that took positions against the communist party. In the summer of 1990, mine workers in the former Soviet Union, now Russia, formed an association of 300,000 members to call for the government to resign because of economic mismanagement.

What is important to understand is that as societies change, associations change. If the United States government requires mandatory military service of all Americans aged 18 to 34, with no exceptions (which has been offered as legislation), all men and women, paraplegics, gays, or wealthy would be inducted. Each would be given a job to perform commensurate with his or her abilities. The induction of all Americans would change the universities, the military, the actions of government (would we be in Iraq if the children of the upper class had to serve?), the occupational recruitment, and all other associations.

Networks

Networks exist based on the complexity of society. In hunting and gathering societies where everyone knows everyone and all needs are met by the group, no networks exist. In large urban societies, elaborate transportation and communication networks are necessary to tie the people together.

The various areas of social organization are interconnected and affected by decisions made at the societal level. Suppose a society decides to sterilize the population (in 1976 India passed legislation—since rescinded—for compulsory sterilization and sterilized over 6 million Indians). Such a decision would have an effect on other organizations within the society. It would not only lower the birth rate but also reduce kinship networks. Certainly, there would be a number of individuals who would attempt to evade such restrictions. Networks tie together social organizations in a society. If social class changes occur, it affects recruitment into various occupations which affects the educational system.

The society is the most important of the social organizations in that it is the most powerful. Any change at the societal level ripples through every other social organization. The presidential election of 2008 has the potential for long term change in every aspect of American life: abortion, military service, healthcare, and NAFTA. The election will ultimately impact all Americans. The effect will be on different population characteristics (e.g. men, women, black, white), collectivities (e.g. protests over abortion, guns), social class (e.g. taxes, jobs), groups (e.g. peers, lovers), families (e.g. blended, extended), communities (e.g. urban, suburban), associations (e.g. schools, hospitals), networks (e.g. economic, political) and ultimately the character of the society itself. What will that do? Changes in social organizations change what all of us *are* and what all of us *will become* in our lifetime. The individual is not as important as the sociological changes causing the outcomes everyone must face daily from losing one's job to paying for the price of gasoline. The individual is impotent and can control very little. The society and its inclusive social organizations are omnipotent and affect a great deal. It is important to understand society since it will affect all future outcomes in our lives and ultimately our deaths.

References

Bonner, J. T. 1980. *The Evolution of Culture in Animals.* Princeton, New Jersey: Princeton University Press.

Cetron, M. J. and O. Davies. 2008. "Trends Shaping Tomorrow's World: Forecasts and Implications for Business, Government, and Consumers (Part One)." *The Futurist*, 42: 35–53.

Christie, P. 2005. "Are Animals More Like Us Than We Dream? Scientists Discovering Culture Not Unique to Humans." Bell Globemedia Publishing.

Retrieved from http://www.rense.com/general62/dream.htm. February 18, 2008.

Durkheim, Emile. 1893. *The Division of Labor in Society.* New York: Free Press. (reprinted in 1964).

Fielden, J. M.and Gallagher, L. M. 2008. "Building Social Capital in First-Time Parents through a Group-Parenting Program: A Questionnaire Survey." *International Journal of Nursing Studies*, 45: 406–417.

Gillies, V. 2008. "Perspectives on Parenting Responsibility: Contextualizing Values and Practices." *Journal of Law and Society*, 35: 95–112.

Helal, A. M., S. A. Malek and E. S. Al-Katheeri. 2008. "Economic Feasibility of Alternative Designs of a PV-RO Desalination Unit for Remote Areas in the United Arab Emirates." *Desalination*, 221: 1–16.

Hinduja, S. and J. W. Patchin. 2008. "Personal Information of Adolescents on the Internet: A Quantitative Content Analysis of MySpace." *Journal of Adolescence*, 31: 125–133.

Lenski, G. et al (1991) *Human Societies: An Introduction to Macrosociology.* New York: McGraw-Hill.

Markert, J. 2008. "The Fading Dream of Retirement: Social and Financial Considerations Affecting the Retirement Decision." *Sociological Spectrum*, 28: 213–233.

Statistical Abstract of the United States: 2008. 127th ed. Washington, D.C.: U.S. Bureau of the Census.

Tonnies, Ferdinand. 1963. "Gemeinschaft and Gesellschaft." (originally published in 1887). *Community and Society.* Translated and edited by C. P. Loomis, New York: Harper & Row.

Weber, Max. 1921. *Economy and Society.* (reprinted in 1968) New York: Bedminster Press.

Wey, T., D. T. Blumstein, W. Shen, F. Jordan. 2008. "Social Network Analysis of Animal Behaviour: A Promising Tool for the Study of Sociality." *Animal Behaviour*, 75: 333–353.

Index